System Design
with Ada

PRENTICE-HALL SOFTWARE SERIES

Brian W. Kernighan, advisor

System Design with Ada

R. J. A. BUHR

Carleton University
Ottawa, Ontario, Canada

PRENTICE-HALL, INC.

Englewood Cliffs, New Jersey 07632

Library of Congress Cataloging in Publication Data

Buhr, R. J. A.
    System design with Ada.

    Bibliography: p.
    Includes index.
    1. Ada (Computer program language)   2. System design.
I. Title.
QA76.73.A35B83   1984   001.64′2   83-13673
ISBN 0-13-881623-9

Editorial/production supervision: Kathryn Marshak and Nancy Milnamow
Cover and jacket design: Edsal Enterprises
Manufacturing buyer: Gordon Osbourne

Printed in the United States of America

10 9 8 7 6 5 4 3 2 1

ISBN   0-13-881623-9   NB21

Prentice-Hall International, Inc., *London*
Prentice-Hall of Australia Pty. Limited, *Sydney*
Editora Prentice-Hall do Brasil, Ltda., *Rio de Janeiro*
Prentice-Hall Canada Inc., *Toronto*
Prentice-Hall of India Private Limited, *New Delhi*
Prentice-Hall of Japan, Inc., *Tokyo*
Prentice-Hall of Southeast Asia Pte. Ltd., *Singapore*
Whitehall Books Limited, *Wellington, New Zealand*

Contents

Part B   INTRODUCTION TO LOGICAL DESIGN

**Chapter 3   Design-Oriented Pictorial System
Description Techniques   37**

Chapter 6   Modularity, Reliability, and Structure: A Communications Subsystem Example   *179*

Preface

The objectives of this book are as follows:

1. To provide a top-down, design-oriented introduction to Ada, accessible to a wide audience

2. To present and to illustrate by example a practically useful, graphical design notation, intended for use at various levels:
   - as an aid to conceptualizing the organization of a system in Ada terms;
   - as an aid to communicating design approaches and decisions in an informal manner among members of a team;
   - as a possible basis for Computer Aided Design of systems, using Ada as the specification and/or implementation language

3. To arm the novice system designer with philosophies, strategies, tactics, techniques, and insights into ways of effectively carrying out the design process in a system life-cycle context

This book should be particularly helpful to all those relatively inexperienced system designers who are currently being or will soon be turned loose to develop microprocessor-based embedded systems. The aim is to provide them with tools, methodologies, and insights to help them succeed in designing quality systems to be implemented by a project team. The recent explosion of available, inexpensive microelectronic technology has produced an extreme shortage of experienced system designers with the right mix of capabilities. Neophyte electrical engineers and computer scientists are thrust into situations where design responsibilities are theirs without having the training or experience to do it right the first time. Old timers in other fields find themselves willy-nilly responsible for system projects. This book is aimed at helping them.

The major part of the book should be accessible to anyone with a modest degree of *computer literacy* who can program in a language such as Pascal, PL/M, or C. The term *computer literacy* is used here to imply some familiarity with the use of computers as embedded components of systems rather than just as vehicles for running application programs written in conventional high-level languages.

The book should be accessible to many second-year and all third-year students in computer engineering or computer science programs and to many third-year and all fourth-year students in electrical engineering programs with computing options, or in data processing programs.

Graduate students and professionals in the work force will find the book useful to fill important gaps in their training by providing a conceptually consistent treatment of approaches to problems they will have already faced in practice. Several advanced design applications are provided toward the end of the book, which will be of particular interest to this group.

The book is aimed at the future through its use of the new programming language Ada to provide abstractions and tools for specifying modular systems. An Ada overview is included. However, the book does not depend on a detailed knowledge of Ada. Indeed, the book may be advantageously read before attempting to acquire such detailed knowledge. In this way, appropriate concepts may be formed before programming habits are developed. For the most part Ada is viewed as if it were Pascal with the addition of the basic features of packages and tasks. The Ada concepts that are required are introduced from the top down in a tutorial fashion. Thus, the book is relatively self-contained. Ada programs may be used as specifications for non-Ada target environments, so that the book is not tied to the use of Ada as an implementation language. Ada may eventually dominate the software world due to the key role being given it by the U.S. Department of Defense. At least one microprocessor manufacturer is supporting Ada at the chip level. However, it is more than the momentum behind Ada that justifies its use for design. The fact is that Ada has the expressive power to describe modular, concurrent systems in terms exactly suited to design.

The expressive power of Ada provides many traps for the uninitiated and unwary. The use of Ada in this book is deliberately constrained, not only to make the material widely accessible but also to arm the reader with an approach to design that can avoid most of the traps. KISS (Keep It Simple Stupid) is the watchword.

The approach of the book to the design process has been inspired by the work of E. Yourdon, L. Constantine, and G. J. Myers on Structured Design.

The graphical notation for Ada evolved naturally while trying to explain and use Ada concepts. Discussion always seemed to center most naturally around pictures drawn on the blackboard or on paper. The details of the notation are the author's own, but the nature of the notation was inspired in part by notations used by Intel to describe iAPX 432 and Ada concepts and by Grady Booch to describe Ada concepts. The idea of using a graphical notation was also inspired by Per Brinch Hansen's structure graph notation for concurrent Pascal which was used and extended by the author and B. A. Bowen in an earlier book.

The graphical notation provides a specific, one-to-one mapping between pictorial descriptions and the key features of the corresponding Ada programs. Thus, pictures are used as a convenient shorthand for Ada programs as well as for design.

A viewpoint of this book is that discussion of structured design in the absence of such a direct relationship between design-level graphical representations of systems and the means by which these representations may be expressed in a programming language can lead to confusion and misunderstanding, unless there is detailed, personal guidance at every step of the way by an experienced practitioner of the art of structured design. Because the object of this book is to present a relatively self-contained, tutorial introduction to design, the need for personal guidance from an expert to interpret it must be avoided. The use of a specific graphical notation for Ada enables this book to discuss structured design at a suitably high level while keeping the reader's feet on the ground.

An aim of this book is to assist readers in harnessing their intuition to think about systems at a logical level. An assumption is that technically-oriented persons usually have a good, intuitive understanding of the ideas of modularization and concurrency which have hitherto lacked a means of expression in a widely-known programming language. Required to harness this intuition are good conventions for visualizing a system composed of interacting modules, a language which can express these visualizations directly and some examples of system design to illustrate the techniques and to provide a basic "parts kit" for assembling new systems. This book aims to assist readers in harnessing their intuition by satisfying these requirements.

The usually difficult subject of concurrency is treated to harness the reader's intuitions about concurrency obtained in day-to-day interactions with other people. The reader is encouraged to think of tasks as analogous to persons and of interactions among tasks via the Ada rendezvous mechanism as analogous to interactions among persons in business offices. The problems of concurrency and the ways of solving these problems are, thus, demonstrated to be old and familiar rather than new and strange.

Both technical system design issues and the design process itself are covered. The approach is to discuss issues and guidelines in both areas in the context of specific examples, rather than in the abstract.

The examples are used as a springboard for attacking problems of wide general concern within the limits of the author's own experience, which includes real time process control, computer communications, office automation, and signal processing systems. The insights obtained from the examples should be transferable to new problem areas.

This book is concerned with the design of systems which may be implemented in a mixture of software and hardware. It is, therefore, more concerned with system structure than with programming per se. The book introduces high-level design abstractions from the top down in a way that will develop the reader's intuition about them without obscuring their fundamental nature behind the complexities of language syntax. Programming examples are provided for all key abstractions in order to keep the reader's feet on the ground. But these examples are provided only after the abstractions have been introduced.

Several substantial design examples illustrate design almost entirely separately from programming.

Design takes place at a higher logical level than implementation and it must accordingly leave out details. Accordingly, the Ada examples in this book are seldom developed as complete programs with all details in place. Rather, they are at the level of skeleton pseudocode, which is the right logical level for design.

The design examples are presented in a stepwise fashion, imitating the way in which they would be presented in design "walk-through" meetings. Figures give system structures as they would be presented in view-graph form by the person conducting the walk-through. The narrative text accompanying the figures describes them in a way they would be described verbally by the person conducting the walk-through. Skeleton Ada programs are then presented at the appropriate level for the first program walk-through. The aim is to show how designs can be developed and discussed using pictorial techniques to enhance communication among members of a project team.

Many of the examples and issues are abstracted from real, difficult implementation projects undertaken by the author and his associates. This provides another reason for informality—the real projects could not be described in detail in the scope of a book such as this. Yet, they provide lessons worth learning.

The material in this book has been tested and refined in the classroom in several undergraduate and graduate courses of the Department of Systems and Computer Engineering of Carleton University and in several short courses given to conference attendees and to industry beginning in 1980.

The book is organized into three major parts. Parts A and B are introductory and should be widely-accessible to readers with minimal background. Part A introduces and motivates the subject and provides an overview of Ada as a design language. Part B provides an introduction to logical design by introducing Ada-oriented, pictorial system description techniques and using them on a variety of simple examples. Part C explores logical design in greater depth. It begins by taking a more detailed look at some features of Ada that affect design. It then tackles questions of modularity, reliability, and structure, using as an example a communications subsystem implementing a simple message protocol. Finally, it tackles the issues in the design of modular, concurrent systems in general, using as an example of the design of a system to implement the X.25 packet switching protocol.

ACKNOWLEDGEMENTS

This book would never have seen the light of day without the flying fingers of Elaine Carlyle at her word processor.

Particular thanks are due to Steve Michell, who contributed criticisms, ideas, and examples for all parts of the book but especially for Chapter 7, and to Ellis Sinyor, whose detailed criticism of the final draft was invaluable.

I would like to thank all of my students who suffered through the development of this material in a number of my courses.

Some of the ideas in this book were developed as a byproduct of research contracts with the Federal Departments of Communications and of National Defense, and of research grants from the National Science and Engineering Research Council. Their support is gratefully acknowledged.

I would never have started without the prodding of my colleague, Archie Bowen.

Discussions with co-workers and students too numerous to mention have shaped my ideas about system design and implementation over the years. Particular thanks in this regard are due to Dennis MacKinnon.

Finally, I would like to thank my family for putting up with Ada's residence in our house for so long.

R. J. A. Buhr

Part A

Background

In this part we give a top-down overview of Ada as a system design language. Advanced readers may proceed directly to Part B.

Chapter 1

Introduction

1.1 MOTIVATION

This book describes an approach to system design with Ada which may be characterized as "object-oriented structured design."

The approach provides for the design and description of Ada systems in "black box" terms using "blueprintlike" pictures, which are easily understandable by all and encourage the formation of intuitive ideas about the nature of a system. The motivation for using the approach is the expectation that improved communication and enhanced intuition will lead to superior design quality in actual projects. For this purpose it seems likely that "a picture is worth a thousand lines of code."

In this book, the term *object* refers to a system component which has the characteristics of a black box. That is, its internal organization is invisible to the user, who only sees its interface specification. According to this use of the term, objects in Ada are packages, tasks, and procedures. Ada objects and their interaction mechanisms provide a metaphor for thinking of systems in a hardwarelike fashion as black boxes connected by cables which plug into sockets. This metaphor aids both communication and intuition.

This chapter is concerned mainly with motivating the approach and placing it in context. Section 1.2 discusses system design in the context of the system life cycle. Section 1.3 explores current problems and future directions in system design and implementation arising from the technology explosion and the software crisis. Section 1.4 summarizes the approach of the book. Impatient readers may skip Sections 1.2 and 1.3 without loss of continuity.

1.2 SYSTEM DESIGN AND THE SYSTEM LIFE CYCLE

This book is concerned with two aspects of the *how* part of design, namely

1. the design process itself; that is, the methodology by which a design for a system is produced
2. technical factors in system design; that is, the factors which affect how the system is to be structured

Design is part of the overall system development process as reflected in the system life cycle. The phases of the system life cycle are as follows, in very high-level terms:

1. ANALYZE
   Analyze the application requirements to determine the feasibility of satisfying the requirements.
2. SPECIFY
   Specify the external requirements of the system.
3. DESIGN
   Prepare a global design in terms of
   (a) user interface
   (b) system functions
   (c) system architecture
   (d) test plan based on the requirements and the global design
4. IMPLEMENT
   Implement the system in the following stages:
   (a) construct the modules
   (b) test and debug the modules
   (c) integrate the modules into subsystems and the final system
5. DELIVER
   Deliver the system to the customer using the following steps:
   (a) validate the system following the test plan
   (b) perform the customer's acceptance test
6. MAINTAIN
   Make changes as necessary to correct errors and to accommodate changing requirements.

The system life cycle applies recursively to life cycles that produce hardware and software portions of the system.

This book is mainly concerned with developing the system logical architecture as part of the global design phase. The remainder of the life cycle is not treated in any detail explicitly. However, throughout the book the influences of other parts of the life cycle on design are continually emphasized.

As presented in the book, the design process is an informal one. It is not possible simply to follow a recipe, turn a crank and produce a system design. Instead of attempting to present a formal methodology, the book concentrates on giving informal guidelines for the steps to be followed in system design and then providing numerous examples to illustrate the use of the guidelines.

Technical factors in logical system design arise in attempting to develop a clean, error-free design which satisfies all of the system requirements. Technical factors may be both qualitative and quantitative. Qualitative factors include modularity, flexibility and reliability. Quantitative factors include external performance in terms of response time and throughput. Factors affecting reliability are considered to be qualitative. With this qualification, we may say that the prime emphasis of the book is on qualitative technical factors in system design. The approach is to discuss these factors in the context of examples.

1.3 REFLECTIONS ON HARDWARE AND SOFTWARE

1.3.1 Introduction

The two components of systems, hardware and software, have had, from a historical perspective, very different characteristics and have been developed by very different methods. The technology explosion is changing all this. The inherent physical modularity of hardware has served as an inspiration for new approaches to software, which in turn are enabling both software and hardware to be designed and specified using software driven techniques. In this sense, software and hardware are moving closer together.

In the software world new development techniques are showing promise of short-circuiting the historical life-cycle approach in certain areas. Furthermore, the arrival of the ubiquitous personal computer has brought software development within the reach of almost everyone.

The purpose of this section is to relate these trends to the material of this book.

1.3.2 Hardware as an Inspiration for Software

Consider for a moment the lucky hardware engineer. The components he designs have an inherent physical reality. These components may be connected together into assemblies, subsystems or systems using cables, plugs and sockets with well defined interface characteristics. Figure 1.1 illustrates the point. A module connected to another module by a plug and cable may be disconnected and replaced by a plug-compatible module with different internal structure without having any effect on the system. Make-or-buy decisions about plug-compatible modules are possible, because plug compatibility permits the growth of a parts industry. Systems are *field reconfigurable* after the power has been turned off or the function performed by the module to be replaced has been disabled.

Another aspect of hardware systems of the kind depicted in Figure 1.1 is the ability

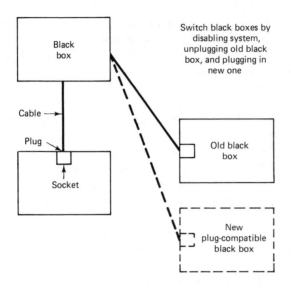

Figure 1.1 Thinking of systems in hardware terms

of one or more of the modules of the system to operate concurrently. In fact any particular module may itself have concurrent components.

The concepts of plug compatibility and concurrency are so natural in hardware terms that it would be quite foreign to think of hardware in any other way. However, historically this has not been the case with software. The widely used traditional programming languages include provision neither for plug-to-plug compatibility of modules nor for support of concurrency. Until recently the few languages that did provide such support were not widely used or widely available. In many cases addition of such features to standard languages has been performed in nonstandard ways by different organizations who recognized the need for these features. The result has been a proliferation of nonstandard, ad hoc approaches.

Ada, however, provides both plug-to-plug compatibility and concurrency in a neatly uniform and consistent fashion. The language supports both sequential modules (packages) and concurrent modules (tasks and active packages, containing tasks). Both packages and tasks have the equivalent of sockets, described by separate specifications. An elegant uniformity results from the fact that the sockets for both packages and tasks look very similar from the outside. This provides for an economy of concepts in describing a system composed of interconnected modules of different types.

Field reconfigurability of an Ada program is very similar to that of a hardware system whose power must be turned off or functionality disabled before unplugging the old module and plugging in a new one. In Ada terms, a software system must be taken down and relinked to install a new, plug-compatible module. In this sense Ada does not provide completely general reconfiguration capability, such as is needed for dynamic installation of a newly created module in a running system. Because of this, Ada is not suitable for writing general-purpose operating systems. However, it is completely suitable for writing special-purpose systems composed of collections of preexisting modules.

6

1.3.3 The Software-Driven System Factory: A Vision of the Future

Having available in Ada a language which can be used to describe systems in hardware-inspired terms, it is possible to think of a system factory in which both hardware and software are designed and specified in the same terms. In these terms, programming becomes more than just generating lines of code. Programming becomes *structured system building* in which programs are built up as structured assemblies of logical black boxes connected together by logical plugs and cables. As such, programs may be used to represent either hardware or software, only becoming lines of code in the bodies of modules which have been committed to software.

Figure 1.2 illustrates a vision of the software factory of the future based on this concept. Figure 1.3 shows how software-driven system design may be performed using a language such as Ada. A key feature of such an approach is the conceptual viewpoint of the system structure that it provides to managers, designers, implementors, suppliers,

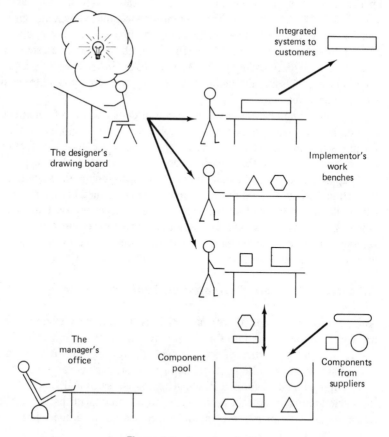

Figure 1.2   A system factory

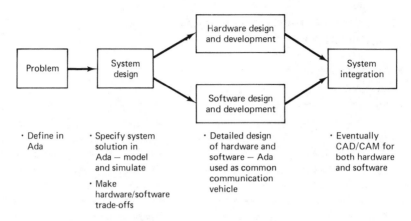

Figure 1.3 Ada in system design

customers, marketers and clients. Discussions of system projects, thus, can take place in the same terms between members of the same interest group and different interest groups in a systems project. The common conceptual viewpoint can be used as a basis for discussing design features, schedules, resource requirements, and so on.

However, it would be too much to ask all of these interested parties to share the same level of understanding of the Ada language. Instead, what is required is a graphical notation for expressing the main features of system structures in terms directly related to Ada language features.

In other engineering fields the pictorial depiction of system structures is known as a blueprint. Of major concern in this book will be the development of a pictorial notation for preparing the equivalent of blueprints for software-driven system designs.

Finally, we note that this software-driven system factory approach implies a life-cycle approach to system development. That is, following the system life cycle described in Section 1.2, system requirements must first be defined before systems can be designed and implemented to satisfy them. However, a different approach to software development which short-circuits the life cycle is emerging for certain types of applications. The significance of these developments and their relationship to the material of this book is discussed in the next section.

1.3.4 New Software Development Techniques

An aspect of the so-called software crisis is the difficulty experienced in practice with translating requirements into satisfactory systems without long lead times and high costs due to inherent properties of the life-cycle approach. The life-cycle approach demands that all significant requirements be defined before results can be seen by clients.

Highly typed, compiled languages such as Pascal and Ada are oriented toward the life-cycle approach. Ada in particular is so oriented, with its support for system modularization and its separation of module specification from the internal details of module implementation. Ada program structures can only be developed based on a detailed understanding of the requirements, and any changed requirements may invalidate them.

However, it may be argued that specification and agreement on all customer requirements for a complex system is humanly impossible in the real world until the customer has seen at least a partial implementation. This impossibility arises from the fact that in the real world human organizations are unavoidably fallible: people are busy, they forget details or are not interested in them, not everyone who knows the requirements is always involved in defining them, and information is lost in human interactions. Even with the best efforts to avoid them, there will be oversights, mistakes and forgotten details. But an Ada program structure to satisfy a requirement may be invalidated by a missing detail. And if the module structure, in terms of data types, packages, tasks, their interfaces and interactions, is invalidated, then every module may have to be modified, or the system will have to be delivered without meeting requirements.

It is certainly desirable in the early stages of a system life cycle to postpone making any design commitments which could later cause major redesign problems. Ideally, all such commitments should be postponed forever, and customers should define their requirements directly by user-friendly interaction with the system which satisfies these requirements. In some application areas, such as data base retrieval, this will become increasingly possible with time.

In such areas, high-level application programs will no longer be written by application programmers and then compiled. Instead, they will be constructed by very intelligent user interface programs, then executed interpretively and finally modified if necessary by further interaction with the user. Strong typing is inappropriate, because program objects may change in nature as the system evolves.

This approach may be called *requirements-by-result,* because the user sees the results of his requirements directly and may refine them interactively to achieve the desired results. It has also been called *interactive prototyping.*

Requirements-by-result contrasts greatly with the more conventional life-cycle development approach in which requirements must be stated in detail long before results become visible. However, the requirements-by-result approach is not applicable, even in principle, to problems which are not of the application-programmer-replacement type. Such problems must be handled for the most part by the life-cycle approach.

Therefore a commitment to Ada as a specification or design language does not impose any more constraints on flexibility than are already present in the nature of real life-cycle projects. Whatever the language of design or implementation, making a change to subsystem interfaces late in a project may affect all subsystems. In a large project, reprogramming or rebuilding the subsystems will be only a part of the cost of such a change.

1.3.5 "Cottage" versus "Heavy" Software Industry

The ubiquitous personal computer has brought software development within the reach of almost everyone. We can all see around us the beginnings of a software "cottage industry," in which people who are not computer professionals are developing applications software on personal computers for their own use or for sale, often with considerable success. Such people are apt to be impatient with talk about software design. The situation is similar with students who have successfully completed a few introductory courses in programming and consequently believe themselves capable of tackling any programming job with similar success. This attitude is natural, because programming can lead to impressive, immediate results with relatively small intellectual effort invested in programming technology per se, apart from that required to learn some arbitrary rules relating to language syntax and system commands. There is, after all, very little computer-related theory actually needed to write programs that work. At its most basic level, programming is a skill like carpentry or house building which may be learned by experience by anyone with an aptitude for it.

The contrast between system designers and cottage-industry programmers is similar to that between professionals (architects and engineers) who design complex buildings and the home handyman who builds his own furniture, summer cottage or house. The home handyman can proceed from the bottom up with a minimum of preliminary design effort, making design decisions as the work proceeds and obtaining required materials (boards, bricks, nails, etc.) as the need arises. The home handyman does not need training in architecture and engineering to do the job successfully.

The cottage-industry programmer can often get away with the home-handyman approach by building programs from the bottom up, a line at a time, making design decisions as the work proceeds. In a sense the job is even easier than the home handyman's, because new materials may not have to be obtained; given a computer of adequate capacity, there is always an ample supply of basic components (computer instructions). The cottage industry programmer does not in many cases need training in software architecture and engineering to do the job successfully.

However, both the home handyman and the cottage-industry programmer will reach a plateau of project size and complexity beyond which it is difficult or dangerous to proceed without training in the relevant architectural and engineering aspects. We may characterize this plateau as marking the dividing line between "cottage" and "heavy" industry.

Heavy industry is characterized by a multiplicity of technologies, workers, and goals, requiring that plans be worked out in detail for any project before implementation work begins. The methods of this book, therefore, are clearly aimed at heavy industry software development. However, it is surely true that working out plans in detail before beginning work will help to avoid mistakes and to increase productivity in any project. Thus, the book should also be helpful to cottage industry programmers.

1.3.6 Software As Black Boxes: A Conceptual Leap

The book encourages the reader to think about software in structural form rather than in flow chart or *lines of code* form. The approach of the book is to develop system structures in black box terms using blueprintlike pictures. Experience shows that the ability to think at this level requires a major conceptual leap for many programmers. This is particularly true of programmers used to working in a conventional application programming environment in which sequential programs run under the control of a monolithic central operating system. A goal of this book is to guide readers over this hurdle. To this end, a considerable amount of tutorial material is presented in Part B to assist the reader in making the necessary conceptualizations.

1.4 APPROACH OF THIS BOOK

The methods of this book are aimed at software-driven system design following the life-cycle approach. The book stands on three legs as illustrated by Figure 1.4:

Structured Design   The methods of the book derive their inspiration from so-called *structured design,* which is a methodology for deriving system structures from data flow patterns in the system.

An Object-Oriented Graphical Notation and Conceptual Model   This notation and model for system components, their interfaces, and interconnection forms the basis of structure graphs developed in structured design; its underlying semantics are provided by the Ada language.

The Ada Language Itself   Only the parts of the Ada language which describe system objects, their interfaces and interactions are of fundamental importance to the material of the book. For the purposes of this book, Ada may be considered as Pascal plus the basic features of packages and tasks. Ada programs are used to illustrate structured design examples, but for the most part the reader with a knowledge of Pascal and a basic knowledge of Ada packages and tasks will be able to follow the examples.

The book first develops each of the three legs of Figure 1.4 in sufficient depth to

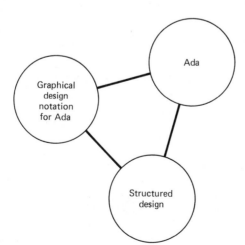

Figure 1.4   Three foundations of this book

begin the discussion of examples. Thereafter, the three legs are used as a basis for the discussion of a number of design examples which illustrate both the design process and technical factors in design. The book is heavily example-driven; issues and principles are developed mainly through examples. The three legs of Figure 1.4 are developed in the remainder of Part A and in Part B. In particular, Chapter 2, which is the last chapter of Part A, provides a top-down introduction to Ada. This introduction should be sufficient to make the book self-contained for the reader familiar with Pascal (or any similar language) and having sufficient "computer literacy" to be comfortable with multitasking concepts.

Chapter 2

Ada
as a System Design
Language

2.1 INTRODUCTION

As discussed in Chapter 1, Ada has a number of new features which support ideas of modularity and concurrency derived from hardware. In particular, Ada supports the metaphor of systems composed of black boxes interconnected by cables which plug into sockets. Black boxes may be packages or tasks or combinations thereof. Sockets are package or task specifications, which are defined separately from their bodies. Concurrency is supported by tasks. Packages and tasks present similar appearing interfaces to the external world. A system may be configured statically by linking together precompiled black boxes through their specifications.

These features of Ada are clearly advantageous for structured design. However, Ada has many other unconventional features. It is useful to classify all the new, important, unconventional features of Ada under the headings of life-cycle features, structured design features, and technical features, as illustrated in Figure 2.1. Life-cycle features are those which assist the entire design and development life cycle. Technical features are those which have been included in the language to meet particular technical requirements. Neither life-cycle features nor technical features are the main concern of this book except as they overlap with structured design features. Structured design features are the ones which are of particular interest in this book.

Consider Figure 2.1, beginning from the center of the figure and moving first to the structured design features. Packaging and separate specification have already been mentioned and discussed briefly. The top-down refinement feature of the language allows nested modules to be included in the first instance in specification form only; their bodies may then be developed separately. This is very useful for presenting the internal design

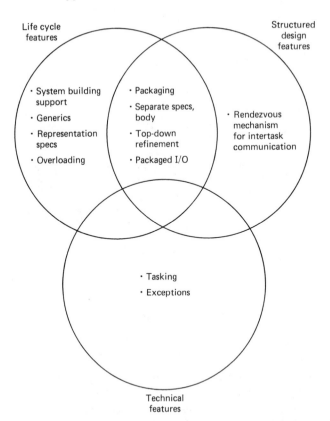

Figure 2.1 Classification of the important new features of Ada

of a complex module without obscuring the essentials with a lot of details. Another widely useful feature is packaged input/output (I/O). Ada has no I/O instructions or statements per se. Instead, I/O is performed by packages; standard I/O packages are included with the compiler, and users may write their own I/O packages for special purposes. A feature of particular significance for structured design is Ada's rendezvous mechanism for intertask communication. This mechanism provides for the uniform nature of package and task interfaces. These five features are the main ones which underlie our methods in this book.

Features which are particularly life-cycle oriented are system building support, which provides for type checking across separate compilations; generic modules, which provide for macrolike parameterized copies of modules to be created; representation specifications, which provide for defining the structure of the hardware environment to the compiler; and overloading, which provides for multiple usage of the same name provided the compiler can distinguish the different usages of the name from the context.

Technical features include tasking and exceptions. Tasking is obviously required for support of concurrency in applications such as real time control. It is not so much the fact that tasking is supported by Ada that is particularly useful to structured design but the particular manner in which intertask communication is handled. Exceptions are technical features which provide for abnormal returns to an exception handler in a caller's environment on occurrence of a designated error condition.

Section 2.2 provides a top-down view of the major new features of Ada of interest to the system designer. Section 2.2 also provides an Ada wrap-up including comments on controversial features of the language and on its appropriateness as a system design or implementation language.

2.2 TOP-DOWN VIEW OF THE MAJOR NEW FEATURES OF ADA OF INTEREST TO THE SYSTEM DESIGNER

2.2.1 Introduction

The major features of interest in this section are those oriented to structured design as depicted in Figure 2.1. In the order in which we shall treat them here, these features are as follows:

- packaging
- separation of specifications and bodies of packages and tasks
- rendezvous mechanism for intertask communication;
- top-down refinement
- packaged I/O
- interrupts

2.2.2 Packaging and Specification/Body Separation

The concept of a package is illustrated in graphical terms in Figure 2.2. A package is a black box which provides services to users through an interface defined by a package specification. The package specification and the package body are distinct components of the program text in Ada and may be separately compiled if desired. The package body is hidden from the user who may only use the package in the way defined by the specification. The specification is the visible part of the package and may include definitions, declarations, and specifications of almost anything that may be in an Ada program. Most often it will contain specifications of subprograms which provide access to the services of the package. However, it may also include data type definitions, data object declarations, nested package specifications, and nested task specifications. The body is the hidden part of the package. Most often it will consist of the bodies of subprograms defined in the visible part and the declarations of package local variables and auxiliary subprograms which are shared between externally visible subprograms. The package may also include nested packages and tasks and initialization specifications.

Figure 2.3 gives a specific example of a black-box view of a simple type of package, namely a STACK package. This example is a modified version of the stack package example presented in the Ada reference manual. This package provides externally ac-

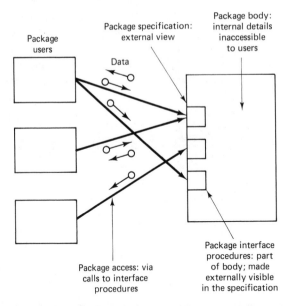

Package users

Package specification: external view

Package body: internal details inaccessible to users

Data

Package access: via calls to interface procedures

Package interface procedures: part of body; made externally visible in the specification

Figure 2.2   Logical view of packages

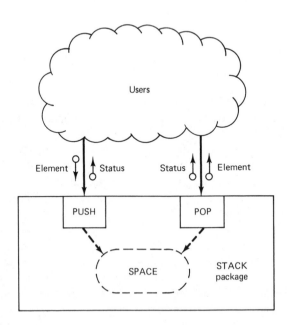

Users

Element | Status   Status | Element

PUSH   POP

SPACE   STACK package

Form of user calls:
STACK. PUSH(ELEMENT, STATUS);
STACK. POP(ELEMENT, STATUS);

Figure 2.3   A stack package

cessible procedures PUSH and POP for elements of fixed, predefined types. The procedures return flags to indicate overflow or underflow. Invisible to the user are the bodies of the PUSH and POP procedures and the stack data structure which is shared between them. The idea is that users of the stack package will not have to change the way in which they use it if the body of the package is changed to accommodate different types of stack data structures, for example, arrays or linked lists.

An Ada program for implementing this package for an array stack data structure is given in Figure 2.4. The first part is a definition of global types used by both the caller and the package. Note that these types could also be defined in the stack package specification, because they are not really *global* but are only relevant to users of the package. They remain global here for later comparison with a stack task.

The stack package specification includes the specification of the procedures PUSH and POP; these specifications consist of simply the name of the procedure followed by its parameter specifications.

The third part is the body of the stack package containing a fixed-size array for the stack and two procedures PUSH and POP which operate on this array.

The procedures PUSH and POP are accessed from outside the package by calling STACK.PUSH or STACK.POP. Simply naming the package by qualifying the call in this way provides access to any program elements inside the package that are made visible in the specification.

Some key points on the packages are as follows:

- Invoking the name of a package provides access to all the elements in it that are named in the specification.
- Package specification has to be declared only once in a program even though there may be many modules using it.
- Almost anything may be packaged.
- Packages and their specifications may but do not have to be separately compiled.

How do Ada packages differ from what we have available in more conventional languages? Let us take "standard" Pascal as an example. Pascal has been extended in many different directions by many different organizations, but in standard Pascal the only *packaging* feature is the procedure. Figure 2.5 illustrates the ways in which procedures could be used to emulate Ada packages. If we insist on separate POP and PUSH procedures, Figure 2.5(a) illustrates that the association of these procedures as part of a stack package must be performed by documenting the association in comments in the program text. The stack space must be declared as global data and PUSH and POP must be declared as separate procedures with no way of associating them by name or even contiguous position in the program text. If we wish to have a single-named stack object, we must make it a procedure with an opcode parameter to indicate which operation is to be performed, as shown in Figure 2.5(b). The stack data structure must still be declared globally. Finally, if we wish to emulate the Ada approach and hide the stack data structure inside the stack package, we arrive at the approach of Figure 2.5(c), which is incorrect

```
— —THIS IS A COMMENT
— —GLOBAL TYPES USED BY BOTH CALLER AND PACKAGE
type ELEM is INTEGER;
type STATUS is (OK, UNDERFLOW, OVERFLOW);


— —THE STACK PACKAGE FOR VARIABLES OF TYPE ELEM
— —SPECIFICATION
package STACK is
   procedure PUSH (E:in ELEM; FLAG:out STATUS);
   procedure POP (E:out ELEM; FLAG:out STATUS);
end STACK;


— —BODY
package body STACK is
   SIZE: constant INTEGER : = 10;
   SPACE: array (1 . . SIZE) of ELEM;
   INDEX: INTEGER range 0 . . SIZE : = 0;

   procedure PUSH (E : in ELEM, FLAG: out STATUS) is
      begin
        if INDEX = SIZE then FLAG : = OVERFLOW
        else
        INDEX : = INDEX + 1;
        SPACE (INDEX) : = E;
        FLAG : = OK;
        end if;
      end PUSH;

   procedure POP (E : out ELEM, FLAG: out STATUS) is
      begin
        if INDEX = 0 then FLAG : = UNDERFLOW
        else
        E : = SPACE (INDEX);
        INDEX : = INDEX − 1;
        FLAG : = OK;
        end if;
      end POP;


end STACK;


— —FORM OF USER CALLS
     STACK.PUSH (ELEMENT, STATUS);
     STACK.POP (ELEMENT, STATUS);
```

Figure 2.4 Ada program for the stack package

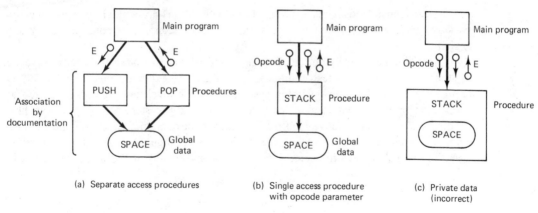

(a) Separate access procedures

(b) Single access procedure
with opcode parameter

(c) Private data
(incorrect)

Figure 2.5   Packages in Pascal

in Pascal. Procedures in Pascal are completely reentrant, and all local data structures disappear on return from the procedure call. There is no way of ensuring that what has been put on the stack will still be there on the next call.

The perceptive reader may observe that Figure 2.5(b) is sometimes exactly what one wants to do with a stack. In Figure 2.5(b) the stack *package* is pure procedure which operates on appropriate global data. This is exactly what processor stacks do in hardware. Although this observation is true, it is beside the point. The fact is that standard Pascal does not provide for the hiding of data in a package in the many cases where that is exactly what is desired.

2.2.3 Rendezvous Mechanism

The next design-oriented feature of Ada we shall consider is the rendezvous mechanism for tasks. Tasks provide a mechanism for concurrent execution. It may be desirable to have concurrent execution in order to exploit the capabilities of multiple processors or because tasks provide a natural model for many real world applications, even if the target environment is a uniprocessor.

The reader familiar with other concurrent programming languages and/or multi-tasking operating systems will wonder whether the term *task* in Ada is equivalent to the same term in those environments or to the term *process* which is also used in those environments. The answer is that Ada tasks have one additional fairly unique feature, namely the capability to provide a procedurelike interface to users very similar to the interface to users provided by a package. Tasks may have entries which may be called by other tasks, and these entries must be specified in a task specification in exactly the same way that package procedures must be specified in a package specification. Although entries are called in the same way as procedures, they are defined and processed differently. Procedures are executed by the caller. Entries are executed by the callee (or acceptor), while the caller waits during a so-called rendezvous.

Thus, considered as black boxes, tasks with entries are similar system objects to packages with visible procedures. This makes for an economy of concepts for system design.

Standard languages such as Fortran, standard Pascal and many others have no multitasking facilities. Instead multitasking facilities, if required, must be provided by an underlying multitasking operating system. The high-level language programs run as application programs which make calls to this operating system for intertask synchronization and communication as required. The calls to the operating system and the intertask communication mechanisms are outside the high level language. This approach is illustrated in onionskin form in Figure 2.6(a). A major difficulty with this approach lies in

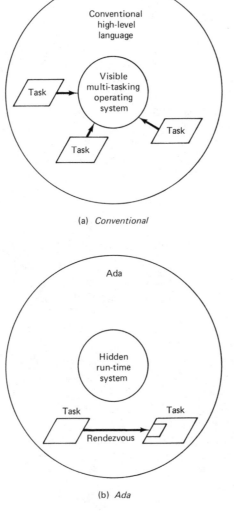

(a) *Conventional*

(b) *Ada*

Figure 2.6 Conventional versus Ada approaches to tasking

its logical complexity. There is no single conceptual model for the entire system consisting of the set of application programs together with the operating system.

In contrast, Ada provides in a single, high-level language a conceptually consistent mechanism for intertask communication which does not rely on explicit calls to an underlying operating system. Instead, as illustrated in Figure 2.6(b), all that is required is an underlying kernel which can support the rendezvous mechanism. This underlying kernel is not visible at the Ada program level. Indeed, the facilities of the kernel can be provided by a complete general purpose multitasking operating system exactly of the kind illustrated in Figure 2.6(a) without having any impact, at least in principle, on the Ada program level. In fact this is the way many initial implementations of Ada will run. The approach in which a complex language runs on top of a complex operating system is obviously undesirable in general and appropriate only as an interim measure. Efficient implementations of Ada will run on top of a minimal kernel or will run directly on hardware supporting the rendezvous mechanism.

To illustrate the nature of intertask communication and the use of the rendezvous mechanism, consider the buffer example of Figure 2.7. This figure shows a black-box view of the interactions between a producer task, a buffer task, and a consumer task. Tasks are shown as black boxes looking somewhat like packages, except that they are drawn as parallelograms rather than rectangles to symbolize their parallel (that is, concurrent) nature. In the figure, the producer and consumer tasks are autonomous tasks without entries. The buffer task, on the other hand, has write and read entries for use by the producer and consumer. The idea is that the buffer task smooths variations between the speed of output of a producing task and the speed of input of a consuming task. The astute reader may ask—why not use a package? Why is a task required? The answer is that otherwise the producer and consumer would not be able to synchronize their accesses to the buffer and might simultaneously interact with the buffer in such a way as to cause inconsistency in its internal data structures. In other words, the buffer task provides mutual exclusion on the buffer data structures.

To readers unfamiliar with Ada tasking, the buffer task may seem a strange form of task. It spends most of its time waiting for other tasks to call it. The reader may object, tasks should be active; they should have work to do, such as controlling a machine or

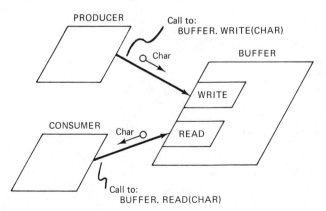

Figure 2.7 The basic format of the structure graph for a three-task producer-consumer system (without using the full graphical notation of Chapter 3)

receiving messages from another computer. However, any task which does work must also communicate with other tasks. The buffer task example serves to illustrate the communication interface mechanism for more general tasks. From this perspective, the fact that it does no work of its own is not important. It could do work and still look the same from the outside. In fact its external interface is a good model for the kind of interface presented to users by many tasks which do work in the examples of later chapters.

Readers familiar with concurrent programming theory and practice will be aware that in other systems there are other ways of ensuring mutual exclusion involving, for example, test-and-set instructions, semaphores, conditional critical regions, monitors, message exchanges, and so on. Ada requires the use of tasks. A positive advantage of this approach from the viewpoint of design is that all task intercommunication and synchronization activities are performed by active program objects at the same logical level. Thus synchronization and intercommunication are explicitly visible in the calls made between program objects. There is no hidden functionality buried in signals or messages. Another positive advantage is the resulting economy of concepts needed to describe a system containing both packages and tasks. Both types of objects present similar external interfaces to users.

Figure 2.8(a) gives the buffer task specification and shows how the producer and consumer tasks call the buffer task. Figure 2.8(b) shows the simplest code for the buffer task body. This version of the buffer task accepts one character from the producer via the WRITE entry and then waits for the consumer to pick up the character via the READ entry before going back to accept another character from the producer. The accept statement is the buffer task's way of saying that at this point it is ready to accept a call on the named entry. If a call has already been made, then a task is waiting in the entry

```
— —PRODUCER
loop
  — —PRODUCE THE NEXT CHARACTER
  BUFFER.WRITE(CHAR);
end loop;


— —CONSUMER
loop
  BUFFER.READ(CHAR);
  — —CONSUME THE CHARACTER
end loop;


— —BUFFER SPECIFICATION
task BUFFER is
  entry READ (C : out CHARACTER);
  entry WRITE (C : in CHARACTER);
end;
```

(a) *Task interfaces*

Figure 2.8   A three-task producer-consumer program in Ada

```
task body BUFFER is
POOL : CHARACTER;
begin
  loop
    accept WRITE (C: in CHARACTER) do
      POOL : = C;
    end;

    accept READ (C: out CHARACTER) do
      C : = POOL;
    end;
  end loop;
end BUFFER;
```

(b) *Simplest buffer task*

Figure 2.8   (continued)

queue and the rendezvous takes place immediately. If the entry queue is empty, then the buffer task waits for a call on that entry. From the caller's viewpoint, if it makes a call on an entry before the buffer task has executed an accept statement for that entry, the caller waits in the entry queue until the buffer task accepts the entry. The buffer task's body must contain at least one accept statement for each entry declared in its specification, otherwise a caller of that entry will wait forever.

Until the rendezvous is finished, the caller is idle. Note that there is no busy waiting in any of these interactions. When the caller waits in the entry queue for the rendezvous to be finished, the caller is not using processing resources. When the acceptor waits to accept a call on an entry, the acceptor is not using processing resources.

To the caller the rendezvous appears syntactically exactly like a call and return from a procedure. The essential difference from a procedure call is that the operation requested by calling the entry is performed by the called task rather than by the calling task, and that a variable delay may therefore be experienced by the caller before returning from the call.

The particular interaction shown in Figure 2.8(b) is obviously inadequate for buffering, because characters cannot accumulate in an internal data structure in the buffer task. Figure 2.8(c) shows a more general program based on the use of an internal ring buffer. To the callers nothing has changed except that idle periods at the buffer task will be shorter. The body of the buffer task has, however, changed significantly. It now contains a so-called *selective wait* statement naming the WRITE and READ entries as alternatives. This selective wait statement (that is, the entire statement between the *select* and *end select* reserved words) should be regarded as a single primitive instruction which sets up a waiting condition in the buffer task for the first call on either WRITE or READ. The producer and the consumer can now proceed independently, leaving it to the buffer task to accumulate any excess of production over consumption. In this example characters are accumulated in a bounded ring buffer. If the producer gets too far ahead of the

```
task body BUFFER is
    POOL_SIZE: constant INTEGER : = 100;
    POOL        : array (1 . . POOL_SIZE) of CHARACTER;
    IN_INDEX, OUT_INDEX: INTEGER range 1 . . POOL_SIZE : = 1;
begin
  loop
    select
      accept WRITE (C: in CHARACTER) do
        POOL (IN_INDEX) : = C;
      end;
      IN_INDEX : = IN_INDEX mod POOL_SIZE + 1;
    or
      accept READ (C: out CHARACTER) do
        C : = POOL (OUT_INDEX);
      end;
      OUT_INDEX : = OUT_INDEX mod POOL_SIZE + 1;
    end select;
  end loop;
end BUFFER;
```

(c) *Buffer task with selective waiting*

Figure 2.8   (continued)

consumer, the ring buffer will wrap around and data will be overwritten before it has been consumed.

This overwriting of the ring buffer can be prevented by using another feature of Ada called a *guard*. Figure 2.8(d) shows the results. The guards are contained in the *when* statements which indicate conditions under which the *selective wait* alternatives are *open* for acceptance. Again, the selective wait statement must be regarded as a primitive instruction which sets up a waiting condition. At the time of execution of this primitive instruction, the guards are evaluated to select open entries which may be accepted. In this particular example, if COUNT is equal to POOL_SIZE, then only the READ entry will be open for acceptance. This means that if the WRITE entry is called, the caller will wait in the entry queue until the entry is opened by a change to the guard. Note that this change to the guard will be caused by acceptance of another entry. A situation in which all entries are closed would be a programming error.

Figures 2.9 and 2.10 provide timing diagrams showing the producer-buffer-consumer interactions for the two cases when all select alternatives are open and when there is one closed select alternative.

Ada has other features associated with the rendezvous mechanism and in Chapter 3 these other features will be introduced together with an expanded pictorial notation to represent all of the alternatives.

Contrast the Ada approach to tasking with that required when using standard Pascal. The first point to note is that standard Pascal does not support concurrency in the language. Standard Pascal can only be used to write concurrent programs by writing special task

```
task body BUFFER is
  POOL_SIZE : constant INTEGER : = 100;
  POOL         : array (1 .. POOL_SIZE) of CHARACTER;
  COUNT      : INTEGER range 0 .. POOL_SIZE : = 0;
  IN_INDEX, OUT_INDEX : INTEGER range 1 .. POOL_SIZE : = 1
begin
  loop
  select
  when COUNT < POOL_SIZE = >
      accept WRITE (C : in CHARACTER) do
        POOL (IN_INDEX) : = C;
      end;
      IN_INDEX : = IN_INDEX mod POOL_SIZE + 1;
      COUNT    : = COUNT + 1;
  or when COUNT > 0 = >
      accept READ (C : out CHARACTER) do
        C : = POOL (OUT_INDEX);
      end;
      OUT_INDEX : = OUT_INDEX mod POOL_SIZE + 1;
      COUNT       : = COUNT - 1;
    end select;
  end loop;
  end loop;
end BUFFER;
```

(d) *Buffer task with guards (following the ADA Reference Manual)*

Figure 2.8   (continued)

procedures which are never called and never execute returns in the high-level language environment. These procedures are made known to the separate run-time kernel which supports concurrency by a Pascal main program which initializes the kernel. From the high-level language view-point, it is all in the programmer's mind. Figure 2.11 provides a structure diagram showing how the various components of a concurrent system written in Pascal interact. This approach may be taken for any standard high-level language which does not support concurrency. The main requirements are that each task procedure has its context maintained by the kernel in such a way that the code generated by the high-level language compiler interacts with the appropriate context for each task. Pascal works fine because its procedures are reentrant and the context is maintained on the stack. Fortran presents a problem because of its lack of reentrancy.

Note that an Ada design in which tasks communicate via rendezvous, can be implemented in a system such as shown by Figure 2.11 by appropriate use of the task synchronization and communication facilities of the kernel. The kernel does not need to support the rendezvous mechanism explicitly because this mechanism is relatively easily implemented using other intertask communication mechanisms.

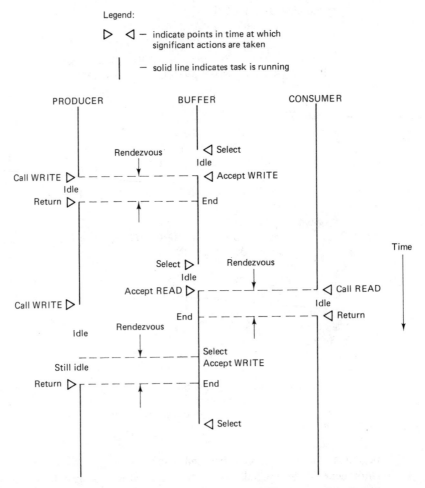

Figure 2.9   Timing diagram for buffer example with no closed entries

2.2.4 Top-Down Refinement

The next design-oriented feature of Ada requiring discussion is the ability to develop Ada programs in a top-down fashion. We have already seen that user programs which must access packages and tasks only need the package and task interface specifications. However, what about nested objects? For example, suppose a package contains internal procedures, packages, and tasks in a nested fashion. The usual rule of program nesting is that an object must be defined before it is used. This rule is also true for Ada. However, the requirement that it be defined before it is used is restricted to the specification. The body may either be defined after it is used in the same context as the specification, or it

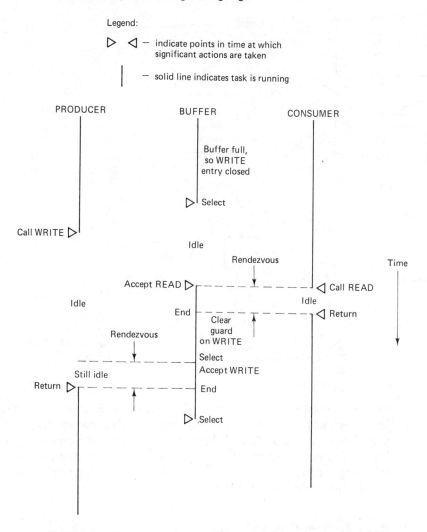

Figure 2.10 Timing diagram for buffer example with a closed entry

may be left as a stub to be defined as a separate compilation unit. The latter approach is illustrated by Figure 2.12. We shall often make use of the approach of Figure 2.12 in examples because of the convenient way in which it provides for explicit partitioning of the program text into page-sized chunks. However, the reader should note that separate compilation is not necessary for top-down refinement in Ada.

How does this differ from conventional languages such as standard Pascal? Standard Pascal has a forward declaration mechanism which makes it possible to write a program in which two procedures call each other. This would be impossible if everything had to

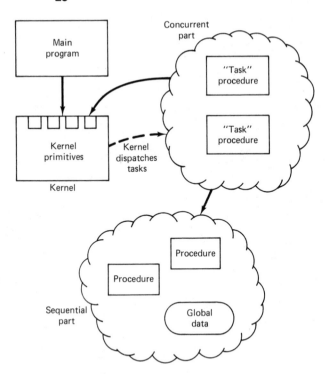

Figure 2.11 Tasking with procedures in Pascal

be fully defined before it was used. The approach is illustrated in Figure 2.13. In this figure, procedure R calls procedure P, which calls procedure Q, which in turn calls procedure P. This is made possible in Pascal, as shown in Figure 2.13, by programming the heading only of Q first, then programming P in full, then programming Q in full, then programming R. However, there is no way of deferring definition of the bodies of P and Q until after that of R in the program text.

2.2.5 Packaged Input/Output

A central feature of Ada which affects not only design but also all other areas of use for the language is that there are no special language statements for input/output. Instead, input/output is performed by packages which may be standard ones distributed with the compiler or special ones written by users. Figure 2.14 provides an example of a package for file input/output. The example is largely self-explanatory except for the new feature in the package specification of the limited private data type. This is a further example of information hiding by packaging. Clearly, in any file input/output package, filenames must be externally accessible. This implies that the structure of the filename type must

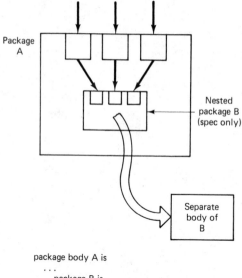

```
package body A is
   . . .
      package B is
       . . .
      end B;

      package body B is separate; — — STUB
      . . .
end A;

separate (A)
package body B is
   . . .
end B;
```

Figure 2.12 Top-down programming with stubs in Ada

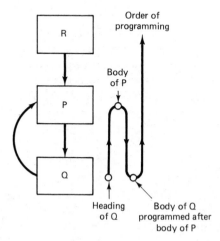

Figure 2.13 Limited top-down programming in Pascal

```
package I__O__PACKAGE is
  type FILE__ID is limited private;
  procedure OPEN  (F : in out FILE__ID);
  procedure CLOSE (F : in out FILE__ID);
  procedure READ  (F : in FILE__ID; ITEM : out INTEGER);
  procedure WRITE (F : in FILE__ID; ITEM : in INTEGER);
private
  type FILE__ID is
    record
      INTERNAL__ID : INTEGER : = 0;
    end record;
end I__O__PACKAGE;

package body I__O__PACKAGE is
  LIMIT : constant : = 200;
  type FILE__DESCRIPTOR is record . . . end record;
  DIRECTORY : array (1 . . LIMIT) of FILE__DESCRIPTOR;
  . . .
  procedure OPEN  (F : in out FILE__ID) is . . . end;
  procedure CLOSE (F : in out FILE__ID) is . . . end;
  procedure READ  (F : in FILE__ID; ITEM : out INTEGER) is . . . end;
  procedure WRITE (F : in FILE__ID; ITEM : in INTEGER) is . . . end;
begin
  . . .
end I__O__PACKAGE;
```

Figure 2.14   File I/O package (following the Ada Reference Manual)

be known in the package specification. However, it is important that users do not generate their own filenames or modify filenames provided by the package. The declaration of filename as a limited private type accomplishes this. A user of the package may obtain a filename only by calling OPEN and may later use it in calls to READ and WRITE. However, it may not access components of a variable of type filename, and it may perform no operations on variables of this type. Therefore it cannot generate its own values of variables of type filename. Such values can only be obtained as parameters of procedures of the package.

Contrast this with languages such as standard Pascal which have imbedded input/output instructions which limit the flexibility of the language.

Obviously this packaging approach to input/output does not at this level address the problem of direct interaction with hardware. The body of this package must somehow perform this interaction either by making calls to an underlying operating system or by directly interacting with hardware. This leads to the next feature.

2.2.6 Interrupts

The final design-oriented feature of Ada which requires discussion is the interaction of interrupts with Ada software. From the Ada software point of view, an *interrupt* is considered an entry call to an interrupt handler task. There are mechanisms called *representation specifications* in the Ada language which allow interrupts to be associated with task entries to accomplish this. For logical design purposes the details of representation specifications are not important at this stage; it is sufficient to know that the capability exists. Figure 2.15 illustrates this approach to interrupt handling for the example of a keyboard handler task.

Contrast this with languages such as standard Pascal which have no low-level mechanisms for interacting with hardware.

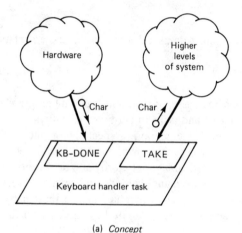

(a) *Concept*

```
task KB-HANDLER is

    entry TAKE (CH : out CHAR);
    entry KB-DONE;
    for KB-DONE use at 8#100 #;
end KB-HANDLER;

task body KB-HANDLER is

    BUF, DBR: CHAR;
    for DBR use at 8#177462#;

begin
    loop
        accept KB-DONE do BUF:=DBR; end;
        accept TAKE(CH : out CHAR) do CH:=BUF; end;
    end loop
end
```

(b) *Ada Code* (*Following Pyle*)

Figure 2.15 Interrupt handling tasks in Ada

2.2.7 Conclusions

The remaining special features of Ada do not have the same critical significance for design as do the features covered in this section, although they of course may be used. We shall introduce them at appropriate points in the text by example. However, we have covered enough in this chapter to proceed with Part B.

It should be emphasized once more that, for design purposes, Ada may be considered to be essentially Pascal with special added features. At the Pascal level, Ada is different in detail from standard Pascal, but its meaning will be obvious to readers familiar with Pascal.

2.3 ADA WRAPUP

2.3.1 Introduction

What are the pros and cons of using Ada as a design and/or implementation language?

2.3.2 Ada for System Design

Ada provides a uniform, black-box view of different types of program modules. It is relatively easy to interpret packages and tasks in hardware or software terms due both to the uniformity of treatment and to the separation of specification and body.

The restriction to the rendezvous mechanism for interaction between concurrent program components offers positive advantages of clarity and uniformity of specification. There are no indirect interactions whose nature is hidden in signals or messages. If direct interaction between interacting tasks is not desirable, then a third party task must be included to handle indirect interactions. The nature of the interactions is thus made clearly visible in an explicit fashion.

Readers concerned with efficiency should note that third party tasks included to handle interactions do not necessarily have to be implemented as tasks in non-Ada target environments. A task which only receives entry calls from other tasks and makes none of its own could be implemented efficiently in a non-Ada target environment as a critical region in shared memory using well known techniques. The desirability of doing so could be indicated by the designer in the Ada description of the system by a *critical region pragma* (formally, a pragma in Ada is an instruction to the compiler—however, it can also be interpreted in a design environment as an instruction to the implementor). The possibility also exists of an Ada compiler using such a pragma to generate efficient code.

Ada supports top-down refinement of nested modules in program text, thereby aiding both the design process and the ease of reading of the program text.

Ada supports the postponement of commitment to the target hardware configuration, subject to the reasonable assumption that the logical architecture is naturally mappable onto all visualized target hardware configurations. For example, a design which includes only two tasks would be very difficult to map onto a hardware architecture consisting of 10 processors. On the other hand, a design which contains 30 tasks might be quite easily mappable onto 10 processors. This would be true independent of the use of Ada. More specific to Ada, a design which relies on sharing packages between tasks would be difficult to map onto a distributed environment. On the other hand, the rendezvous mechanism is quite easily mapped into a distributed environment. We shall have more to say on these matters in Part C.

The expected high level of standardization of the language and of its penetration into the computing community are both positive features.

2.3.3 Ada for Implementation

Considered as an implementation language, there is a certain amount of controversy surrounding Ada. The major substantive criticisms are concerned with complexity, reliability, and real time processing.

There is no doubt that the language has many features, is very powerful, and is consequently more difficult to learn than most current languages. However, it is surely easier to learn than existing combinations of standard languages and multitasking operating systems. Furthermore, if not all features are required, then subsets may be defined by convention; that is, programming organizations using Ada may establish standards for the use of Ada which restrict normal use of certain features of the language. Such restrictions might be enforced by the use of preprocessors.

Questions concerning reliability arise in part because of the language's size and complexity and in part because some particular features of the language may interact in ways which may prove unreliable. For example, dynamic tasking and exceptions are in themselves complex, and it seems likely that using them in combination in an unrestricted fashion will produce programs whose correctness is difficult to guarantee.

Questions concerning Ada's capability to support real time interactions arise from the fact that the rendezvous mechanism is the only mechanism for interaction between concurrent system components. There are no explicit test-and-set or semaphorelike memory locks which can be used for efficient sharing of memory-based critical sections between concurrent components. The concern is that in an environment in which several tasks are running on a single processor, the forced overhead of task context switching to make a rendezvous places a limit on real time response. In the author's opinion, this is unlikely to be a significant problem in the long term. Intelligent compilers, aided perhaps by suitable pragmas, will be able to generate efficient code for particular environments.

An extreme, negative view of Ada as an implementation language is advanced by Hoare in his famous (or infamous) address to the ACM (Association of Computing Machinery), where he says that it should not be used for applications where human safety is at stake. This seems to the author to be an unfair criticism of a programming language, given the present state of the art in practice. Much more than merely the programming language is involved in ensuring the safety of a complex engineering system. In the final analysis, no matter what programming language is used, the safety of such systems depends on the foresight and competence of their designers and implementors in a wide variety of areas, of which software is only one. The programming language is simply a tool for implementing the software part of the system. As with all tools, it can be used poorly or well.

Used well, Ada seems likely to be a better software implementation tool than we have had previously. But the real advantage of Ada, in the author's opinion, is the contribution it makes to bringing system design and implementation closer together conceptually. Surely this can be expected to yield, in the hands of competent professionals, positive results with respect to system safety and reliability.

2.3.4 Conclusions

Ada's high-level concepts form an excellent basis for system design. Ada's high level of standardization and its expected wide dissemination provide further good reasons for using it for system design. Avoidance of details of the language inappropriate for design may be accomplished by following a design methodology based on a subset of Ada. The remainder of this book is concerned with presenting such a methodology, centering around the use of a graphical notation which captures the essential concepts of Ada while avoiding non-essential details.

Part B

Introduction
To Logical Design

In this part we first explore Ada system structures using graphical techniques. Then we describe an informal system design methodology and use it, together with our knowledge of system structures, to develop designs for three example systems which are simple enough to be relatively easy to follow but which nevertheless illustrate key issues.

Chapter 3

Design-Oriented,
Pictorial
System Description
Techniques

3.1 INTRODUCTION

Everyone knows that "a picture is worth a thousand words." Mathematicians know that a good notation may assist in suggesting solutions to problems. This chapter describes an approach to the description of system architectures which employs pictures and a good notation. The approach is based on the Ada language. However, only superficial knowledge of Ada is required to read this chapter, which introduces the concepts by analogy with familiar, nonprogramming examples. The description technique includes concurrency. However, the treatment of concurrency is tutorial in nature and should be accessible to readers without substantial background in concurrent system principles.

Section 3.2 provides a pictorial notation to describe system architectures. It includes a tutorial section on a dynamic metaphor for Ada tasking in terms of human activities and interactions (Section 3.2.2), which may be skipped by the advanced reader.

Section 3.3 develops a "parts kit" of canonical system structures using the pictorial notation of Section 3.2. It covers both sequential and concurrent systems. For concurrent systems it covers solutions to the basic problems of mutual exclusion, synchronization, scheduling and deadlock.

Section 3.4 reviews the relationship of the material of this chapter to Ada.

Section 3.5 provides conclusions.

3.2 INTRODUCTION TO PICTORIAL DESCRIPTIONS OF SYSTEM ARCHITECTURES

3.2.1 Pictorial Notation

Figure 3.1 provides the basic pictorial symbols: boxes represent packages and tasks; arrows represent access connections and data flow; and a special oval symbol represents data. It is also useful to have a special cloud symbol for a module whose nature has not yet been defined.

These symbols may be used to construct data flow graphs and/or structure graphs. Data flow graphs identify modules and show data flow interactions among them, without showing the control interactions. Structure graphs show both data flow and control interactions.

The major difference between packages and tasks is symbolized by the different way in which the boxes representing them are drawn. Packages are rectangles. To symbolize their parallel nature, tasks are parallelograms.

The symbols for packages and tasks indicate not only their differences but also their similarities. Boxes are used to symbolize the black-box nature of both packages and tasks. Smaller boxes at the edges are used to symbolize "sockets" which users may use to "plug into" the black boxes. Note that *sockets* is not an Ada term. The term is used to symbolize the common aspects of package and task interfaces. For both packages and tasks, plug compatibility is required. That is, users of packages or tasks as well as bodies of packages or tasks must meet the requirements of the interface specification defining the nature of the sockets.

An access connection from a user to either a package or a task is indicated by an arrow drawn from anywhere on the user box to the appropriate socket of the accessed box. Note that *access* here is a pictorial concept indicating a connection from one module to another. It does not imply use of access variables in the Ada sense.

In both cases, the interface specifications describe only how to connect *to* black boxes. Neither connections *from* black boxes nor identities of users are given in the interface specifications.

Connections to packages may be procedural or nonprocedural. Procedural connections indicate calls to ordinary procedures declared in the package specification. Nonprocedural connections indicate access to other internal aspects of a package, such as internal variables which are declared in the package specification.

Isolated procedures are depicted as rectangular boxes without sockets. They may be visualized as degenerate packages.

Sockets of tasks, known in Ada as entries, behave, from the user's viewpoint, very much like package procedures. Indeed, a task with an interface which is never accessed by more than one other task can be replaced functionally by a package, with procedures replacing the entries. Conversely, a package whose procedures may be accessed by more than one task in a non-overlapping fashion can be replaced functionally by a task, with entries replacing the procedures.

The significant difference between procedural access to packages and entry access

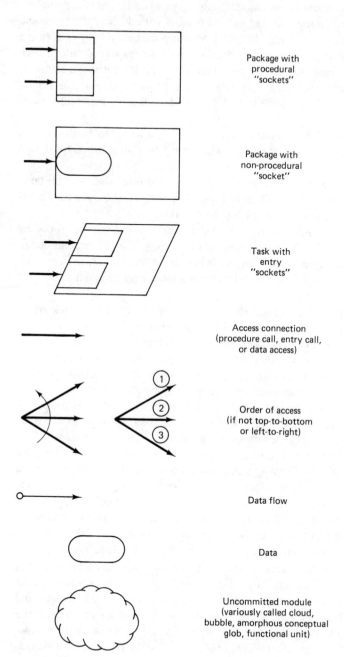

Package with
procedural
"sockets"

Package with
non-procedural
"socket"

Task with
entry
"sockets"

Access connection
(procedure call, entry call,
or data access)

Order of access
(if not top-to-bottom
or left-to-right)

Data flow

Data

Uncommitted module
(variously called cloud,
bubble, amorphous conceptual
glob, functional unit)

Figure 3.1 Basic pictorial conventions for describing architectures

to tasks lies, from the user's viewpoint, in mutual exclusivity and timing, not functionality. The rendezvous mechanism requires the calling task to *meet* with the accepting task and then wait while the accepting task services the call. If an accepting task is busy performing its own work or interacting with another task, then it cannot accept a new call. In such circumstances, new callers must wait in a queue associated with the entry. This ensures mutually exclusive processing of entry calls from different tasks. It also has timing implications for the caller, who may have to wait for an unpredictable length of time to return from the call.

The symbols of Figure 3.1 are not sufficient for all purposes. In particular, the rendezvous mechanism has a number of options which must be distinguished for design purposes by different symbols.

In what follows, the reader should assume, unless stated otherwise, that all tasks loop forever and never terminate. The calling and accepting patterns shown in the figures then may be interpreted as patterns for one cycle of the loop.

Figures 3.2 and 3.3 illustrate the various rendezvous options and the corresponding pictorial symbols. As illustrated by these figures, entry calls may be unconditional, conditional, or timed, and acceptances of entry calls may be in fixed order, in time order (first-come-first-served), or conditional. As well, the acceptor may time out if no calls occur for a predefined time interval.

With reference to Figure 3.2, we introduce a new symbol with a bent-back arrow to indicate refusal by a caller to wait indefinitely for acceptance. The refusal can take two forms. If no delay is permissible, then the call is said to be conditional, and an alternative action indicated by an *ELSE* statement must be specified. If a delay T is permissible, then the call is said to be timed, and the permissible delay T must be specified in an *OR* statement. In either case an alternative action may be performed.

As shown by Figure 3.3(a), entries accepted in fixed order are indicated pictorially either by an arrow drawn across the access arrows in the structure graph in the fixed order of acceptance or by numbering the arrows in that order. As shown by Figure 3.3(b), a set of entries accepted on a first-arrival basis (in other words in time order) by selective waiting is indicated pictorially by drawing a line around or across the corresponding set of entry sockets. As shown by Figure 3.3(c), entries ignored until a guard is cleared are indicated by a dot adjacent to the access arrow. As shown by Figure 3.3(d), the possibility of timeout from a selective wait condition is indicated by including a delay alternative, as a pseudo-entry socket in this task. Such an alternative is like another entry from the acceptor's point of view. It is effectively an entry called by the run-time system.

In Figure 3.3(b), the selective accept clause indicates that the acceptor task wishes to wait for the first entry call of any of entries A or B; if calls on A and B occur simultaneously, then one of them is to be picked at random. When a call is made and accepted, the rendezvous lasts until the acceptor reaches the END statement. This is the so-called *critical section*. Further processing may be performed by the acceptor relative to an entry after the end of the critical section but before leaving the selective wait clause.

With reference to Figure 3.3(b), it is essential to understand that waiting for an entry call in a selective wait clause is not *busy* waiting. The form of the selective wait

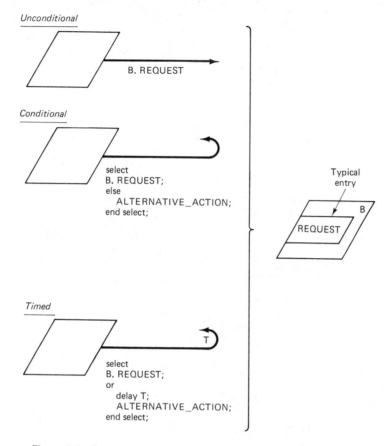

Figure 3.2 Structure graph symbols for different types of entry call

clause, with its list of select alternatives separated by *or*, can mislead the reader into thinking that these alternatives are tried one after the other in an iterative fashion until one is found on which a call is pending. Nothing could be further from the truth. In fact, the entire selective wait clause, with all its select alternatives, should be regarded as a primitive instruction to set up a compound waiting condition. During the waiting period, the accepting task is in a suspended state.

In Figure 3.3(c), the *WHEN* statement uses a guard variable X to defer acceptance of a call on entry A until X is true. In practice a guard will be cleared during processing of another entry in the same selective wait statement or as a result of an entry call to another task.

With reference to Figure 3.3(c), it is essential to understand that guards are set when the select clause is invoked and do not change dynamically while the task is waiting.

With reference to any of Figures 3.3(b)–(d), it is essential to understand that only one entry call is accepted in a single invocation of a selective waiting clause. After

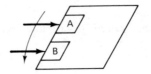

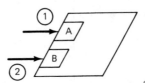

```
accept A; do . . . end; - - CRITICAL SECTION
OTHER_A_PROCESSING;
accept B; do . . . end; - - CRITICAL SECTION
OTHER_B_PROCESSING;
```

(a) *Fixed Order*

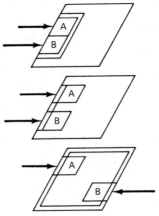

```
select
    accept A do . . . end; - - CRITICAL SECTION
    OTHER_A_PROCESSING;
or
    accept B do . . . end; - - CRITICAL SECTION
    OTHER_B_PROCESSING;
end select;
```

(b) *Time Order* (*Selective Waiting*)

Note:
Dots indicate
guards.
Annotated dots
indicate
entry-closed
condition.

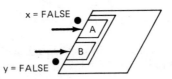

```
select
    when x = >
        accept A do . . . end; - - CRITICAL SECTION
        OTHER_A_PROCESSING;
or
    when y = >
        accept B do . . . end; - - CRITICAL SECTION
        OTHER_B_PROCESSING;
end select;
```

(c) *Conditional*

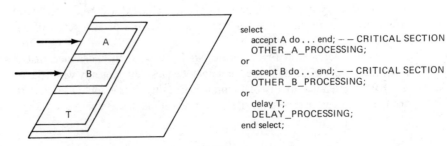

```
select
    accept A do . . . end; - - CRITICAL SECTION
    OTHER_A_PROCESSING;
or
    accept B do . . . end; - - CRITICAL SECTION
    OTHER_B_PROCESSING;
or
    delay T;
    DELAY_PROCESSING;
end select;
```

(d) *Timeout*

processing this entry, the acceptor will typically invoke the clause again to wait for another entry call, on the next cycle through its infinite loop.

It will be useful to distinguish the types of delays which can occur in task interactions as follows:

1. A calling or accepting task may experience *structural delays* resulting from either fixed order of acceptance or conditional acceptance. Structural delays depend on the structure of the interactions between tasks. The possibility of their occurrence is visible in the structure graph.

2. A calling task may experience *congestion delays* due to entry queueing. Congestion delays depend on the number of tasks calling a single acceptor and on the frequency of their calls. The possibility of congestion delays is thus also visible in the structure graph.

3. A calling or accepting task may experience latency delays, even in the absence of structural delays or congestion delays. This may occur either because the accepting task has not yet reached the point in its internal logic where it accepts an entry which has already been called or because the calling task has not yet reached the point in its internal logic where it calls an entry which has already been accepted. Latency delays must be assumed to be small in any sensibly designed system. Their nature is not visible in the system structure graph.

Figure 3.4 illustrates how some of these symbols may be used to depict systems. Figure 3.4(a) is a *data flow graph,* which shows only data flow between modules. It does not show access connections. It may include any of the module types of Figure 3.1.

Figure 3.4(b) is a *structure graph,* which shows the actual access connections between modules. A structure graph also shows the data flow between modules. It presents a static picture of the structure of the system, including both control and data interactions. It also gives some information about the sequencing of interactions.

To a large extent, packages and tasks may be freely interconnected and nested as illustrated by Figure 3.5. Care must be taken to ensure that where a package is accessed by more than one task, the tasks will not interfere with each other. This is a design problem covered in Section 3.2.

As illustrated by Figure 3.5, it is useful to distinguish between *passive* and *active* packages. A passive package contains no nested tasks. An active package contains nested tasks, which may be hidden by the package interface specification.

Our pictorial notation provides a hardwarelike metaphor for systems as collections of black boxes connected together by plugs and sockets. However, this is primarily a static metaphor, helpful mainly for visualizing relationships.

Figure 3.3 Structure graph symbols for different types of entry acceptance (*note:* Dots indicate guards. Annotated dots indicate entry-closed condition.)

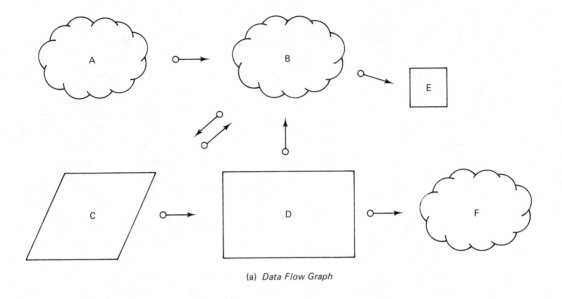

(a) *Data Flow Graph*

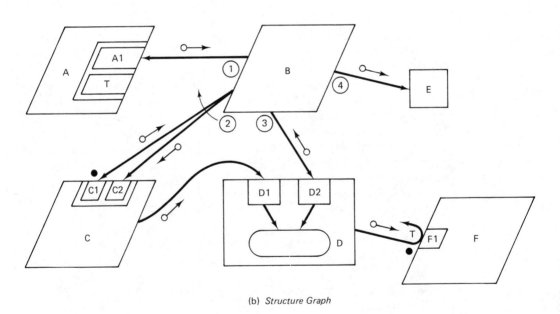

(b) *Structure Graph*

Figure 3.4 Examples of use of pictorial notation

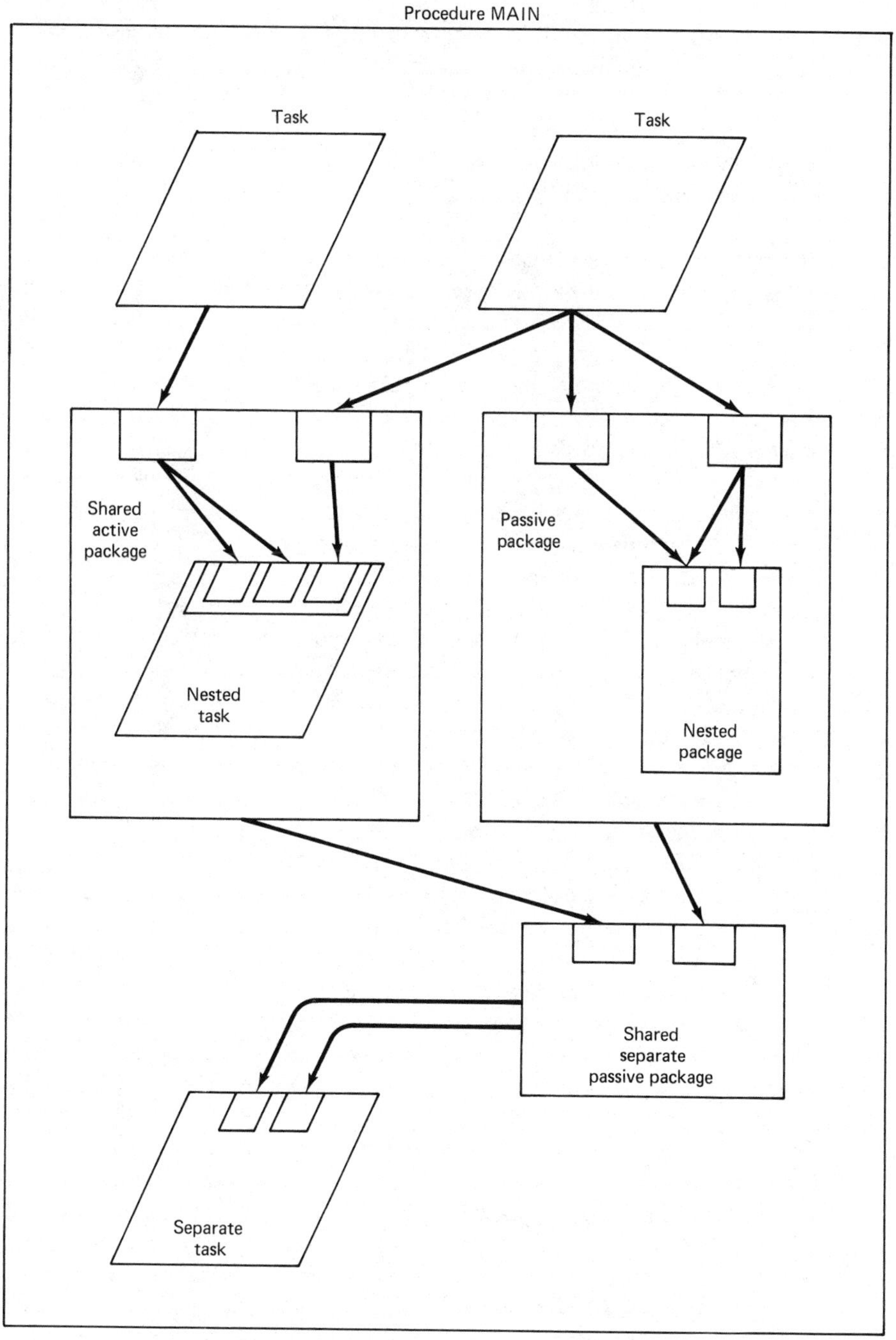

Figure 3.5 Nested, separate, and shared packages and tasks

A dynamic metaphor of system operation is required for visualizing operation of the system as a dynamic entity with possible concurrent activities. This requirement is addressed in Section 3.2.2, following.

3.2.2 Dynamic Metaphor of Ada Tasking: Human Interactions

Our purpose here is to assist the reader in harnessing his or her intuition about human interactions and organizations to develop a dynamic metaphor of Ada tasking.

Think of the structure graph of a system as describing the static, physical structure of a business office. People in offices are connected by corridors and doorways. People correspond to tasks. Corridors correspond to access connections. Offices with their doorways correspond to interfaces of tasks or active packages. Walking down a corridor to another office corresponds to a task entry call or an active package procedure call. Waiting outside the office for service and then receiving service corresponds to the rendezvous mechanism. Using a passive resource such as a dictaphone, word processor, or filing cabinet corresponds to accessing a passive package.

A small portion of the structure of a business office is depicted by the structure graph of Figure 3.6. Figure 3.6(a) provides an informal view, using stick figures for people, and Figure 3.6(b) provides a corresponding Ada view. This graph shows an incomplete set of possible access and rendezvous relationships among several persons (tasks) and passive black boxes (passive packages) in a typical office environment. Note that this structure is not necessarily a good one; it is simply one of many possible structures. Shown are five persons: the vice president, two managers, a secretary, and an assistant to one of the managers. Also shown are three passive black boxes, all of which are filing cabinets in this particular example. Because, in the sense we shall be developing it, the analogy between black boxes and packages and between persons and tasks is exact, for clarity we shall henceforth refer only to packages and tasks. We shall now proceed to describe the relationships in this figure informally.

First consider the vice-president task. He accesses his private filing cabinet at his own pleasure without any need to coordinate this access with any other task. He may also choose to access a more public filing cabinet, such as the company personnel file, and then perform a rendezvous with one of his managers to hand over control of that file to the manager. The access arrow from the vice-president task to the personnel manager indicates a visit by the vice president to the personnel manager's office to make a rendezvous. Here the rendezvous is used to request the acceptor to perform a service on behalf of the caller. The caller names the service requested, in this case *process personnel file,* and may also pass parameters to the acceptor such as the name of the person whose file is to be processed and the type of processing required. In general a rendezvous may be used to pass parameters and data in either direction. While a rendezvous is in progress, the caller waits, and either task may have to wait for the rendezvous to commence. For example, the vice-president may have to wait for the manager to accept his request, or the manager, who may be expecting a request from the vice-president, may have to wait for his request to arrive before it can be accepted.

In this particular example, the vice-president task accesses three modules, namely

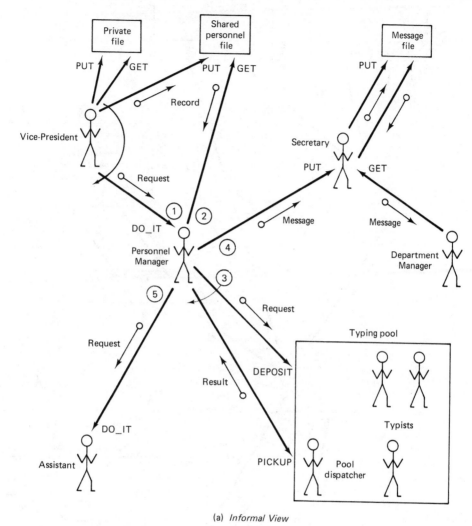

(a) *Informal View*

Figure 3.6 Partial structure graph of an office

two passive packages and one task. The structure diagram can give considerable information on the time ordering of these accesses as shown.

An Ada program skeleton for the vice-president task is given in Figure 3.7. The term *skeleton* implies that only the major logical features of the program are given, omitting details. Program skeletons of this kind are sometimes useful design and specification tools. Note in this case, however, how the information contained in the program skeleton is also contained in more compact form in the structure graph.

Now consider the personnel manager. He waits for a call from the vice-president and then processes the named personnel record. Interactions of the type depicted here which involve a shared package are tricky in programming terms, as they are in real life, because control over the shared package must be very carefully handed over from task

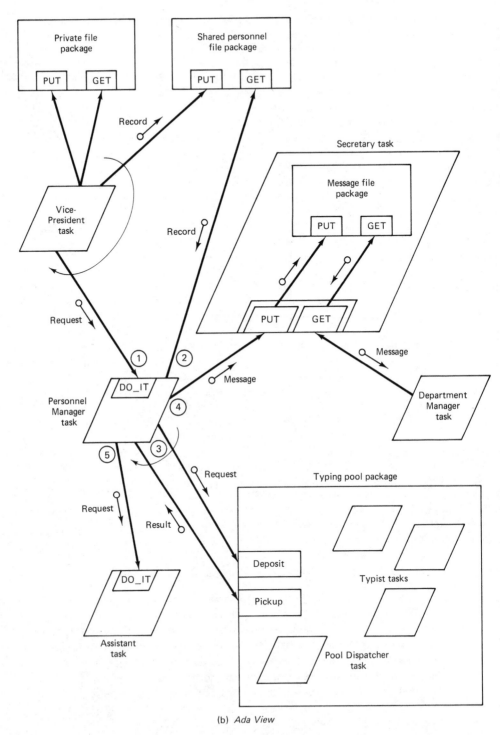

(b) *Ada View*

Figure 3.6 (continued)

```
task body VICE__PRESIDENT is
  . . .
begin
  loop
    . . .
    PRIVATE__FILE.GET ( . . . );
    . . .
    PRIVATE___FILE.PUT ( . . . );
    . . .
    PERSONNEL__FILE.PUT ( . . . );
    PERSONNEL__MANAGER.DO__IT ( . . . );
    . . .
  end loop;
end VICE__PRESIDENT;
```

Figure 3.7   Ada program skeleton for the vice-president task

to task. For example, the vice-president must be careful not to modify the particular record in the personnel file after he has asked the personnel manager to process it and before the personnel manager has informed him that the work is done.

To process the file, suppose the personnel manager has the following operations to perform: he must pick up the designated record, have a report typed based on the record, pass the report to the manager of the department concerned, and request his own assistant to keep track of further developments. He may be happy to interact directly with the typing pool and with his assistant, knowing they will not keep him waiting, but direct interaction with the departmental manager, who is not always available, may be inconvenient. Therefore he may decide instead to perform a rendezvous with a secretary to deposit a message for the departmental manager. Whether the departmental manager performs a rendezvous with the secretary to pick up messages before the message is deposited or after the message is deposited does not matter to the personnel manager; in either case, the personnel manager expects that the message will get there eventually.

An Ada program skeleton for the personnel manager task is given in Figure 3.8.

The secretary performs message-drop services for a number of managers depositing these messages in a message file as they arrive from some managers and handing them over to other managers as they are requested. The secretary initiates no rendezvous but participates in a number of rendezvous by accepting calls for service.

An Ada program skeleton for the secretary task is given in Figure 3.9.

The assistant to the personnel manager simply waits for orders from the personnel manager and then executes these orders. This execution is not shown.

The departmental manager picks up messages from the secretary by initiating rendezvous with the secretary and then performs his own functions not shown in the structure diagram.

Consider now the interaction of the personnel manager and the typing pool. The personnel manager needs to be able to assign typing of the report to any free typist in

```
task PERSONNEL__MANAGER is
  entry DO__IT( . . . );
end PERSONNEL__MANAGER;

task body PERSONNEL__MANAGER is
  . . .
begin
  loop
    . . .
    accept DO__IT ( . . . ) do . . . end;
    PERSONNEL__FILE.GET ( . . . );
    . . .
    TYPING__POOL.DEPOSIT ( . . . );
    . . .
    TYPING__POOL.PICKUP ( . . . );
    SECRETARY.PUT ( . . . );
    ASSISTANT.DO__IT ( . . . );
    . . .
  end loop;

end PERSONNEL__MANAGER;
```

Figure 3.8 Ada program skeleton for the personnel manager task

```
task SECRETARY is
  entry PUT ( . . . );
  entry GET ( . . . );
end SECRETARY;

task body SECRETARY is
  . . .
begin
  loop
    . . .
    select
      accept PUT ( . . . ) do . . . end;
    or
      accept GET ( . . . ) do . . . end;
    end select;
    . . .
  end loop;

end SECRETARY;
```

Figure 3.9 Ada program skeleton for the secretary task

the pool. Similarly, free typists in the pool need to be able to signify their readiness to do work for users of the pool. There are two approaches to these types of interactions in human organizations:

- third party coordination by another person, acting as a dispatcher for the pool, or
- direct multiway interactions between the multiple persons in the pool and the multiple potential users.

Third-party coordination is easy to describe. The clients and the typists both rendezvous with a pool dispatcher who accepts typing requests and allocates work to free typists. The dispatcher and typists are together regarded by users as a resource with its own office. This resource is an analogy for an active package.

Direct multiway interactions between users of the typing pool and the typists in the pool are more complex to describe. In human terms, a user may walk into the pool and, in effect, broadcast a request to all typists in the pool. This may be done by shouting, ringing a bell, visual scanning and making eye-to-eye contact, or other similar means. If there are many free typists, they will require a method of agreeing among themselves who will volunteer to perform the service. Alternatively, they may all volunteer, and the user will accept one and reject or ignore the rest. In the latter case, typists not explicitly rejected will have to recognize that they have been ignored. If the pool is very busy, then many users may be waiting for service, and a method for matching users to typists is required.

Clearly, the Ada rendezvous mechanism provides a good metaphor for systems as groups of persons interacting on a one-to-one basis. Multiway interactions must be reduced to sets of one-to-one interactions to be described in rendezvous terms. Third-party coordination of multiway interactions is directly and easily described in this way; direct multiway interaction is not.

There are two ways of looking at Ada's restriction to one-to-one interactions between tasks:

- as a welcome application of the KISS (Keep It Simple Stupid) principle, or
- as a limitation.

On the one hand, if Ada provided a mechanism by which a rendezvous could occur with any free member of a selected pool of tasks, then the multiway direct interaction could be more simply described in Ada. There would need to be a method for queueing multiple tasks wishing to avail themselves of this mechanism for the same pool. On the other hand, as was discussed earlier, such a mechanism can be easily specified in Ada by packaging a number of worker tasks and a dispatcher task to form such a pool. Thus there do not appear to be any limitations imposed on design freedom by the one-to-one nature of the rendezvous mechanism.

We defer the detailed consideration of structure graphs and program organizations for active packages and for pools of tasks until Section 3.3.

The relationships shown by the structure graph of Figure 3.4 and the program skeletons of Figure 3.5, although incomplete, are representative both of real operations in an office and of interactions between program modules in an Ada program. There are a number of aspects omitted from this particular example diagram which give rise to further questions. For example, how, later on, can the vice-president check or be notified that the correct action has been performed? This question and others like it lead, in programming terms as in real life, to a need for multiple rendezvous between the vice-president and the personnel manager and, indeed, between other tasks in the structure diagram. However, we shall leave these questions to Section 3.3.

We now need to examine the rendezvous mechanism in more detail.

3.2.3 Human-Interaction Metaphor for the Ada
Rendezvous Mechanism

A metaphor for the rendezvous mechanism in human interaction terms for the simplest type of rendezvous is illustrated in Figure 3.10. The caller leaves his office and goes to the acceptor's office, where he finds the acceptor's door open. He gives a request *form* providing the nature and parameters of the request to the acceptor and then goes to sleep outside the acceptor's office. The acceptor, who has been waiting for a call with his door open, accepts the request form and processes the request while the caller is asleep. At the end of the rendezvous, the acceptor reopens his door and awakens the caller, who then returns to his office.

Life is not always as simple as in Figure 3.10 and in general, either the acceptor must wait with his door open for a call, or the caller must wait outside the closed door for acceptance before rendezvous can begin. Figure 3.11 illustrates both of these cases. In either case the progress of the rendezvous after it begins is the same as shown in Figure 3.10.

Figure 3.12 illustrates the general case. Multiple callers queue in first-in-first-out (FIFO) order outside the acceptor's door (multiple doors symbolize multiple entries). In Ada terms there is a separate entry queue for each entry, organized in first-in-first-out order. Not all doors may be open while the acceptor is waiting; closed doors correspond to closed entries (closed by guards).

Where no parameters are associated with the call of an entry, it is appropriate to think of each request form as simply a token to indicate that the service provided by that entry is required. In general terms, the request form includes input parameters and a tear-off sheet containing spaces to fill in returned parameters. The caller picks up this tear-off sheet from the acceptor before walking away from the rendezvous.

An acceptor may close his door again immediately after terminating a rendezvous, even if someone is waiting outside the door, in order to finish processing the request associated with the terminated rendezvous, or to perform other internal actions.

Structural delays are experienced by callers when a door is closed even when the acceptor is not busy and other doors are open. Congestion delays are experienced when a queue forms in front of a door which the acceptor is servicing as fast as possible. Latency delays are experienced when all doors are closed while the acceptor performs

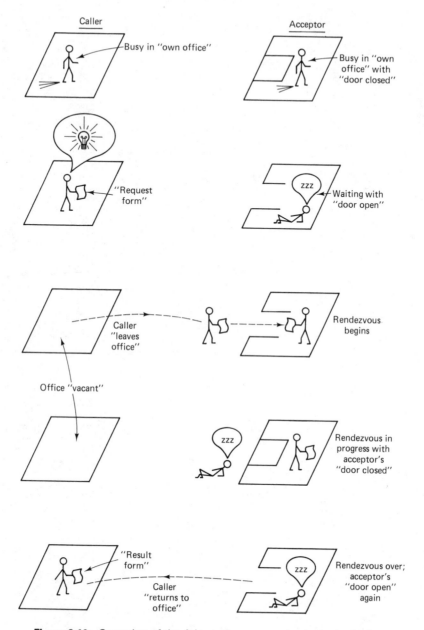

Figure 3.10 Operation of the Ada rendezvous mechanism: simplest case

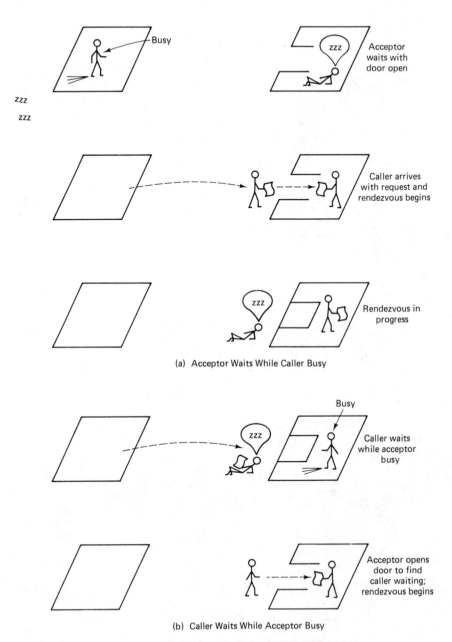

(a) Acceptor Waits While Caller Busy

(b) Caller Waits While Acceptor Busy

Figure 3.11 Some rendezvous examples

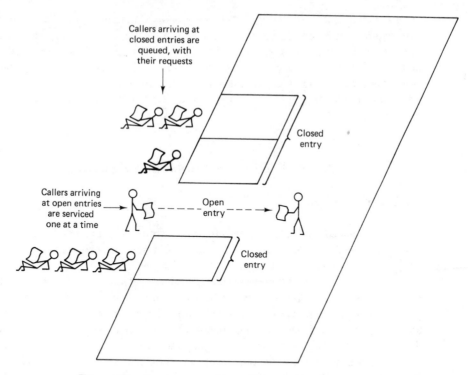

Callers arriving at closed entries are queued, with their requests

Closed entry

Callers arriving at open entries are serviced one at a time

Open entry

Closed entry

Figure 3.12   Rendezvous with multiple-entry queues and guards

his own internal work even though no guards are set. Note that an acceptor's own internal work might require him to visit other offices. Therefore, when a door is closed, the acceptor might not even be in his office.

Thus, visits to other offices may waste time in unpredictable ways. And while absent from his own office, a person may miss important events. Other things being equal, a person in an office will usually prefer to interact with other persons by being visited rather than by making visits. Then there is never any need to waste time waiting for other persons unless there is nothing else to do.

Obviously, this selfish viewpoint would result in no interactions at all if every task adopted it. As we shall see, in Section 3.3, the problems of designing interaction structures for interacting tasks center around deciding which tasks have roles which require minimal interference with their other work. Only in the simplest systems is the rendezvous direction unimportant; for example, if two tasks interact only with each other then it is not important who calls whom.

As a final remark on the rendezvous mechanism, any impression that may have been formed that a rendezvous restricts callers and acceptors from concurrent activities while the acceptor is servicing a request made by an entry call should be dispelled. The restriction on concurrency exists only during the actual rendezvous when the entry call itself is being processed. A rendezvous may be used simply to deposit a request which may require further processing by the acceptor after the rendezvous has terminated. An example is the rendezvous performed by the vice-president with the personnel manager in Figure 3.6, to hand over a file for processing. The vice-president may continue to work independently after the rendezvous has terminated, while the personnel manager processes the file. In this case, the rendezvous itself is used only to pass the request to process the file.

3.3 DEVELOPING A PARTS KIT OF CANONICAL ARCHITECTURES

3.3.1 Introduction

Having introduced tasks and packages from an informal viewpoint and having considered a few examples of their use, we now proceed to a more general viewpoint in which we present and classify various ways of structuring parts of systems using these building blocks. A goal of this section is to develop a basic set (or *parts kit*) of canonical, structured system parts. Various types of canonical parts are obviously possible, and our concern here is to classify these types, discuss their properties, and provide guidelines for selecting appropriate types for particular circumstances. Note that the term *type* in this context does not mean *data type* in the Ada language sense.

Because most of the problems arise in concurrent systems, the concern here will be mainly with concurrent systems.

First, we need a few definitions.

System parts may be composed of tasks of the following functional types:

1. *Slave:* a task which interacts with only one other task (called its master) to receive work to do; may call its master to get the work and to report on its completion or vice versa; may also be assigned by its master to perform work for others.
2. *Server:* a task which performs services in response to calls from a number of user tasks; never calls other tasks, either autonomously or in response to requests; has no control over other tasks; always accepts calls immediately, subject only to the usual constraint of accepting one caller at a time.
3. *Scheduler:* a task whose only purpose is to delay the acceptance of calls on particular entries, subject to prevailing conditions.
4. *Buffer:* a combined server/scheduler used for deposit and pickup of items.
5. *Secretary:* a task with greater autonomy than a server/scheduler, which not only provides services and performs scheduling, but also makes calls to other tasks to report results.
6. *Agent:* an autonomous task which not only performs as server, scheduler, and secretary, but also does its own work involving autonomous calls to other tasks

(note that, in these terms, many so-called *secretaries* in human organizations are actually *agents*).

7. *Transporter (or messenger):* a task whose purpose is to transport items between other tasks; makes calls to other tasks to pick up and deliver items but has no other control over the activities of other tasks.

8. *Users, managers, etc.:* autonomous tasks which interact with tasks of the other types to perform some overall system function.

We have seen that tasks may be grouped into functional units in active packages, just as persons in human organizations may be grouped into functional units in offices. Such active packages behave in many ways like tasks and, like tasks, may be classified into the same functional types as above. Thus system parts may be composed not only of tasks, but also of active packages of these functional types.

Tasks and active packages may also be usefully classified according to the directions of their data and control interactions with other tasks and active packages. Such a classification is provided in Figure 3.13.

With respect to data interactions, a module (task or active package) may be classified as a *sender* or a *target* (or both). With respect to control interactions, a module may be classified as a *caller* or an *acceptor* (or both). For example, an item may be passed from a caller-sender to an acceptor-target via a call in the direction of the data flow. Alternatively, an item may be passed from an acceptor-sender to a caller-target by a call in the opposite direction to the data flow. It may sometimes be convenient to use the term *middle-man* to denote modules which are both senders and targets or both callers and acceptors.

Let us now consider some basic types of system architectures involving packages and tasks.

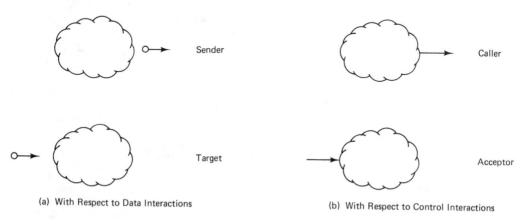

(a) With Respect to Data Interactions

(b) With Respect to Control Interactions

Figure 3.13 Classification of system modules with respect to directions of both data and control interactions with other modules

3.3.2 Architectures Involving Shared Packages

Sequential system structures involving passive packages were briefly discussed in Section 3.2. Such structures present few technical or conceptual difficulties, and accordingly, further discussion of them will be postponed until we discuss design examples in subsequent chapters.

Consider now the interaction of many tasks with a shared passive package; such interaction presents coordination problems which may be solved as shown in Figure 3.14. This figure uses the STACK package of Chapter 2 as a convenient example of a package whose visible procedures access shared internal data. Whether or not a stack would be shared in practice between many tasks is irrelevant to the points we wish to make here. The figure illustrates both structure graphs and program skeletons for the major components of the structure graphs.

Several tasks may share a package without further coordination if the package procedures are reentrant and there is no shared internal data or if the package provides read-only access to shared internal data as shown in Figure 3.14(a). Uncoordinated sharing is also possible if timing conditions in the system ensure that calls to the package can

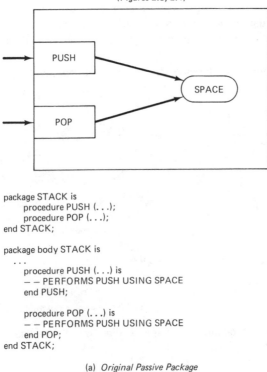

Original passive
stack package
(Figures 2.3, 2.4)

PUSH

SPACE

POP

```
package STACK is
     procedure PUSH (. . .);
     procedure POP (. . .);
end STACK;

package body STACK is

   . . .
     procedure PUSH (. . .) is
     − −PERFORMS PUSH USING SPACE
     end PUSH;

     procedure POP (. . .) is
     − −PERFORMS PUSH USING SPACE
     end POP;
end STACK;
```

(a) *Original Passive Package*

Figure 3.14 Shared packages: stack example

never overlap; however, this approach is unsafe in general, because timing conditions may change with time. Otherwise some coordination is required.

One form of coordination, shown in Figure 3.14(b), is to change the package into a server task whose entries provide the same services as the procedures of the original package.

Another approach, shown in Figures 3.14(c) and 3.14(d), is to change the package into an active one with a nested scheduler task to enforce mutual exclusion.

A final approach, shown in Figure 3.14(e), is to leave the original package untouched and to use a separate scheduler task which allocates the package to user tasks as required; the user tasks must agree that they will use the package only after calling the scheduler.

Is one of the solutions of Figure 3.14 preferred? The solution of Figure 3.14(b), which uses a single server task, is attractive because it combines intuitive clarity with safety. The solution of Figure 3.14(c) is attractive because it preserves the facade of the original package. Finally, Figure 3.14(e) provides a more complicated interface to user

```
task STACK is
    entry PUSH (. . .);
    entry POP (. . .);
end STACK;


task body STACK is

    . . .
    procedure INTERNAL_PUSH is
    - - PERFORMS PUSH USING SPACE
    end INTERNAL_PUSH;

    procedure INTERNAL_POP is
    - - PERFORMS POP USING SPACE
    end INTERNAL_POP;

begin
  loop
    select
      accept PUSH (. . .) do INTERNAL_PUSH; end;
    or
      accept POP (. . .) do INTERNAL_POP; end;
    end select;
  end loop;
end STACK;
```

(b) *Equivalent Task*

Figure 3.14 (continued)

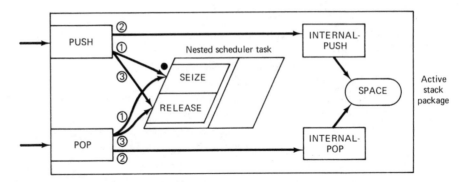

(c) *Equivalent Active Package*

Figure 3.14   (continued)

tasks than seems desirable and is potentially unsafe because of the lack of direct protection of the package contents from use by unauthorized tasks.

3.3.3 One-Way Interaction Architectures

In preparation for the data-flow-based design technique used in subsequent chapters, the development of appropriate architectures for canonical system parts in this and subsequent sections of this chapter is based on data flow.

```
separate (STACK)
task body SCHEDULER is
  BUSY : boolean := FALSE;
    begin
      loop
        select
          when not BUSY =>
            accept SEIZE
            do BUSY := TRUE; end;
        or
          accept RELEASE
          do BUSY := FALSE; end;
        end select;
      end loop;
end SCHEDULER;
```

(d) *Scheduler Task*

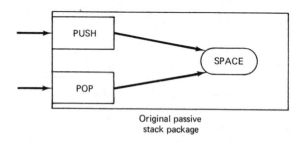

Original passive
stack package

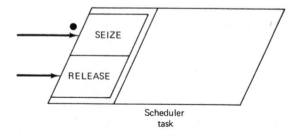

Scheduler
task

(e) *System with Original Package Unchanged — Users Must Schedule
Themselves using the Scheduler Task*   **Figure 3.14**   (continued)

Consider how tasks may interact to pass items (requests or data) in one direction. We have seen several examples of such direct interactions in Figure 3.4. In such inter-actions, the item being passed may flow in the direction of the rendezvous or in the opposite direction. For example, in Figure 3.4, the request from the vice-president to the personnel manager flows in the direction of the rendezvous, but the message from the secretary to the department manager flows in the opposite direction.

In Section 3.2.3, several types of delays in task interactions were distinguished. In considering the performance characteristics of various candidates for our parts kit of interaction architectures in this chapter, we shall be concerned mainly with structural delays; that is, those which involve conditional waiting.

Structural delays have the interesting property that their average duration tends to increase with decreasing interaction activity and vice versa (interaction activity measures the rate of flow of items between pairs of tasks). For example, when a task is waiting for an item, the average length of time it must wait is inversely dependent on the average rate of flow of items. Thus a high level of interaction activity may reduce structural delays effectively to zero. It follows that different interaction structures may be appropriate for different levels of activity.

The possibility of congestion delays will affect our thinking in this chapter only through the principle stated earlier that a busy task will always prefer to act as an acceptor rather than a caller in its interactions with other tasks. One reason for this preference is that a call to another busy task risks a congestion delay.

Following the discussion of Section 3.2.3, we shall ignore the possibility of latency delays.

Suppose a single sender task wishes to send something to a single target task as shown in Figure 3.15(a). Then two main possibilities are clearly apparent: the sender may send it via an unconditionally accepted call directed to an acceptor target, as shown in Figure 3.15(b), or a caller target may request it via a conditionally accepted call directed to the sender, as shown in Figure 3.15(c). Clearly the first approach will be preferable to the target and the second to the sender; no choice can be made without further information.

The further information that is needed is the nature of the roles of the two tasks in a system context. If two tasks interact only with each other via a single rendezvous, then the direction of the rendezvous is unimportant. If, however, the sending task has other interactions (for example, due to its role as a server, scheduler, buffer, secretary, or agent), so that unnecessary interference is intolerable, then configuring the target task as a caller as in Figure 3.15(c) is preferable. In these circumstances, the target task must be prepared to put up with postponing its other work while waiting for the sender to accept its call.

If the target task cannot afford to do this and interaction activity is low, then this configuration is unsatisfactory. On the other hand configuring the target task as an acceptor, as in Figure 3.15(b), ensures minimal interference with its other activities but may be unacceptable to the sender.

If neither the sender nor the target can tolerate interference with their activities, then a solution is to use a *transport* task, as shown in Figure 3.15(d). The figure shows this structure as appropriate for communication between tasks which also have other entries, so that the entry called by the transport task may be included within a single selective accept clause in the called task.

A transport task may be regarded as the target's stand-in or partner, which does the target's waiting for it.

Because a transport task calls both the sender and target instead of them calling it, it provides minimal interference with their other activities, and by definition it has no

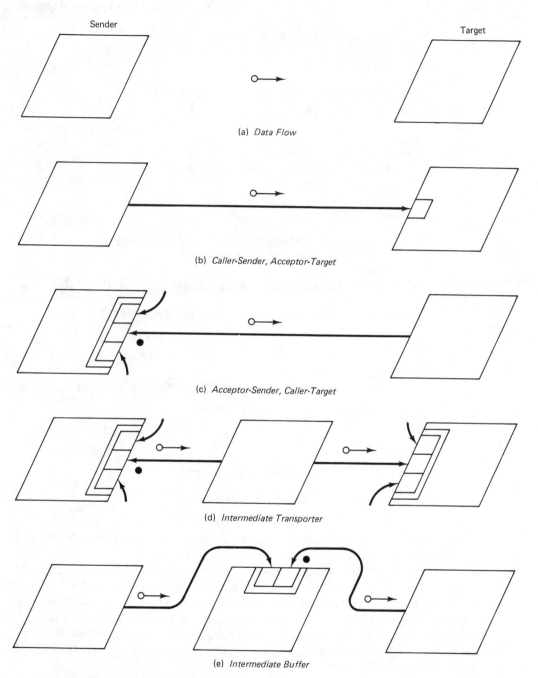

Sender

Target

(a) *Data Flow*

(b) *Caller-Sender, Acceptor-Target*

(c) *Acceptor-Sender, Caller-Target*

(d) *Intermediate Transporter*

(e) *Intermediate Buffer*

Figure 3.15 Canonical structures for one-way interaction between a pair of tasks

```
— —A TRANSPORT TASK HAS NO ENTRIES
task TRANSPORTER is
end TRANSPORTER;

— — A TRANSPORT TASK FOLLOWS A GET-PUT CYCLE
task body TRANSPORTER is

  begin
    loop
      SENDER.GET (ITEM); — —CONDITIONAL WAIT
      TARGET.PUT (ITEM);
    end loop;
  end TRANSPORTER

— —SENDERS AND TARGETS USUALLY HAVE MANY ENTRIES
— —OTHERWISE WHY USE A TRANSPORT TASK?
task SENDER is
  — —ENTRIES GROUPED INTO A SINGLE SELECTIVE WAIT STATEMENT
  . . .
  entry GET (ITEM : out ITEM_TYPE); — —CONDITIONAL WAIT
  . . .
end SENDER

task TARGET is
  — — ENTRIES GROUPED INTO A SINGLE SELECTIVE WAIT STATEMENT
  . . .
  entry PUT (ITEM : in ITEM_TYPE);
  . . .
end TARGET;
```

(f) *A Transport Task Example*

Figure 3.15   (continued)

other activities to be interfered with, so it can afford to wait. This solution is often one that is adopted in human organizations in similar circumstances.

For high levels of interaction activity, the transport task of Figure 3.15(d) will seldom or never have to wait for items. A possible approach in this case is to eliminate guards and have the transport task operate on a fixed schedule. It may do so by delaying itself on each cycle of its infinite loop. Note also that for high levels of interaction activity, the sender may need buffer storage for items being produced at a higher rate than they can be picked up by the transport task. For this case, the transport task may be designed to carry more than one item.

As shown in Figure 3.15(e), an alternative approach for high levels of interaction activity is to provide a buffer task between the sender and target which can handle any temporary excess of items produced by the sender, thus, removing the need for buffer storage from the sending task. This will be an appropriate solution only if the target task interacts with other tasks only through the buffer task. We shall have more to say on this later.

A buffer task was illustrated by an Ada program example in Chapter 2.

An Ada program skeleton showing the typical interactions of a sender and target task via a transport task is provided in Figure 3.15(f). Note the assumption that the entries called by the transport task are members of a selective wait group at either end.

What if several tasks may send something, as shown in Figure 3.16(a)? Again, two main choices for direct interaction are possible, with the target task as a caller, as shown

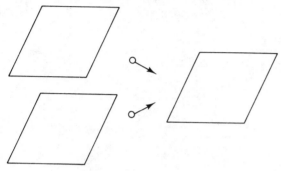

(a) *Data Flow — Many Senders, One Target*

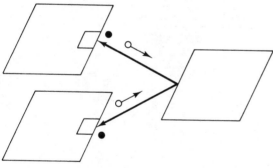

(b) *Acceptor-Sender, Caller-Target*

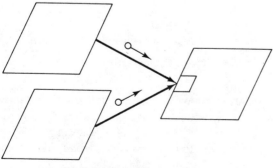

(c) *Caller-Sender, Acceptor-Target*

Figure 3.16 Direct, one-way interaction involving many tasks

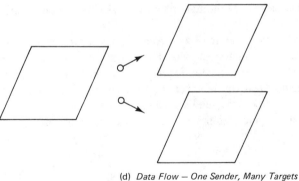

(d)　*Data Flow — One Sender, Many Targets*

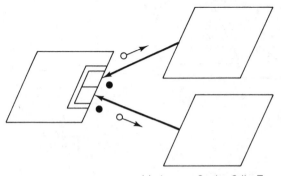

(e)　*Acceptor-Sender, Caller-Target*

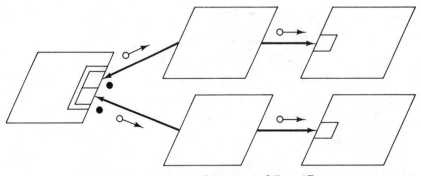

(f)　*As for* (e)　*with Transport Tasks between Caller and Target*

Figure 3.16　(continued)

in Figure 3.16(b), or as an acceptor, as shown in Figure 3.16(c). Unlike Figure 3.15, there is a clear difference between the acceptor and caller approaches even when further information about the roles of the tasks in a system context is not available. A caller target task must choose which sending task to call, and once it has made the choice, it is stuck with it until the called task has something for it; in the meantime an item may come along from another sending task which it could pick up if it wasn't waiting elsewhere. Furthermore, it must know all its senders.

On the other hand an acceptor target task may pick up the first call from any sender, as shown in Figure 3.16(c), and it does not need to know all its senders. Therefore it seems wise to configure the target as an acceptor in these circumstances with a proviso that senders must not be made to wait unnecessarily due to other activities of the target task.

However, if the target task is configured as an acceptor, as recommended above, and if it is often otherwise occupied so that it is not always able to accept the entry calls in question quickly, then all senders may be unnecessarily blocked, waiting for a rendezvous. In these circumstances, neither of the approaches of Figure 3.16(b) or 3.16(c) is satisfactory.

Now consider the circumstances of Figure 3.16(d), where one task sends to many targets. If the targets are acceptors, then problems arise similar to those of Figure 3.16(b). In these circumstances it is better to configure the target tasks as callers and the sender as an acceptor, as shown in Figure 3.16(c). The sender needs an entry for each target so that it can apply guards appropriately to force targets to wait when it has nothing for them. This approach assumes that the target tasks can afford to wait in the sender's entry queues. If not, then a transport task must be introduced between the sender and each of its targets, as in Figure 3.16(f).

Of course, the problems of unnecessary delays either in picking up items sent or in unblocking senders in both Figures 3.15 and 3.16 can be solved by using conditional or timed calls. However, the calling tasks must be prepared to retry failed calls. They may also have to resort to polling a number of tasks before a successful call is made. This is a messy solution when a clean mechanism for selective waiting is available, as it is in Ada. Programs with retry and polling will tend to be both more logically complex and less efficient than programs without it.

What if there are many senders and many targets? Then a solution is to introduce one or more buffer tasks, as shown in Figure 3.17.

The buffer task of Figure 3.17(b) has a single SEND entry for all senders and a RECEIVE entry for each target. It is configured as an acceptor. It is not configured as a caller or a middleman for the following reasons. The caller choice can be rejected immediately for the same reasons as for Figure 3.16(b) when there is more than one sender. Configuring it as a middleman in the direction of data flow has the undesirable effect that it must decide when to attempt to rendezvous with each target task. If a target is otherwise occupied at the chosen time, then unnecessary, indirect blocking of sending tasks may occur. A way around this problem is to poll the targets using a conditional or timed entry call. However, as discussed previously, polling is undesirable and should be avoided. Configuring it as a middleman in the opposite direction to the data flow is also undesirable, for the same reasons that the caller choice was rejected in Figure 3.16(b).

Note that the approach of Figure 3.17(b) for providing a receive entry for each target is suitable only when all targets are well known. Otherwise, a single entry without conditional waiting may be used (implying that callers may have to keep trying).

The solution of Figure 3.17(b) assumes that the target tasks do not have to worry

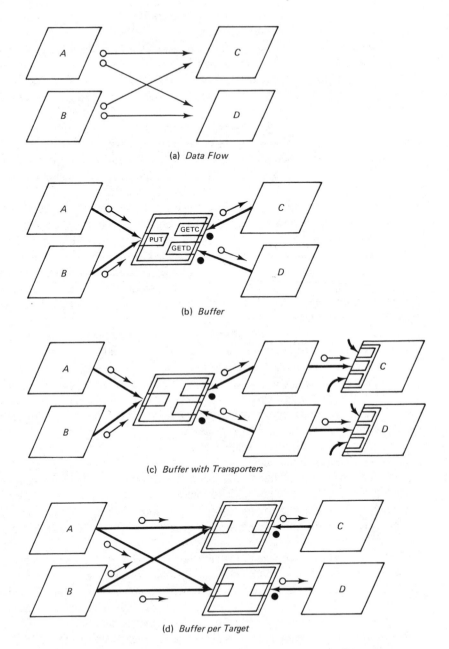

(a) *Data Flow*

(b) *Buffer*

(c) *Buffer with Transporters*

(d) *Buffer per Target*

Figure 3.17 Indirect, many-many interactions using a buffer task

about missing other events while waiting in the buffer's entry queue. The assumption will be valid if the targets have no entries of their own.

To provide more flexibility, a transport task can be used between the buffer and each of its targets, as shown in Figure 3.17(c). This allows the target tasks to wait for other entry calls while the transport tasks are waiting for items to arrive at the buffer task. This solution is a generalization of that of Figure 3.13(d).

A solution with more tasks than Figure 3.17(b), but with desirable modularity properties, is shown in Figure 3.17(d). Instead of a single buffer task, there is a buffer task associated with each target task. Each such buffer task provides a single pipeline to its associated target task. Any task may use this pipeline to send items to the target task. The target task, for its part, receives all its interaction with other tasks through this pipeline. Thus it never needs to worry about missing other events while waiting in the buffer task's entry queue.

The price paid for using the structures of Figures 3.17(b) or (d), compared to Figure 3.17(c), is a loss in flexibility. In Figures 3.17(b) or (d), the target task must process items in the order in which they are supplied by the buffer task. In contrast, in Figure 3.17(c), the target task can place guards on its own entries to control the order of processing.

This loss in flexibility could be avoided at the price of additional complexity, by placing the appropriate entries and selective accept mechanisms in the buffer task. However, a complicated interaction may then be required between the buffer and the target because the application logic is distributed between them.

An Ada program skeleton for the buffer task of Figure 3.17(b) is provided in Figure 3.18.

3.3.4 Out-of-Order Scheduling

A requirement often arises for requests made in entry calls to be serviced in a different order (in time) from that in which they are made. This may be termed *out-of-order scheduling*. Such a requirement may arise when certain requests need to be treated differently at different times due to changing conditions or when certain requests have fixed higher priority than others. The best way of handling out-of-order scheduling in Ada is by providing separate entries to differentiate requests requiring different treatment. This enables out-of-order scheduling to be handled by the called task alone using guards. Entries are treated differently at different times due to changing conditions. The entry names must provide all the information required for the server to decide which entries to close until they can be serviced. This approach may in some cases require that a large number of entries be defined. For this purpose, arrays of entries, known as *entry families* in Ada, may be used.

Out-of-order scheduling may also be based on a parameter of the entry. However, this requires cooperation between tasks to accomplish the scheduling. The calling task must be prepared to have its request rejected if it cannot be serviced at the time its entry call is accepted. This is because the nature of the Ada rendezvous mechanism is such that the parameters of an entry call cannot be examined until after the call is accepted

```
task BUFFER is
  entry PUT (ITEM: in ITEM_TYPE)
  entry GETC (ITEM: out ITEM_TYPE)
  entry GETD (ITEM: out ITEM_TYPE)
end BUFFER;

task body BUFFER is
  . . .
  begin
   loop
     select
       accept PUT (ITEM: in ITEM_TYPE)
         do
         — — STORE ITEM
         — — CLEAR APPROPRIATE TARGET'S GUARD
         end;
     or
       when SOMETHING_FOR_TARGET_C = >
       accept GETC (ITEM: out ITEM_TYPE)
         do
         — — HAND OVER ONE ITEM
         — — SET GUARD IF NO MORE ITEMS
         end;
     or
       when SOMETHING_FOR_TARGET_D = >
       accept GETD (ITEM: out ITEM_TYPE)
         do
         — — HAND OVER ONE ITEM
         — — SET GUARD IF NO MORE ITEMS
         end;
     end select;
   end loop;
 end BUFFER;
```

Figure 3.18 Code of a buffer task serving many senders and targets

and there is no explicit mechanism for blocking a calling task at that point. Implicit blocking can be performed by nesting accept statements, but such an approach does not solve the out-of-order scheduling problem, because the nested rendezvous can only be terminated in the reverse order from that in which they were initiated. Therefore, if the parameters are such that the request cannot be immediately serviced, the acceptor usually has no alternative but to terminate the rendezvous and return a parameter indicating rejection of the request. The caller must then be prepared to try again. To ensure fair treatment of retries, the acceptor will need one or more retry entries which it preferentially accepts. But if extra entries are required anyway, why not provide separate entries in the first place to differentiate requests requiring different treatment insead of using parameters? Indeed, this is the proper approach.

A server task with some entries having fixed higher priority than others is illustrated in Figure 3.19. The figure shows a special structure diagram notation combining fixed-order and selective acceptance. The reason this notation was not introduced earlier is that it is not directly supported in Ada; it must be programmed, as shown in the figure. The server is always open to the highest priority entry. Lower-priority entries are open only if no one is waiting for higher-priority service. When no one is waiting on any entry, any entry at any priority level will be accepted. Thus, callers of lower-priority entries suffer longer congestion delays.

This solution assumes callers do not use timed entry calls. Otherwise a delay alternative would be required to prevent deadlock resulting from a high priority caller timing out after his entry count attribute has been checked but before his call has been accepted.

In an actual Ada run-time environment, there may be a slight, unavoidable anomaly if several calls occur "simultaneously," when all entries are open, because the selective accept mechanism will pick one at random. However, the practical implications of this anomaly will not be great if the time *window* during which simultaneous calls can occur is small. In any case only one anomalous call will be accepted, after which the guards

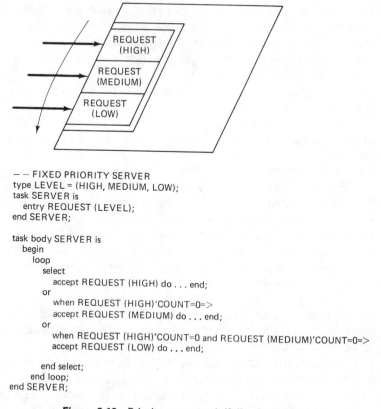

```
- - FIXED PRIORITY SERVER
type LEVEL = (HIGH, MEDIUM, LOW);
task SERVER is
    entry REQUEST (LEVEL);
end SERVER;

task body SERVER is
    begin
        loop
            select
                accept REQUEST (HIGH) do . . . end;
            or
                when REQUEST (HIGH)'COUNT=0=>
                accept REQUEST (MEDIUM) do . . . end;
            or
                when REQUEST (HIGH)'COUNT=0 and REQUEST (MEDIUM)'COUNT=0=>
                accept REQUEST (LOW) do . . . end;

            end select;
        end loop;
end SERVER;
```

Figure 3.19 Priority server task (following Wegner)

will be readjusted. The practical difference is negligible between, first, a high-priority call hitting this window and then not being accepted and, second, missing this window and having to wait for completion of servicing of a lower-priority call.

An example of when such a priority server might be needed is when low-priority background tasks and high-priority real time tasks both use the server.

3.3.5 Two-Way and Multi-Way Interaction Architectures

Two-way interaction between two tasks occurs when items may flow in both directions between them.

A degenerate case of two-way interaction occurs when items are exchanged during a single rendezvous. This case is effectively one-way interaction; it will not be considered further here.

Many mechanisms involving multiple rendezvous and/or multiple tasks may be devised for two-way interaction between a pair of tasks. As we shall see, the alternatives have varying degrees of acceptability for various purposes. However, several alternatives can immediately be discarded as unacceptable, because of the danger of deadlock. Figure 3.20 provides examples. Deadlock may occur due to a direct structure graph cycle (Figure 3.20(a)), or due to an indirect structure graph cycle (Figure 3.20(b)). It may also occur when there are no apparent cycles in the structure graph, as shown in Figure 3.20(c). Figure 3.20(c) contains a possible mutual waiting cycle, due to improper closing of an entry by a guard. Figure 3.20(d) provides timing diagrams showing how deadlock can occur for all of these cases.

Figure 3.21 shows a number of deadlock-free ways of structuring two-way inter-actions between a pair of tasks.

As shown by Figure 3.21(a), direct structure graph cycles can be used safely by careful ordering of each task's sequence of call and accept statements. One task must make the first call, the other task must make the first accept, and thereafter each task's calls and accepts must alternate. However, this is a very restrictive approach.

Figure 3.21(b) illustrates another way of making a direct structure graph cycle safe, by using a conditional entry call in one direction. This concept is simple but requires additional logic to decide what to do if the call fails and when and how often to call again. The overall system is also conceptually complex, because return from a rendezvous does not mean the work was done. It also makes use of a unique feature of Ada, namely the conditional entry call, when other good solutions which do not require this feature are available. Both the KISS principle and the goal of using Ada as a design language suggest that the other solutions might be preferable.

In Figure 3.21(c), separate rendezvous in the same direction are used for the different directions of data flow. Pickup can be performed polling or by conditional waiting, neither of which is satisfactory in general.

Figure 3.21(d) has rendezvous in both directions but avoids deadlock by using a transport task in one direction. The sender in that direction accepts calls from the transport task only when it has something to be picked up. In the other direction the sender calls the other task directly. This solution is good if the direct call between the two primary

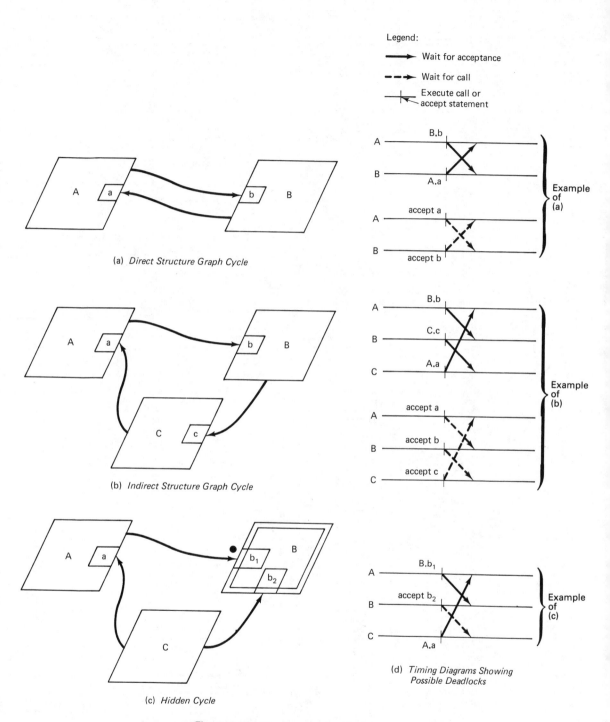

Legend:

➤ Wait for acceptance

┅➤ Wait for call

Execute call or accept statement

(a) *Direct Structure Graph Cycle*

(b) *Indirect Structure Graph Cycle*

(c) *Hidden Cycle*

Example of (a)

Example of (b)

Example of (c)

(d) *Timing Diagrams Showing Possible Deadlocks*

Figure 3.20 Rendezvous deadlock

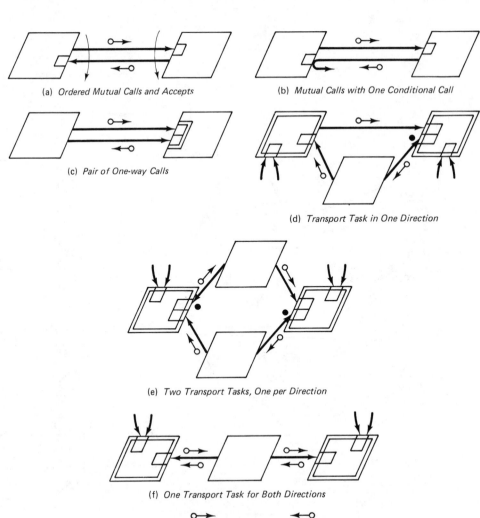

(a) *Ordered Mutual Calls and Accepts*

(b) *Mutual Calls with One Conditional Call*

(c) *Pair of One-way Calls*

(d) *Transport Task in One Direction*

(e) *Two Transport Tasks, One per Direction*

(f) *One Transport Task for Both Directions*

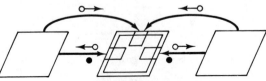

(g) *Single Buffer Task*

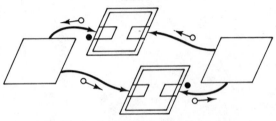

(h) *One Buffer Task for Each Target*

Figure 3.21 Two-way interaction architectures

tasks does not result in undue interference with the caller's other activities. The call should, therefore, not involve conditional waiting. This solution has the advantage over the next one of using fewer tasks but the disadvantage of providing an asymmetric solution to a symmetric problem.

The solution of Figure 3.21(e) uses two transport tasks, one in each direction, each of which conditionally waits for items to transport. This solution is flexible because it imposes no constraints on either of the primary tasks with respect to their interactions with other tasks, and as with all transport task solutions, it minimizes interference with the other activities of the primary tasks.

Figure 3.21(f) mimics a solution one often sees in human organizations for batched transport of items, where immediate delivery is not of concern but transport costs are of concern. A single transport task performs both pickup and delivery services for batches of items in both directions, on a scheduled basis, without conditional waiting. For high levels of interaction activity in both directions, such a single transport task handling both directions and running on a regular schedule performs as well as two transport tasks, one for each direction, each running on the same schedule. It seems questionable that constraints will often arise in computer programs leading to a requirement for such batched transport of items.

Transport task solutions have great flexibility, but suffer from two disadvantages in certain circumstances:

- the number of transport tasks required is proportional to the number of pairs of interacting tasks, which could be high if each task interacts with many others;
- there may be a need for internal buffering of items in the sender or target tasks, if interaction activity is high.

The buffer task solutions of Section 3.3.4 can be used for two-way, as well as one-way, interactions, to avoid these disadvantages, at the cost of some loss of flexibility. Figures 3.21(g) and 3.21(h) illustrate the approaches, which are identical to those for one-way interactions, except that primary tasks may be both senders and targets. The loss of flexibility was discussed in Section 3.3.4.

In terms of efficiency, both transport and buffer approaches require the same number of rendezvous to transfer data between a pair of primary tasks. However, this may be somewhat misleading, because the number of task context switches may be higher in certain circumstances for the transport task approach, simply because there are more tasks.

Multi-way interaction structures among many tasks may be handled by piecing together pairwise interaction structures from Figure 3.21 in a consistent fashion.

To be avoided are ad-hoc combinations of different interaction structures for the same set of tasks. Such combinations could contain hidden deadlocks due to pernicious combinations of entry calls and guards, even when entry call cycles are not present in the structure graph. An example of this kind of deadlock was given in Figure 3.20(c). We leave it as an exercise to the reader to show that ad hoc combinations of different interaction structures for the same set of tasks can lead to deadlock due to this kind of circular waiting.

3.3.6 Intertask Flow Control

We have seen how tasks can arrange to send items to other tasks and to wait for items from other tasks, using a wide variety of canonical structures. We have also seen in passing how sometimes a sending task may be blocked by the unavailability of room for the item. Our first contact with this possibility was in the first example of tasking in the book, namely the buffer task of Chapter 2, in which a guarded WRITE entry provided the blocking. Such blocking is one way in which a target task may control the incoming flow of items. However, other ways are also possible, as described below.

Caller-target tasks may exercise flow control very simply by not calling for items. Acceptor-target tasks face a more complex situation.

In general, an acceptor-target task may exercise flow control in the following ways:

- block the item by blocking the sending task, using a guard;
- block the item by refusing to accept it from the sending task during the rendezvous but release the sender from the rendezvous;
- discard the item during the rendezvous;
- call potential senders to tell them when a flow control condition has been imposed;
- give credit to senders in advance of sending.

The first three approaches require that senders be prepared to try to send first and then either wait or fail, if flow control is being exercised, thus possibly tying up resources unnecessarily or losing data.

The fourth approach is not satisfactory because the warning may not get there in time and because it can result in deadlock due to simultaneous mutual calls.

The approach of giving credit in advance has attractive advantages. With this approach, a sender can always be sure that items it sends will not be blocked, and a target can always be sure that items it receives will be acceptable. In its simplest form, *credit* would take the form of a count of the number of items which the target can accept. The sender would agree not to exceed its current credit allocation. When its current credit allocation was exhausted, the sender would have to wait for additional credit before sending more items.

How should sender/target interactions be arranged to manage credit effectively? This depends on the canonical structure chosen for task interaction. Some possibilities are shown in Figure 3.22.

If interaction is direct or via transport tasks, then the approaches of Figures 3.22(a) –(b) are possible.

Figures 3.22(a)–(b) assume that, while credit is available, it is returned as an *out* parameter of the SEND entry (initial credit could be obtained by calling SEND with a null item). The differences between these figures relate to different ways of getting more credit after no more credit is available via SEND.

The target could call the sender back when credit becomes available, as shown in Figure 3.22(a). This is safe from deadlock because of the order of the calls and accepts.

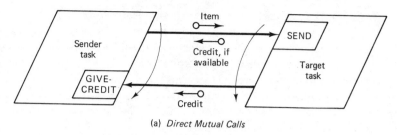

(a) *Direct Mutual Calls*

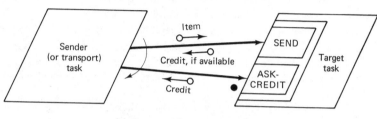

(b) *Separate ASK.CREDIT Entry in the Target Task*

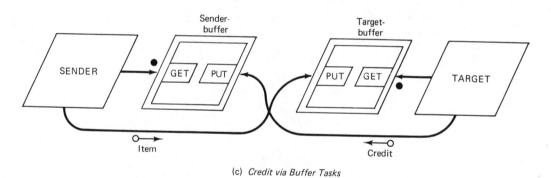

(c) *Credit via Buffer Tasks*

Figure 3.22 Task interaction structures for flow control by credit

However, this introduces excessively tight (and, therefore, unmodular) coupling between sender and target.

As shown in Figure 3.22(b), the target could provide a separate, guarded ASK__CREDIT entry, where the sender may wait for credit after it has sent an item, if no more credit is available. If the sender cannot wait directly, a transport task could be introduced for this purpose.

If buffer tasks are chosen as the interaction mechanism, then the approach of Figure 3.22(c) is appropriate. The PUT entries may be used by many senders. Each GET entry is used only by the target task which *owns* the buffer task. Each sender may also be a target.

3.3.7 Packaged Sets of Tasks: Active Packages

As mentioned in our discussion of the business office analog of concurrent programming, it may often be desirable to view a collection of tasks which are cooperating to provide services to other tasks as an active package which provides these services. Active packages may perform the same roles as tasks (recall the roles of slave, server, secretary, agent, transporter, etc., defined in Section 3.3.1). They may also perform new roles such as service pools, as we shall see.

A simple, real-life example allows us to describe the active package approach without being concerned with details of the problem. Consider the example of customers queueing for service from one of a number of tellers in a bank. A common solution is to have a single queue from which customers are dispatched to be serviced by tellers at particular wickets. A particular approach will be described here in which customers wait at a dispatching window in the bank for a dispatcher to provide the name (i.e., wicket number) of a free teller. Customers then move to the assigned wicket to obtain service from the teller.

The dispatcher is the manager of the single customer queue. During operation each teller informs the dispatcher that it is free by giving it the name of its wicket to be passed on to a customer. Each customer waits for a wicket name and then goes to the wicket to be serviced.

Figure 3.23 provides a simple description of this example in structure graphs and

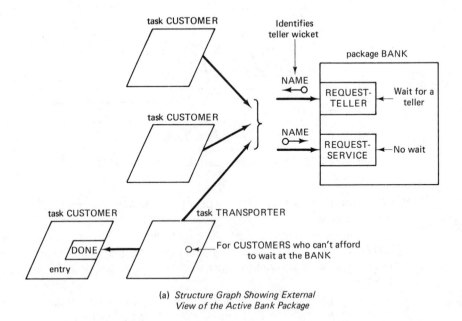

(a) *Structure Graph Showing External
View of the Active Bank Package*

Figure 3.23   The bank example of an active package

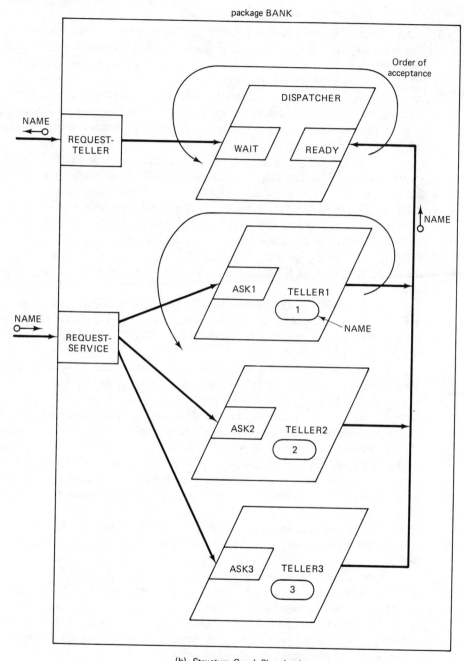

(b) *Structure Graph Showing Internal Details of the Bank Package*

Figure 3.23 (continued)

Ada, avoiding sophisticated features of tasking (Chapter 5 removes this restriction). Figures 3.23(a) and 3.23(b) show the tasks and the bank package in structure graph form. The customers, the dispatcher, and the tellers are tasks, and the bank is an active package whose services are provided to customers by procedures. The dispatcher performs the role of scheduler. The tellers perform the roles of slaves who are assigned by their master (the dispatcher) to perform work for customers. They are assumed to interact with other tasks in the bank, not shown in the figure, to perform this work; otherwise there would be no need to make them tasks.

In Figure 3.23(b), the entry queue of the dispatcher's WAIT entry serves as the customer queue. The dispatcher task accepts a WAIT call only after it has rendezvoused with a free teller who has made a READY call. It thus cycles between acceptance of calls on READY and WAIT, assigning a teller to a customer on each cycle. Each teller cycles between calling READY and accepting ASK. Each teller knows its wicket number and passes it to the dispatcher when ready. Each customer given a wicket number is expected immediately to make a call on the ASK entry of the appropriate teller via the REQUEST SERVICE procedure. Failure to do so is an error which will tie up that teller.

Thus, a customer calling REQUEST__TELLER may have to wait to return from a WAIT call. The dispatcher itself may have to wait to receive a READY call or a WAIT call. A teller may have to wait to return from a READY call and then may have to wait for an ASK call.

Figure 3.24 gives an Ada program skeleton corresponding to these structure graphs. Note again how a structure graph aids in conceptualizing the organization and operation of a program. The program skeleton of Figure 3.24 is not really necessary for this purpose. Design-level discussions can be conducted entirely in terms of the structure graph. The program is only necessary to resolve details such as the method of identifying teller tasks. Here the method is simple to the point of naivety—each TELLER task is separately coded with its own internal wicket number initialized prior to run time. This number is passed around as shown in the figure and finally used in a case statement to select the right teller. Better ways of defining and identifying members of task pools will be covered in Chapter 5.

Finally, Figure 3.25 fills in the deferred details of the skeleton package. The task bodies were left as stubs in the BANK body; their internal details are defined separately here.

Although in this particular example, no interactions by tellers with packages or tasks outside their own package are shown, in real life such interactions are quite common. In general, active packages may not only be called, but may also call others.

The particular type of active package illustrated by this example may be called a service pool. A *service pool* is an active package which provides the services of one of a number of identical tasks to individual callers.

Active packages may also be used as bi-directional transport entities and as generalized servers or agents of various types, as we shall see in subsequent chapters.

```
package BANK IS
  type T__TYPE is (DEPOSIT, WITHDRAW, CHECK__ACCOUNT, PAY__BILL);
  type R__TYPE is . . . — — RESULTS REPORTED HERE;
  type WICKET is integer range 1 . . 3;
  procedure REQUEST__TELLER (NAME : out WICKET;
  procedure REQUEST__SERVICE (NAME        : in WICKET;
                              TRANSACTION : in T__TYPE;
                              RESULT      : out R__TYPE);
end BANK;

package body BANK is
  NAME : WICKET;

  task TELLER1 is
    entry ASK(TRANSACTION : in T__TYPE;
              RESULT       : out R__TYPE);

    end TELLER1;
  task body TELLER1 is separate;

  task TELLER2 is
  . . .
  task TELLER3 is
  . . .
  task DISPATCHER is
    entry WAIT   ( NAME : out WICKET);
    entry READY ( NAME : in   WICKET);
    end DISPATCHER;
  task body DISPATCHER is separate;

  procedure REQUEST__TELLER ( NAME : out WICKET) is
    begin DISPATCHER.WAIT ( NAME );
  end REQUEST__TELLER;

  procedure REQUEST__SERVICE ( NAME        : in WICKET;
                               TRANSACTION : in T__TYPE;
                               RESULT      : out R__TYPE);

  begin
    case NAME is
      when 1 = > TELLER1.ASK (TRANSACTION, RESULT);
      when 2 = > TELLER2.ASK (TRANSACTION, RESULT);
      when 3 = > TELLER3.ASK (TRANSACTION, RESULT);
    end case;
  end REQUEST__SERVICE;
end BANK;
```

Figure 3.24 The BANK package with task stubs

```
— —TASK BODIES OF BANK PACKAGE—
separate (BANK )
  task body DISPATCHER is
    NAME: WICKET;
      begin
        loop
          accept READY (NAME : in WICKET );
          accept WAIT   (NAME : out WICKET);
        end loop;
      end DISPATCHER;

separate (BANK)
  task body TELLER1 is
    NAME : WICKET : = 1;
      begin
        loop
          DISPATCHER.READY ( NAME );
          accept ASK( TRANSACTION : in T__TYPE;
                      RESULT        : out R TYPE)
          do WORK;
            end;
          CLEAN__UP__AFTER__WORK;
        end loop;
      end TELLER1;
— —AND SO ON, FOR THE OTHER TELLERS
```

Figure 3.25   Task bodies for the BANK package

3.3.8 Conclusions

Many further design issues with respect to system architecture could be explored but would take us into too much detail at this stage. In this section we have illustrated how to describe system architectures assembled from the high-level Ada building blocks of packages and tasks. The description techniques have been presented in such a way that they should be accessible to readers without specific detailed knowledge of the Ada language. All that is needed is an informal understanding of the meaning of the symbols in the structure diagrams and an appreciation of the nature of the rendezvous mechanism. Given this informal and intuitive understanding, system organizations may be described simply as collections of persons cooperating to achieve an end, and system architectures may be designed based on our knowledge of human organizations.

We have also introduced some useful system parts in the form of slaves, servers, schedulers, buffers, secretaries, agents, transporters, and pools.

We have generally avoided discussing the efficiency of the various structures we have introduced. Efficiency is of particular concern in multi-tasking systems in which third-party tasks are required for transport and/or buffer purposes. We defer specific discussion of efficiency to postmortem discussions of system design examples in Part C.

The next section makes some concluding remarks on the relationship between the material of this chapter and the Ada language.

3.4 DISCUSSION: STRUCTURE GRAPHS AND ADA PROGRAMS

3.4.1 Introduction

The old adage "a picture is worth a thousand words" can only be true in a design context if everyone seeing the picture is confident that it can be translated into a thousand words if necessary. To aid the reader's development of this confidence, Ada programs for selected examples were provided in Section 3.3. Section 3.4.2 provides a brief retrospective discussion of the mapping mechanism.

Two issues which are not at this stage of great concern to the novice reader, but which will be of interest to the more advanced reader, are raised in Sections 3.4.3 and 3.4.4. These sections may be skipped on first reading without loss of continuity. Section 3.4.3 discusses some deficiencies of Ada with respect to the ability of the specification parts of Ada modules to reflect the intent of the designer. Section 3.4.4 discusses how in this chapter we have implicitly and deliberately restricted the designer's freedom with respect to the full power of Ada.

3.4.2 Mapping Structure Graphs into Ada Programs

Section 3.3 showed by example that mapping structure graphs into Ada programs is straightforward and mechanical.

Interface sockets in the boxes representing packages and tasks translate directly into declarations in module specifications. Socket names become procedure or entry names. Names adjacent to data flow arrows become parameters. Access arrows directed at packages translate into procedure calls. Access arrows directed at tasks translate into entry calls. The different symbols for different types of rendezvous access all translate directly into Ada. Socket names do not have to be globally unique, because in Ada a call to a procedure or entry is qualified by the package or task name. Module bodies are programmed separately from module interfaces and internal details are invisible across the interface, enforcing the black box nature of packages and tasks. Modules with the same interface but implemented differently are interchangeable.

Certain aspects of structure graphs are, however, not represented in Ada module specifications.

3.4.3 Limitations of Ada with Respect to the Specification of Structure

Ada does not support the declaration of structure graph interconnections at the specification level. There is no requirement in a module's specification to name either which modules it accesses or which modules access it. Therefore it is not possible in general for the compiler to check that the designer's interconnection constraints are met. It is possible for a module to access an incorrect module, in error. The only apparent exception is when modules are separately compiled. Then, *with* clauses are required to name the separately compiled modules which are to be accessed. However, such clauses may occur in module bodies and do not represent a specification-level declaration of structure. Furthermore, *with* clauses cannot name tasks.

What such a structure graph declaration might look like is shown in Figure 3.26. It may often be appropriate to include such structural information in a package or task specification in comments.

There is no semantic information of any kind in the specification part of a task or package. Such information must be conveyed in comments. This applies not only to the functionality of procedures and entries but also to the nature of the interactions between tasks, including interactions with tasks nested in active packages. The nature of such interactions is often important to both the calling and called tasks, as illustrated by Figure

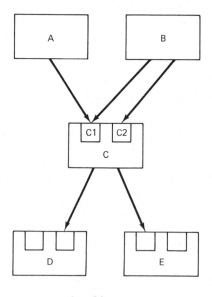

```
package C is
    required (D, E);
    is required by (A, B);
    procedure C1 (...);
    procedure C2 (...);
end package C;
```

Figure 3.26 What a package specification with a structure graph declaration capability might look like

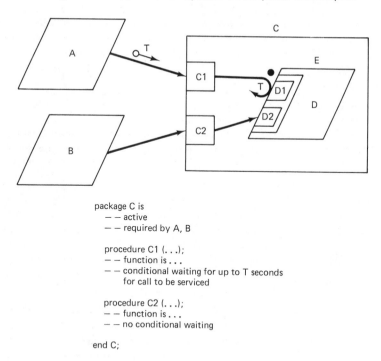

```
package C is
   − − active
   − − required by A, B

   procedure C1 (. . .);
   − − function is . . .
   − − conditional waiting for up to T seconds
        for call to be serviced

   procedure C2 (. . .);
   − − function is . . .
   − − no conditional waiting

end C;
```

Figure 3.27   Nature of comments required

3.27. The reader is encouraged to use such comments in task and active package specifications.

These limitations do not impede the straightforward translation of structure diagrams into Ada program bodies; but they do impose a requirement to document the designer's intent in comments in the specifications.

3.4.4 Have We Restricted Designer Freedom?

The structure diagram notation and approach of this chapter is very simple. The advanced reader may object that its simplicity is likely to make it inadequate to express all the possibilities inherent in Ada. The objection is a valid one, but it misses the point.

There are possibilities for system structuring in Ada which are not covered by the notation and approach of this chapter. However, the remaining possibilities are subjects for more advanced discussion. The architectural possibilities discussed so far are easily described pictorially, cover a broad range of requirements, and are all straightforwardly mapped into actual Ada programs. An attitude of this book is that architectural possibilities not easily described pictorially should be considered only as a last resort.

The approach to tasking in this chapter has been the simplest possible one. An implicit assumption has been made that systems are composed of a fixed number of tasks activated at startup which thereafter loop forever. No functionality is lost, and considerable simplicity is gained by such an approach. However, Ada allows more generality; tasks may be dynamically created and terminated. One of the more complex features of tasking in Ada is the task termination rules. By avoiding dynamic task creation and termination, concern for these rules is eliminated, and system conceptual clarity is enhanced at a single stroke. In many circumstances where a variable number of tasks need to be assigned to a varying number of activities, a fixed-size pool of tasks can be created to fulfill the need. Idle tasks in the pool simply wait to receive calls or to have their calls accepted. Often, the disadvantage of occupying memory space with stacks and descriptor tables for idle tasks will be a small price to pay for simplicity.

The more general approach to tasking is discussed in Chapter 5.

In this chapter, packages and tasks are assumed to have similar access interfaces. Packages are assumed to provide only procedural access, just as tasks provide only entry access. In fact, in Ada the package access interface can provide for direct access to almost anything in as nonuniform a fashion as desired. However, it contributes to design simplicity if a single, uniform type of interface is assumed. We shall retain this view throughout the book.

Exceptions have been omitted from this chapter. In general, the philosophy of this book is that exceptions should be relegated to the level of internal details within modules, with errors at module interfaces handled by parameters of calls. This is a simple and sufficient approach. Chapter 5 will provide a broader view of exceptions.

In this chapter, data flow arrows have been used freely to indicate parameter passing between modules, as if all such passing of parameters was by value (that is, by copying the parameter values into the target module's context). Thus, the problem of pointers (access variables in Ada) has been ignored.

The problem with pointers is that they point to dynamic objects which may be deallocated or reused for other purposes whereas some program modules incorrectly still retain reference to them. This is because a caller's copy of a pointer is not destroyed when it is passed to another module. If the caller tries to reuse the pointer in error, after the object it points to has been deallocated or reused, unpredictable results may occur.

Unfortunately, in the absence of mechanisms in Ada for doing certain desirable things without pointers, their use is unavoidable. For example, in implementing a communications package, pointers to messages, packets and the like appear unavoidable. Pointers will be discussed further in Chapter 5.

Finally, the whole subject of generics has been ignored in this chapter. Our philosophy is that the use of generics is more closely related to implementation than system design. Accordingly, there will be no treatment of generics in this book.

3.5 CONCLUSIONS

Based on this chapter, it should be possible both to understand and to generate system descriptions in terms of structure diagrams showing interactions between Ada packages and tasks without needing detailed knowledge of Ada.

A perspective has also been provided on some system design issues and a start made on developing a parts kit of basic architectures.

In general, Ada provides great freedom of expression for the programmer. The restrictive assumptions which have been made or implied in this chapter constrain this freedom in order to provide systemization of the design process. A viewpoint of this book is that Ada provides too much freedom to create excessively complicated and potentially unreliable system structures. Restricting this freedom is unlikely to do harm and likely to do good. The KISS principle has dominated our thinking.

Chapter 4

Introduction to Architectural Design (with Examples)

4.1 INTRODUCTION

The purpose of this chapter is to describe the design process, to illustrate it using some simple examples, and to raise further technical design issues in the context of these examples. The chapter draws on the material of Chapter 3 and reinforces it by using it on simple examples.

The design portion of the system life cycle is shown in Table 4.1. It is preceded by the analysis and requirements definition phases and followed by the implementation phase. The design phase itself may be broken into three major subphases, namely, global design, test plan design, and detailed design. The primary concern in this chapter is the global design subphase.

Global design is concerned with definition of the user interface, identification of the system functions, and development of the system architecture. The user interface design is part of the design phase because it is very closely coupled to the system architecture. That is, certain features of a user interface may dictate certain approaches to system architecture and vice versa. Therefore it is important that system designers and not just end users participate in this phase. This phase describes in complete detail all the features of the system which are visible to its users, including all commands, command syntax, command parameters, error messages, startup procedures, error recovery procedures, and so on.

The system function subphase is required as a checklist for allocating functions to system modules during development of the architecture. The system functions specification provides a listing and description of all functions without any explicit or implied commitment to any particular grouping of these functions into modules.

TABLE 4.1 DESIGN PORTION OF THE LIFE CYCLE

Life cycle phase	Explanation
Global design • User interface • System functions • System architecture	Down to the level of subsystems and major or critical modules inside major or critical subsystems
Test plan	In terms of user interface and architecture defined to this point
Detailed design	*Level 1* Down to the module level *Level 2* Internals of each module

The system architecture phase of global design is concerned with identifying modules, allocating functions to modules, and defining interaction between modules to determine overall system operation.

The test plan phase of design is concerned with defining test data, test modules, test procedures, and testing philosophies for the system. Testing is concerned with exercising the system to ensure first, that it operates without failure and second, that it meets the requirements. Debugging is a separate activity from testing which involves looking for the sources of problems when they are found during testing and fixing them. The test plan is an important phase of design because the act of developing it can lead to greater insight into actual operation of the system and can often reveal inadequacies in the user interface and system function specifications. Because of this mutual influence, development of the global design and of the test plan tend to proceed in an interleaved fashion in actual projects.

Of course, the final phase of design is detailed design. In this phase details are defined to the point that the remaining work can be assigned to implementors.

For a large system the design phase may proceed recursively for subsystems, sub-subsystems, and so on.

In this chapter we are concerned with design methodology and technical issues for system architecture design for simple problems in a simple target environment. To this end, we shall attack the design of three simple example systems intended for implementation on desk-top microprocessor systems of the type illustrated in Figure 4.1. This type of system is assumed to have a video character display refreshed directly from memory by hardware, a keyboard for entering commands and data, and a printer for producing

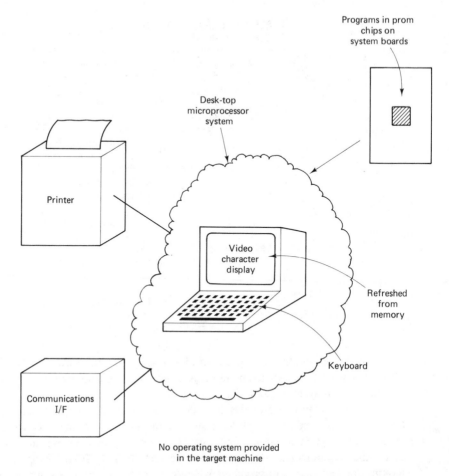

Figure 4.1　Basic target environment for the examples of Chapter 4

hard copy output. Programs and fixed data are contained in PROM (Programmable Read Only Memory) chips on system boards which plug into the back of the system. RAM (Random Access Read-Write Memory) is available for scratch-pad use at run time. There is no on-board general-purpose operating system so that programs developed for this desk-top microprocessor system must do all the device handling and interfacing, as well as controlling and synchronizing internal activities associated with keyboard input, video output, and printer output.

The desk-top system will be referred to as the target system. Programs for the target system are assumed to be developed on a separate development system with an Ada compiler and a PROM chip loader. Ada multitasking mechanisms are assumed to be supported by an appropriate PROM-based kernel in the target system. Such an arrangement will support the direct implementation of Ada programs in the target system. An alternative approach would be to use another language such as Pascal or PL/M in the development system and to augment the language by an appropriate set of programming conventions and an appropriate run time kernel in the target system to support the package and task concepts of Ada.

The three examples chosen for development are the following:

1. LIFE—a system to enable the operator to play the game of LIFE using the keyboard and video character display.
2. FORMS—a system to allow the operator to enter data via the keyboard into the fields of a form on the video display and to have the form printed as quickly as possible on a line-by-line basis as fields are completed without waiting for data entry for the entire form to be completed.
3. DIALOGUE—a system to allow operators at geographically separate locations to interact via messages prepared and displayed on their screens.

The simplicity of the assumed target system obviously limits the usefulness of these systems. A particular disadvantage is the lack of peripheral storage. However, we have deliberately kept the target configuration simple so that the examples will be as simple as possible. Even these simple examples provide a variety of design issues for discussion, and, as will be shown, the approaches which emerge can be easily applied to more general target systems.

This chapter develops design methodologies and technical design issues by developing the software architectures of these three simple applications. Section 4.2 gives an overview of design strategies and methodologies. Section 4.3 provides preliminary guidelines for an informal, practical design process. Sections 4.4, 4.5, and 4.6 discuss the design examples.

4.2 DESIGN STRATEGIES

4.2.1 Introduction

We use the term *design strategy* to indicate a starting point, a direction of approach, and a philosophy for developing the system architecture. For example, one design strategy is *top-down functional decomposition*. In contrast, we use the term *design methodology* to include, in addition to the design strategy, the systematic procedure by which the designer describes, refines, and records his design decisions.

Strategies relating to the direction of development of the system design include top-down, bottom-up, middle-out and edges-in.

Strategies which relate to the philosophical basis for development of the system design include functional decomposition, data-flow-driven structure design and data-structure-driven design. These strategies are described and illustrated in the next sections.

4.2.2 Functional Composition/Decomposition Strategy

Figure 4.2 illustrates top-down functional decomposition. The system is first thought of as an amorphous, conceptual glob which must perform all of the functions described in the functional specifications. This set of functions is regarded as a single composite function F; top-down functional decomposition then proceeds by breaking F into subfunctions, those subfunctions into further subfunctions, and so on.

A problem with top-down functional decomposition is that it does not naturally lead to identification of common functionality at the bottom-most levels of the hierarchy. It is a fact that many systems naturally emerge from the design process as diamond-

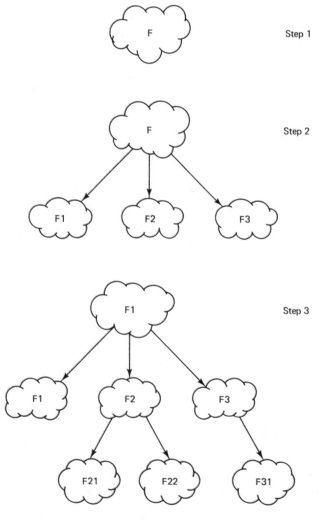

Figure 4.2 Top-down functional decomposition

shaped with a bulge in the middle rather than as triangular with the peak at the top and the base at the bottom. It is often true that the common functions at the bottom levels can be identified in advance.

Figure 4.3 shows the strategy of bottom-up functional composition, which is applicable when bottom-level functions can be identified in advance. This strategy groups functions into higher and higher-level composite functions until it reaches the *top* of the system, which is viewed as a single composite function.

In some cases it may be easier to identify functional units at the *middle* of the hierarchy first. Figure 4.4 shows the strategy of middle-out functional composition/ decomposition, which is appropriate in this case. It is a combination of the two previous strategies; it is bottom-up from the middle-up and top-down from the middle-down.

There are a number of problems with top-down functional decomposition, bottom-up functional composition, and their variations.

The first problem is that they assume that there exists a definite top to the system. The top of a system is usually thought of as a place where control is handed over to the system via some interface to an external autonomous agent. Embedded systems are characterized by a proliferation of external autonomous agents, such as human operators,

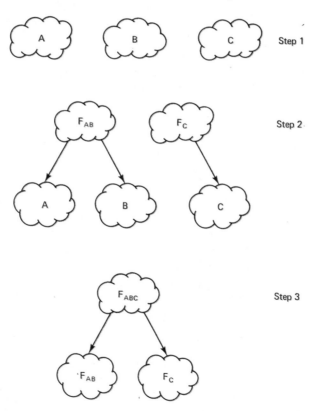

Figure 4.3 Bottom-up functional composition

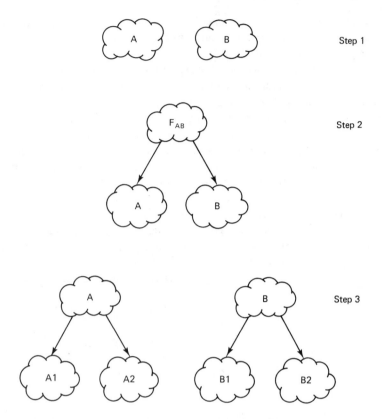

Figure 4.4 Middle-out functional composition/decomposition

communication networks, measuring devices, and so on, which are more logically thought of as being at the edges rather than at the top or bottom of the system.

The second problem is that these strategies do not take account of data. Data passing, data sharing, and data embedding are left as details to be cleaned up after the functional decomposition or composition has been performed. Data flow and data structure thus become subservient to control. However, it is more natural in many, if not most, systems to begin by considering data.

A final problem with the functional composition/decomposition strategies is that criteria for evaluating the resulting structures are very difficult to define. Therefore different designers will usually emerge from the design phase with very different functional decompositions.

4.2.3 Data-Structure-Driven Design Strategy

Where functional decomposition concentrates on the control structure of the program to the exclusion of its data structure, an alternate approach concentrates on the data structure first and builds the control structure around that. This approach may be called *data-*

structure-driven. Data-structure-driven design seems most appropriate for business-data-processing applications where problems of system architecture are left to the operating system and all that remains is to process structured files and structured records in these files. This book is concerned more with system design in which system architectural problems are paramount. Accordingly, we shall bypass data-structure-driven design.

4.2.4 *Data-Flow-Driven Structured Design Strategy*

The design strategy which shall be used throughout the remainder of this book may be called *data-flow-driven structured design*. This strategy begins by identifying the key components of data flow in the system. It then performs a form of functional decomposition by identifying transformation functions at nodal points in the data flow. The result is a data flow graph. The next step is to develop from this data flow graph a structure graph which describes the system control structure to implement the data flow. The strategy is then applied to subsystems, sub-subsystems, and so on. Throughout these steps, details of data structures are deliberately postponed.

Figure 4.5 illustrates data-flow-driven structured design for the case where there is a single thread of data flow. The overall system is thought of as performing a composite function F to transform input data into output data, as shown in Figure 4.5(a). Then internal components of data flow are identified and a data flow graph is developed to show this internal data flow, as shown in Figure 4.5(b).

The functional units F1, F2, and F3 are transformation units, the nature of which is uncommitted at this stage. The uncommitted nature of the functional units in the data flow graph is indicated here by drawing them as clouds, following Figure 3.1. Data flow graphs are also sometimes drawn using circles for the nodes and are correspondingly sometimes known as *bubble charts*. We shall usually refer to the nodes in data flow graphs as *modules*.

The data flow graph makes minimal commitments to the nature of either the data flow arrows or the modules.

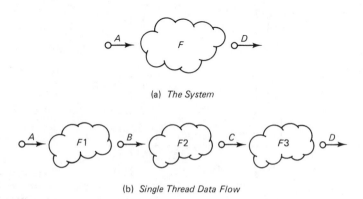

(a) *The System*

(b) *Single Thread Data Flow*

Figure 4.5 Single-thread data flow

The data flow arrows may represent application-level data or control data, such as requests, notifications, responses, confirmations, etc. They may represent transmission by value or by reference. They may represent destructive or nondestructive readout. There are no separate symbols for these different forms. If important at this stage, the distinction must be made clear by the graph documentation. Otherwise the commitment may be postponed until later stages.

The modules in the data flow graph of Figure 4.5(b) could be packages, tasks, procedures, functions, or isolated data structures. The modules themselves could provide the necessary control for data flow, or auxiliary control external to these primary modules might be required. Additional components of data flow might be required to indicate the nature of the control interactions between modules. These possibilities are explored further in Figures 4.6 through 4.10.

Figure 4.6 shows the most straightforward way of turning a data flow graph into a structure graph. In this approach the data flow graph is simply *hung up* from either the input end or the output end and used directly as a template for a vertical structure graph which provides completely hierarchical control. The resulting structure diagram is viewed as representing cascaded procedure calls. If the graph is hung up from the input end, then the procedure calls are in the direction of the data flow; if the graph is hung up from the output end, then the procedure calls are in the opposite direction to data flow. In either case auxiliary procedures GET and PUT are required to control the getting of input and the putting of output.

An alternative to vertical control is horizontal control, as shown in Figure 4.7. In this approach a separate control unit controls the flow of data between the modules.

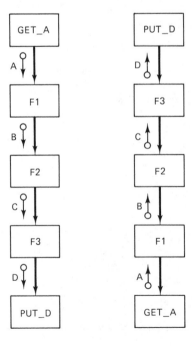

Figure 4.6 Vertical control of single-thread data flow ("vertical" structure diagram derived directly from the single-thread data-flow diagram by "hanging it up from one end")

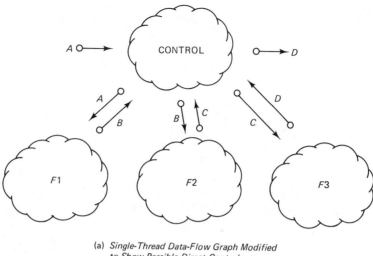

(a) *Single-Thread Data-Flow Graph Modified to Show Possible Direct Control*

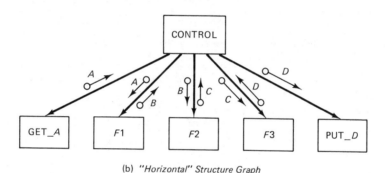

(b) *"Horizontal" Structure Graph*

Figure 4.7 Horizontal control of single-thread data flow

Although one can move directly from the original data flow graph to the horizontal structure graph of Figure 4.7(b), it seems best as a general practice first to redraw the data flow graph to include a control module, as shown in Figure 4.7(a).

Another approach is to use hierarchical control, as shown in Figure 4.8. Figure 4.8(a) shows a redrawn data flow graph including a control module which manages only the central part of the data flow graph; the ends are managed directly by the F1 and F3 modules. A hierarchical structure graph to implement this data flow graph is shown in Figure 4.8(b); in this structure graph the F1, F2, and F3 modules are implemented as packages with appropriate GET, CONTROL, and PUT interface procedures. The transformation functions F1, F2, and F3 are embedded in the bodies of the packages.

A mixed approach is shown in Figure 4.9, embodying aspects of horizontal, vertical, and hierarchical control.

One of the nice features of the data-flow-driven approach is that data flow graphs imply no commitment by themselves to implementation as sequential or concurrent sys-

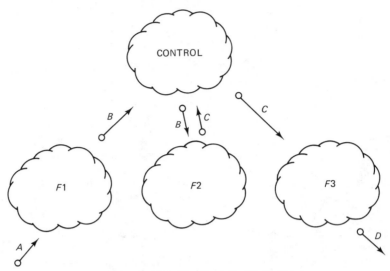

(a) *Single Thread Data-Flow Graph Modified to Show One Possible Form of Hierarchical Control*

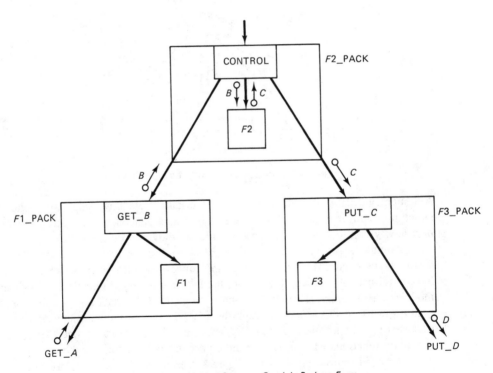

(b) *Hierarchical Structure Graph in Package Form*

Figure 4.8 Hierarchical control of single-thread data flow

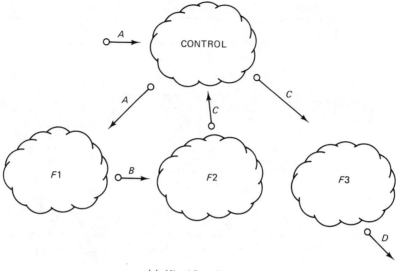

(a) *Mixed Data Flow Graph*

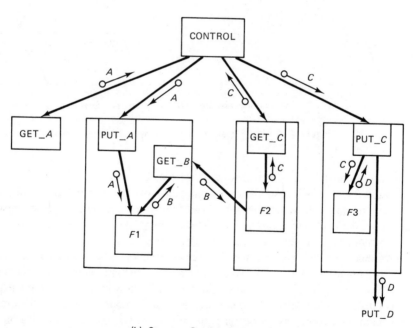

(b) *Structure Graph in Packaged Form*

Figure 4.9 Mixed control of single-thread data flow

99

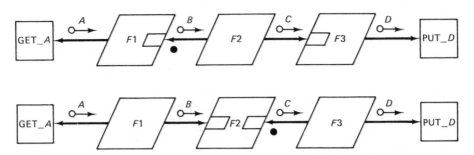

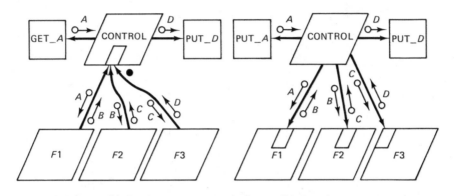

(a) *Because tasks are autonomous, control in a concurrent system may be implicit, no matter which way the interactions are directed between individual tasks.*

(b) *Concurrent systems may also have explicit control.*

Figure 4.10 Concurrent structure graphs for single-thread data flow

tems. A great deal of design can, therefore, be carried out before this commitment is made. Our examples so far in this chapter have shown structure graphs for sequential systems only. However, the same data flow graph can be used as the basis for either a sequential or a concurrent system. In fact, it may often be more straightforward to develop a structure graph for a concurrent system from a data flow graph than to do so for a sequential system, because there is often no need for an explicit, separate control function.

Figure 4.10(a) gives two examples of a structure diagram for a concurrent system which directly implements the single-thread data flow graph without any explicit separate control. This is possible because tasks are autonomous and there is therefore no need in general to enforce any particular control hierarchy on the structure diagram connections. The method of connection between pairs of tasks can, therefore, be determined by the requirements of the application.

Of course, as shown in Figure 4.10(b), separate control may be implemented in a concurrent system just as in a sequential system. In this figure, the functions of the F1, F2, and F3 modules are implemented by slave tasks.

Two approaches to control of slave tasks in this example are shown:

1. Slave tasks call a control task to request something to transform.
2. A control task calls the slave tasks to request that the transformations be performed.

The first approach would be used when it was desired to perform each transformation function concurrently with other transformation functions. In this case, transformed data would be returned by the slave task via a call to the control task to request more work. The second approach is to have the control task call the slave tasks. If the control task waits for the transformation to be completed, then this is logically no different from a procedure call in sequential system.

Of course, a far richer variety of concurrent system architectures is possible than has been illustrated in Figure 4.10. We shall leave further discussion of the possibilities to the examples.

The operation of embedded systems is unlikely to be characterized only by single thread data flow. More likely is multi-thread data flow as illustrated by Figure 4.11. Here are shown the first two steps in the development of a multi-thread data flow graph: the first step is to identify the data flows across the edges of the system; the second step is to develop the internal data flows on an edges-in basis. We shall have more to say on this in the examples.

4.2.5 Design Strategies and Testing Strategies

As was mentioned earlier, the design phase of the system life cycle is concerned not only with development of the system architecture but also with the system test plan. Each of the design strategies has a corresponding test strategy. Thus, testing may be performed from the top-down, from the bottom-up, from the middle-out, or from the edges-in. Testing may also follow particular control paths or particular data flow threads.

Top-down testing requires the use of *dummy* lower-level modules. Bottom-up testing requires the use of *driver* higher-level modules. Middle-out testing requires both driver and dummy modules. Edges-in testing is similar to bottom-up testing. All testing must be done in integration steps in which fully tested modules are integrated with untested modules and other tested modules on a progressive basis for further testing.

Testing is a separate subject, and further discussion here would take us beyond the scope of this chapter.

4.3 DOODLING WITH DATA FLOW: GUIDELINES FOR STEP-BY-STEP DEVELOPMENT OF A SYSTEM DESIGN

This section describes an informal design methodology based on the data-flow-driven structured design strategy.

There are a number of major steps in the development of a system design by the data flow approach which are of general enough applicability to summarize here as

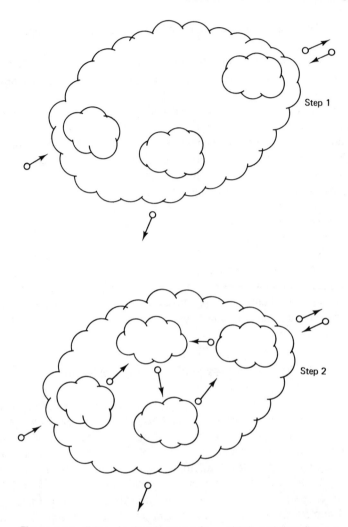

Figure 4.11 Edges-in development for multi-thread data flows

guidelines. The informality of this methodology justifies the term *doodling with data flow*
to describe it. The steps are as follows:

1. Make a first pass at identifying the major obvious subsystem modules at the system
   edges. Treat the central part of the system as a single central module. At this stage,
   functions should be assigned to the modules only in the broadest, most informal
   sense without being too concerned yet about completeness or whether the modules
   are exactly the right ones. The objective of this first step is only to provide a starting
   point for the design process. Further steps in that process can be expected to identify
   required changes to the starting point; this is natural and inevitable and, therefore,

too great a commitment to the first starting point is undesirable. Design is always in part a trial-and-error process and should be willingly accepted as such.

2. On a blank piece of paper sketch these modules, for design doodling purposes. Begin thinking about the nature of the data flows between them and of the need for consequent components of data flow internally. Based on this thinking, arrive at a trial identification of internal modules which seems sound on both functionality and modularity grounds.

3. Use the data flow sketches and the thinking that went into them to refine the view of both modules and data flows. The need for further modules and data flows may become apparent, for example to include control and error handling functions.

4. To the extent possible at this stage, assign functions in detail to modules, using the functional requirements specification as a check list. Again, refine the data flow graph based on this assignment. Perform a walk-through of the system design at this point, and make changes as necessary.

5. Develop one or more structure graphs defining candidate system architectures in terms of packages and tasks for the view of the system developed so far; based on the function assignments, define the package and task interfaces from a functional viewpoint omitting details of data structures and types. For tasks, decide on rendezvous directions, guard conditions, third party tasks, transport tasks, conditional and timed calls and so on, following the guidelines of Chapter 3. Again, perform a walk-through, and make changes as necessary.

6. Define the system interfaces in detail, including details of data types and structures, and perform a walk-through again.

7. If the system is sufficiently large and complex, it may be necessary to proceed recursively with this approach to develop subsystem designs.

8. *Walk-throughs* should be performed from as many different viewpoints as are necessary to satisfy key members of the project team of the quality and completeness of the design; these walk-throughs should be in meeting form with all key team members participating—a presentation followed by a question and answer session is best. Criteria for evaluating designs are discussed later in this chapter and in Chapter 6.

These guidelines are illustrated by example in the following sections.

4.4 FIRST DESIGN EXAMPLE: LIFE

4.4.1 Introduction

This section describes the design of a system to play the game of LIFE on an interactive, desk-top computer of the type described in Section 4.1. The main reason for choosing the game of LIFE for this first example is its simplicity; by choosing such a simple example, we can proceed with the problems of design without having them obscured by the problems of the application.

The main contribution of this example is to show how the design for a system with an interactive command decoding requirement can be developed using the data flow approach and implemented using finite state machines, Ada tasks, and Ada packages.

The game of LIFE is not really a game in the normal sense of the word. Rather it is just a set of rules for displaying interesting sequences of patterns on a *board,* consisting of a grid of squares like a checkerboard. Counters are placed on each square and live or die at each generation according to certain rules relating to the presence or absence of other counters. Successive generations of boards may present interesting dynamic patterns. In our system the board will be displayed on a video screen. The dimensions of the board are assumed predefined in the program. The player sitting at the keyboard may use a series of commands to initialize the first generation on the video screen and may then ask the system to play a given number of generations. Our primary concern in this chapter is with the design of the interactive part rather than the game playing part of the LIFE system.

The rules of the game of LIFE have no significant bearing on our design. However, for the curious, here they are. The rules are based on the relationship of each counter to its neighbors. Each counter may have up to eight neighbors in the eight squares surrounding it. The game begins with any number of counters on the board in any pattern. This is known as the initial generation. The next generation is determined by applying the following two rules to all squares on the board simultaneously:

- If a counter is on a square, then it survives if it has exactly two or three neighbors.
- If a square has no counter on it then one is born if it has exactly three neighbors.

Let us assume that the user manual has defined a set of commands composed of strings of words formed into command lines. Commands are entered on a character-by-character basis from the keyboard, and the end of a command line is denoted by a special character, for example, carriage return. Command words are separated by blanks. Commands are processed only at the end of each line. A special line on the screen is reserved for displaying the current command as it is entered.

Assume there are seven possible commands with word sequences defined by the finite state machine (FSM) of Figure 4.12. Commands 1 and 2 fill all the squares or empty all the squares to provide a starting point. Commands 3 and 4 set up the way in which pairs of numbers in commands 5 and 6 will be interpreted as row or column numbers. Commands 5 and 6 add or remove counters in the square at the coordinates specified by the number pair. Command 7 plays a given number of generations. Our problem now is to design a system which will recognize these commands when entered, reject sequences of characters and words which do not form recognizable commands and arrange for execution of the appropriate operations of filling or emptying the board, placing the counters on the initial board to create the initial generation, adding or removing counters on a displayed board to create a new, initial generation board, and playing a designated number of generations.

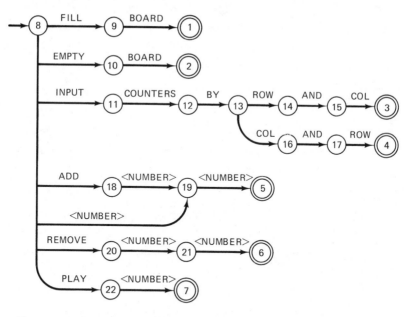

Figure 4.12   Finite state machine for word sequences in LIFE command lines (*note:* Actions are null except for transactions associated with ⟨NUMBER⟩. Then the action is to save the number in one of two possible save locations.)

4.4.2 Data Flow

The following development of the LIFE system data flow graph follows the recommended doodling with data flow procedure of Section 4.3.

At the system edges, the following modules are needed:

- a keyboard input module to receive characters from the keyboard hardware
- a line holder/decoder module to hold partially completed command lines for display in the special area on the screen and to decode the completed command lines
- a board holder module to hold the information required to display the current board and to generate new boards for display

The essential elements of internal data flow are as follows:

- input characters for assembly into command lines
- decoded commands
- display requests for prompts, lines and responses
- display requests for new board configurations

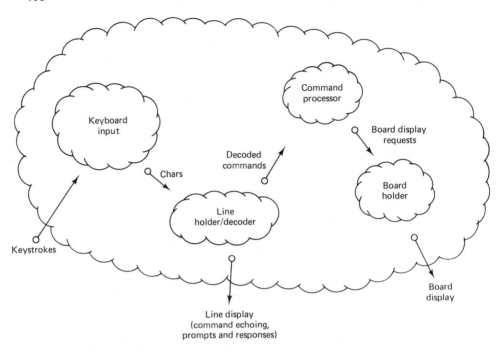

Figure 4.13   LIFE system data-flow graph

To string these data flow elements together, at least one additional module is required, namely a command processor to transform decoded commands into board display requests. The previously identified line holder/decoder module performs the transformation of characters into decoded commands. The result is shown in Figure 4.13.

Having arrived at a clean, overall data flow graph, refinement of the line holder/decoder module is appropriate. Command lines are decoded on a word-string basis. Therefore it seems appropriate to partition the line holder/decoder into a line holder and word-string decoder. Figure 4.14 shows the result. A command-word dictionary is assumed to be part of the line holder module to translate a string of characters delimited by blanks into a word code. The word-string data flow element between the line holder and the word-string command decoder could be a single word-string variable or a sequence of word-code variables; this is a design detail which can be postponed at this stage.

4.4.3 Structure

It is quite straightforward to derive a structure graph from this data flow graph. The first problem is to decide the nature of the modules in the data flow graph. The keyboard input module must be a task if characters on the keyboard are to be fielded on an interrupt basis. The line and board holder modules can be packages, because the screen is refreshed from memory by hardware and does not require a task to drive it. Note that, from a broader perspective, a screen driver task should be specified as part of the system design

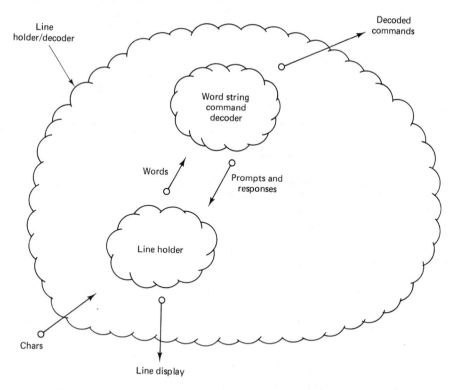

Figure 4.14   Stepwise refinement of the LIFE system data-flow graph

even if it is to be implemented in hardware; however, here we are assuming the hardware is given. Because, in general, interrupt service tasks should be kept as simple as possible, the control of the system should not be left to the keyboard input task. Therefore, we need one other task internally in the system to interface with the keyboard task and to provide system control. Several approaches are possible. A particularly simple approach is to hang the data flow graph from some point near the middle. An appropriate point is between the line-holder/decoder and command processor modules. A task may be inserted at this point to provide overall control. Note that this task introduces no new functionality; it simply realizes the data flow path. Thus, no corresponding module is required in the data flow diagram. The word-string decoder module is now appropriately committed as a package. This result is illustrated in Figure 4.15.

The intended operation of the system described by this structure graph is as follows. When the LIFE task starts up, it first calls GET__COMMAND in the line holder/decoder package, which in turn calls GET__CHAR in the keyboard task repeatedly until all characters in the line are assembled and stored internally in the line holder package; the command is then decoded and the code returned as an out parameter of the GET__ COMMAND call together with any parameters of that command (such as the number of generations to play).

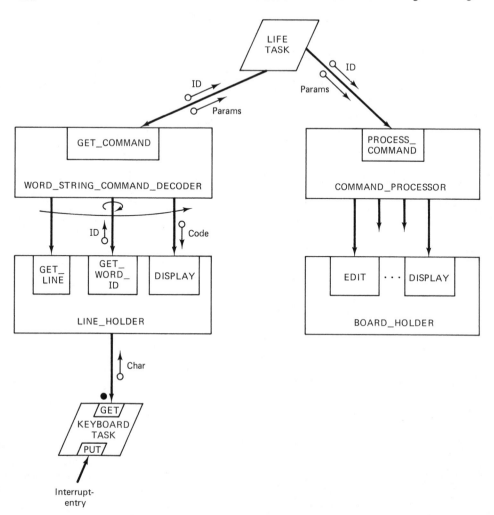

Figure 4.15 LIFE system structure graph

Note that the LIFE task may be held up waiting for the next character.

Internally, when the decoder package returns from the NEXT__LINE call, it calls GET__WORD__ID repeatedly until it gets a recognizable or an unrecognizable command. Command error messages and next command prompts are handled internally via the DISPLAY procedure.

When the command is decoded, the LIFE task calls the command processor package, passing the appropriate command id and parameters. The command processor package then takes care of performing the function requested by the command by accessing the board holder package as appropriate.

The next step in design is to develop the internals of the various modules. It will be sufficient for illustrative purposes to develop structure graphs for the internals of the line holder package and the command decoder package. Figures 4.16 and 4.17 show possible internal structures of these packages.

In the line holder package of Figure 4.16, the GET__LINE procedure repeatedly calls GET__CHAR. An internal marker indicates the position of the next word available for retrieval by GET__WORD__ID. The GET__WORD__ID procedure retrieves this next word (moving the marker at the same time), matches the word against the internal dictionary, and passes the resulting word ID to the caller. Because no explicit error handling is indicated in this package, there must be at least one value of the word ID reserved for the condition *unrecognizable word*.

The internal development of the command decoder package is shown in Figure 4.17 in both structure graph and skeleton program form. This package contains an internal FSM package which encapsulates the current state, the FSM tables and the NEXT procedure for accessing the tables to update the state, given the event. Returned as parameters of the NEXT procedure are state and action codes which are used by the GET__COMMAND__ID procedure to decide whether the command has been decoded yet and whether there are any parameters to be saved.

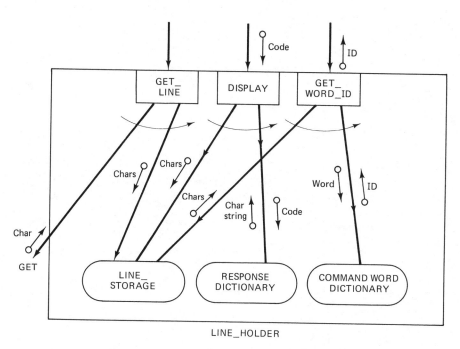

Figure 4.16 Internal development of line holder

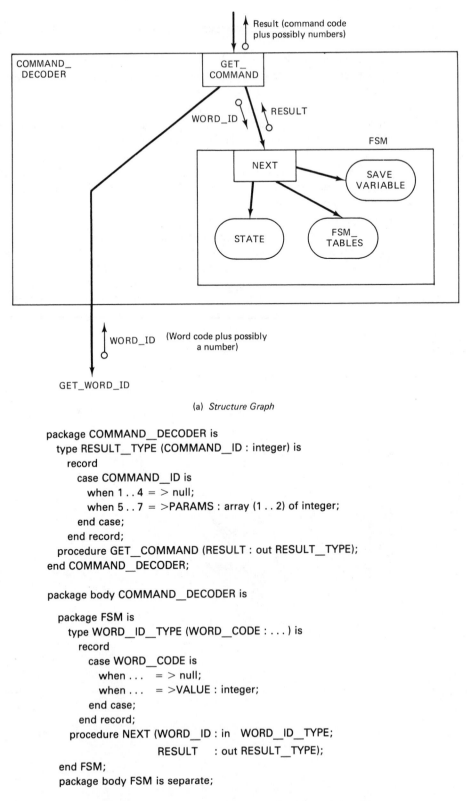

(a) *Structure Graph*

```
package COMMAND__DECODER is
  type RESULT__TYPE (COMMAND__ID : integer) is
    record
      case COMMAND__ID is
        when 1 .. 4 = > null;
        when 5 .. 7 = >PARAMS : array (1 .. 2) of integer;
      end case;
    end record;
  procedure GET__COMMAND (RESULT : out RESULT__TYPE);
end COMMAND__DECODER;

package body COMMAND__DECODER is

  package FSM is
    type WORD__ID__TYPE (WORD__CODE : ... ) is
      record
        case WORD__CODE is
          when ...  = > null;
          when ...  = >VALUE : integer;
        end case;
      end record;
    procedure NEXT (WORD__ID : in  WORD__ID__TYPE;
                    RESULT   : out RESULT__TYPE);
  end FSM;
  package body FSM is separate;
```

Figure 4.17 Internal development of command decoder

```
        procedure GET__COMMAND (RESULT : out RESULT__TYPE) is
        . . .
          begin
            loop
              LINE__HOLDER.GET (WORD__ID):
              if WORD__ID.WORD__CODE = NO__MORE
                then exit; end if;
              FSM.NEXT (WORD__ID, RESULT);
            end loop;
            if RESULT.COMMAND__ID = . . . then. . . ;— — ERROR
          end GET__COMMAND;

  end COMMAND__DECODER;

  separate COMMAND__DECODER

    package FSM is
      STATE : integer : = 8;
      EVENT, ACTION : integer;
      SAVE : array (1 . . 2) of integer;
      S__TABL : array (EVENT, STATE) of integer
        : = . . . ; — — ARRAY AGGREGATE OF STATES
      A__TABL : array (EVENT, STATE) of integer
        : = . . . ; — — ARRAY AGGREGATE OF ACTIONS
      procedure NEXT (WORD__ID : in   WORD__ID__TYPE;
                       RESULT    : out RESULT__TYPE) is
        . . .
        begin
          EVENT  : = WORD__ID.WORD__CODE;
          ACTION : =    A__TABL (EVENT, STATE);
          STATE  : =    S__TABL (EVENT, STATE);
          case ACTION is
            when 1 = > null;
            when 2 = > SAVE(1): =WORD__ID.VALUE;
            when 3 = > SAVE(2): =WORD__ID.VALUE;
          end case;
          RESULT.COMMAND__ID : = STATE;
          if STATE in 5 . . 7
            then RESULT.PARAMS : = SAVE;
          end if;
      end NEXT;

  end FSM;
```

(b) *Ada Program Skeleton*

Figure 4.17   (continued)

4.4.4 Design Evaluation

Some typical questions concerning design quality which might be raised in a design walk-through are as follows:

1. Could this design easily handle type-ahead of characters? Type-ahead is a feature allowing a fast typist to get ahead of the system without loss of characters. The lack of type-ahead in this simple system is unlikely to be a problem, but it can be a problem in systems where processing of a character is sometimes slow, perhaps due to the need to access peripheral storage.

2. Could the system easily be modified to provide immediate notification to the operator of an incorrect character sequence up to the current character position without waiting for the end-of-line?

3. Does the system design make it easy to change the words of commands, the allowed word sequences in command strings, and the semantics of commands? Such changes are often required during the normal lifetime of any system.

With respect to type-ahead, it would obviously be quite easy to place a type-ahead buffer in the keyboard task for accumulation of characters under conditions when the system does not call GET__CHAR fast enough to remove each character before the next one arrives.

Immediate notification of errors is more of a problem. The internal design of the line holder/decoder package must be modified to produce a system which is capable of notifying the operator of command errors as soon as an incorrect character is typed in the context of the command string entered up to that point. The main modification required is to replace the word-string command decoder by a character-string command decoder.

The system is not particularly easy to modify to accommodate changes in commands because of the separation of the command-word dictionary in one package and the word-sequence FSM tables in another package. It would be better from this point of view to put these data structures in the same package. In this respect the character-string command decoder suggested above provides a better starting point for a quality design.

Note, however, how the design of Figure 4.15 emerged as a result of an explicitly stated user interface requirement that commands would be processed one line at a time. Thus, the user interface definition has resulted in a design which limits the flexibility of the system. As a general rule, if flexibility is important, then it must be stated as part of the requirements; otherwise, the designer may be led to meet specific requirements with a system of limited flexibility.

Finally, is the particular structure as clean as possible? Are there any logically unnecessary extra interfaces or extra modules? Reexamining Figure 4.15, the overall design might be tidied up a bit by eliminating the somewhat redundant GET__COMMAND call made by the LIFE task to the word-string command decoder package. This could be accomplished by eliminating the latter package and instead imbedding its functionality in the body of the LIFE task. This approach amounts to hanging the data flow graph of Figures 4.13 and 4.14 from the word-string command decoder module and making that module a task. Whether the resulting structure is better or not is probably a matter of taste in this example. However, it is important to explore such questions as part of the design process.

4.5 SECOND DESIGN EXAMPLE: FORMS

4.5.1 Introduction

The purpose of this design example is to introduce an additional level of complexity over that of the very simple LIFE example. This additional level of complexity arises because of the need to coordinate foreground activity seen by the operator with a concurrent background activity spawned by this foreground activity.

The FORMS system is required for the preparation, editing, and printing of business forms. To keep the system simple, there is assumed to be no file storage device available, so that all that can be done is to prepare one business form on the screen and print it directly from its resulting representation in primary memory.

Editing the form is a foreground activity in the sense that the operator specifically initiates all form edit activities and waits for them to be completed. On the other hand, printing a form could be a foreground or a background activity. As a foreground activity, the operator would request printing of a completed form displayed on the video screen and then wait for printing to be completed.

As a background activity, printing could take place while edit operations were in progress on the screen. One approach would be to arrange that more than one form could be stored in primary memory so that edit operations could proceed on one form while another completed one was being printed. Another approach, taken in this example, is to arrange that foreground editing and background printing take place concurrently on the same form but that editing can only access the incomplete parts of the form and printing the complete parts. In this way we can arrange that the form is printed as quickly as possible without having the operator wait to complete the form before printing begins. With this approach an interesting coordination problem arises between editing and printing because of different logical views of the form by these two activities. Editing views the form as a collection of fields. Printing views the form as a collection of lines of full-page width.

With reference to Figure 4.18, for the purposes of this example, a business form may be viewed two quite different ways.

- As a collection of rectangular fields of different sizes and shapes, each with a defined position on a page, and each containing lines of text within the confines of the field *(field-lines)*
- As a set of lines on a page *(page-lines)*

Fields may be narrower than a full-page width, and they may, therefore, include parts of several page-lines. A page-line may contain several field-lines. Field boundaries are assumed to consist of rows and columns of asterisks. Field titles are assumed to be

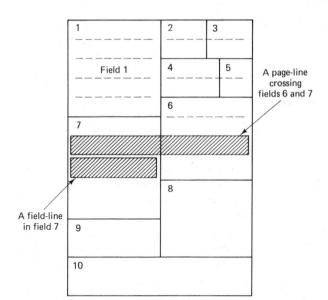

Figure 4.18 Fields in a form (*note:* Field numbers are not part of the field text.)

part of the text in the field. Pages are assumed to be filled with fields; that is, there are no empty spaces between fields and the fields all line up at the page edges.

To provide for simultaneous editing and printing of the same form, fields are numbered sequentially, first from left to right and then from top to bottom; a field may only be edited in this sequence, and once a particular field is edited, it may not be reentered for further editing until the field edit sequence is completed. Page-lines of the form are printed as soon as they are inaccessible to further editing without waiting for the entire form to be complete. Because the form is prepared fieldwise, a page-line is complete when all the fields it crosses have been completed.

Editing is controlled by two special function keys, as follows:

1. A special START-EDIT function key is followed by the entry of a three-character integer specifying the form number to be edited. This results in a blank form being displayed with field #1 ready for data entry; the special form number 000 indicates reedit of the current form. The START-EDIT keystroke will be recognized only when the system has just been turned on or when printing of the current form is complete.

2. A NEXT-FIELD function key is used by the operator to indicate completion of the current field and to request movement of the cursor to the beginning of the next field in the field number sequence. Thus, the system knows that editing of a field is completed when it sees the NEXT-FIELD keystroke.

The current edit position is always indicated by a cursor. Display of the cursor is controlled automatically from the hardware. The position of the cursor is controlled by software separately from the entering of data characters.

Within a field, data entry and editing are accomplished by entering data characters at the current cursor position and by using a BACKSPACE function key to move the cursor backwards within a field. As characters are entered, the cursor position moves to the right one character position at a time. Use of the BACKSPACE key simply moves the cursor backwards one character position at a time without modifying the field contents. For software simplicity, insertion is simply handled by typing the material to be inserted over top of what already exists and then retyping the remainder of the field; deletion is accomplished by backspacing and then typing blanks.

The system takes care of enforcing field boundaries and of performing the correct operations at these boundaries. When moving to the right at the right field boundary, the cursor position moves to the beginning of the next field-line, and when moving to the left at the left field boundary, it moves to the end of the previous field-line, under software control. At the uppermost left and bottommost right cursor positions in the field, the cursor has nowhere further to go. Any attempt to move it in the wrong directions at these points is an error, except for use of the NEXT__FIELD key.

If an error of any kind occurs, the system will ring a bell and stop processing the command that caused the error.

The above user interface has been kept simple, for pedagogical purposes, and is not particularly good in some respects. However, it will be sufficient for our purposes for the moment. We shall reserve criticism of it until the design evaluation.

Tables describing different forms are required. In the absence of peripheral storage, they must be stored in primary read-only memory so that they are available as soon as the system power is turned on. The START__EDIT command identifies a particular one of these form tables to be used in displaying a blank form on the screen and to be used subsequently in editing. The form tables must contain information about the dimensions and position of each field on the form and about the sequence of fields for editing purposes. The form tables must also contain, for each field, a list of the page-lines freed for printing. For example, in Figure 4.18, fields 1 and 2 free no page-lines; field 3 frees page-lines 1 and 2; field 4 frees no page-lines; field 5 frees page-lines 3 and 4; field 6 frees page-line 5 and so on. Such lists of page-lines for each field are inherent, fixed properties of the form and can therefore be part of the form tables.

4.5.2 Data Flow for Editing

Following the guidelines of Section 4.3, a data flow graph for this system can be developed from the edges in. Figure 4.19 shows the first step. Flowing into the middle of the system from its edges are keystrokes from the keyboard, form shape and attribute data from the current form table, and characters or page-lines from the video display storage for printing. Flowing out from the middle of the system to its edges are ring requests for the bell, characters to be displayed in the video display storage (note that this includes the cursor display function), and page-lines for the line printer subsystem. Also flowing out from

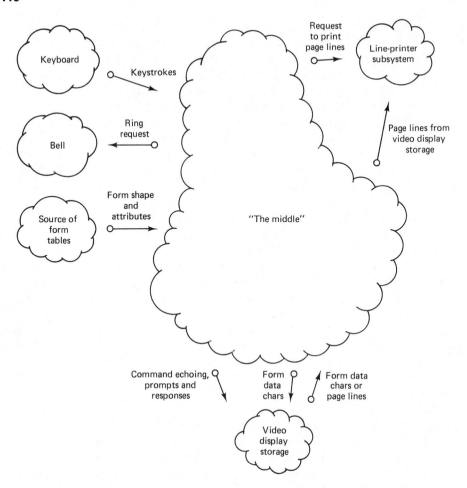

Figure 4.19   First data-flow graph of the FORMS system

the middle of the system are requests to print page-lines. The assumption here is that the actual page-lines to be printed come directly from the video display storage via a different mechanism from that which makes requests to print page-lines; this is a logical assumption in light of the way in which page-lines are freed for printing by successive field visits.

It now remains to develop the internal details of the data flow graph for the middle of the system. However, unlike the LIFE system, the data flow graph will not be single-thread. Multiple threads arise from the fact that multiple functions are being performed. As general strategy it is a good idea to consider such multiple threads separately at first. In this case the logical place to start is the foreground form editing thread.

Figure 4.20 provides an expanded data flow graph of the form edit/display foreground activity. The essential principle around which this data flow graph is constructed is the separation of logical and physical display management. Logical display management

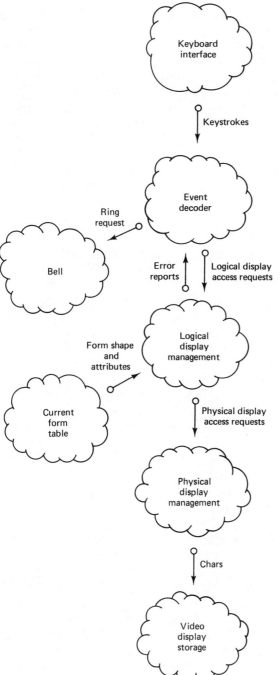

Figure 4.20 Expanded data-flow graph of the form edit/display foreground activity

117

is concerned only with the processing and editing of forms. At this level, forms are treated as logical entities without regard for how they are physically displayed. Physical display management, on the other hand, is concerned only with such items as the cursor's position on the screen, the entry of characters at absolute screen positions, the retrieval of physical lines for printing, and so on. Physical display management is not concerned with the logical interpretation of what is displayed. Given this basic separation, the data flow graph naturally evolves by inserting an event decoder module between keystrokes and logical display access requests, a display management module between the latter and physical display management requests and, at the end of the thread, a physical display management module. We use the term *event decoder* here rather than *command decoder*, because we wish to include the possibility of interaction of this module also with the printing background activity. As such, it will eventually be concerned not only with operator commands but also with events in the printer system.

4.5.3 Structure for Editing

It is quite straightforward to translate this data flow graph into an appropriate structure graph. Following the discussion in Section 4.4.4, we shall make the event decoder module a task. Logical display management does not need to be a task because it is exclusively used by the event decoder for the foreground edit activity. There is never any interaction of logical display management with the background printer activity. Therefore we can immediately decide that logical display management will be a passive package.

Provided that the event decoder task handles all the coordination between the foreground and background activities with respect to the printing of lines, there can never be any possible conflict between access to physical display management for editing purposes and access to it for retrieving lines for printing. This is the only situation in which it is possible at this stage to decide that physical display management will be a passive package. Otherwise there might arise an unacceptable conflict. For the moment, we shall assume that physical display management is a passive package and return to the question of whether conflict can arise later.

Figure 4.21 provides external and internal views of a logical display management package. It has three interface procedures, namely, NEW__FORM, NEXT__FIELD, and EDIT__FIELD. Calls to NEW__FORM must provide a form number as a parameter. Internally, the NEW__FORM procedure accesses the form table identified by the form number to display a blank form (if the form number is not 000) and moves the cursor to the upper left corner of the first field in the form (home position). An incorrect form number results in an error parameter being returned. The NEXT__FIELD procedure takes no input parameters because the next field is determined by the form tables. The body of the NEXT__FIELD procedure gets the required cursor position from the form tables and moves the cursor to that position. It also passes the field number to an internal field edit package which will handle the details of editing within that field.

The EDIT__FIELD procedure takes a character code as an input parameter (any alpha numeric character or the backspace character) and returns an error code when the input character is invalid or field boundaries would be violated by performing the edit

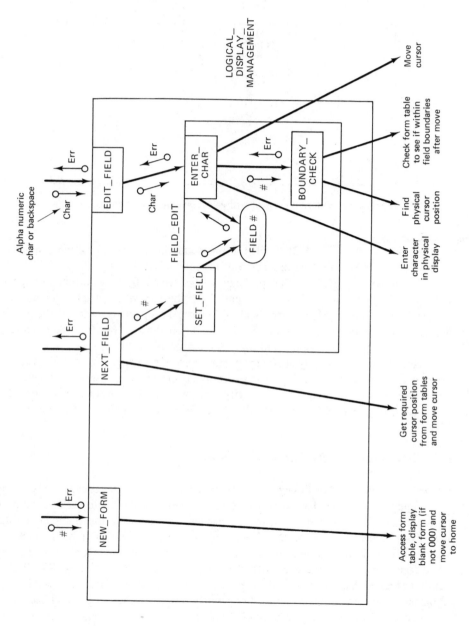

Figure 4.21 External and internal views of a logical display management package

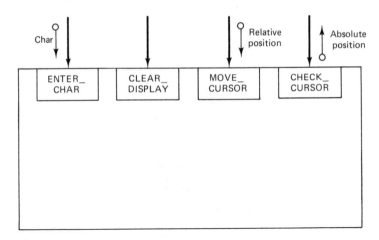

Figure 4.22 External view of a physical display management package

function. The body of the EDIT__FIELD procedure simply passes on the character to the ENTER__CHAR interface procedure of the internal field edit package.

The internal FIELD__EDIT package knows which field is current through the SET__FIELD procedure and can therefore check the current form table for boundary violations via an internal boundary check procedure. This package relies on the physical display management package to find the current physical cursor position and to enter the character in the physical display and move the cursor.

Turning now to the physical display management package, Figure 4.22 presents a minimal external view of this package to provide the necessary services required for logical display management. These services are provided by interface procedures EN-TER__CHARACTER, CLEAR__DISPLAY, MOVE__CURSOR, and CHECK__CUR-SOR.

4.5.4 Data Flow for Background Printing

Figure 4.23 refines the data flow graph based on the requirements for background printing.

Figure 4.23 shows that no new modules are required to handle background printing but that some additional data flows are needed. Omitted from this figure are all data flows associated only with editing. Let us follow a NEXT__FIELD request. First, the NEXT__FIELD keystroke interrupt is picked up by the keyboard interface, and a keystroke code is passed to the event decoder. The event decoder sends a NEXT__FIELD request to logical display management. Following lookup of the current form table, logical display management sends a page-line number range (N. .M) for printing back to the event decoder. The event decoder forwards this page-line number range to the page-line printer, which retrieves the actual page-lines from the physical display management package, prints them, and then reports back to the event decoder with a MORE__LINES notification.

The reason for using the term *event decoder* instead of *command decoder* now

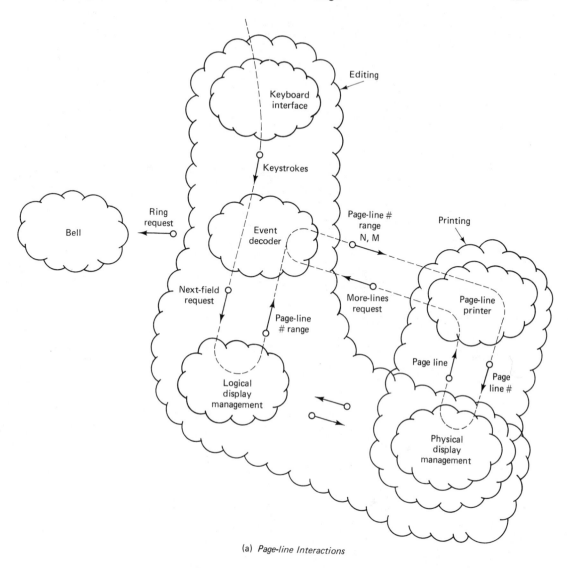

(a) *Page-line Interactions*

Figure 4.23 Data-flow graph refinement

emerges; the decoder must be responsible for processing two events, namely, keystrokes arriving from the keyboard interface and MORE__LINES notifications arriving from the page-line printer.

The event decoder has moderately complex responsibilities. It must perform both command recognition and command processing, each of which involves correct handling of different kinds of event sequences. Accordingly, a further refinement of the event decoder module seems desirable.

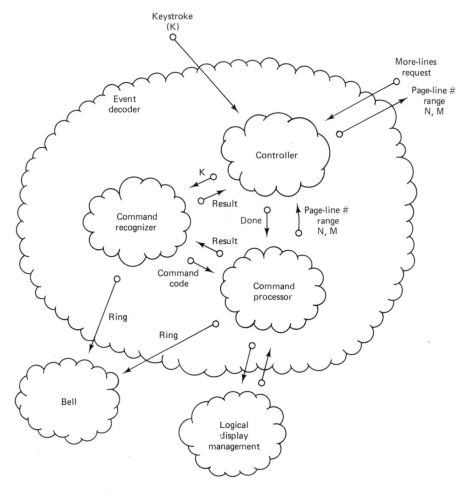

(b) *Event Decoder Internal Data Flow*

Figure 4.23   (continued)

Figure 4.23(b) provides this refinement. Separate command recognizer and command processor modules perform these functions with a single controller module acting as an overall coordinator. The controller sends keystrokes to the command recognizer which in turn sends command codes to the command processor when printing is done. The command processor in turn provides the controller with a range (N . . M) of lines to be printed upon field exit. The controller interfaces with the keyboard interface and page-line printer modules. The command processor interfaces with the logical display management module. Note that the controller must know when there are no more lines.

Figure 4.24 provides finite state machines (FSMs) for the command recognizer and command processor modules. Edit commands are single keystrokes and are therefore immediately recognized. START__EDIT commands involve multiple keystrokes and

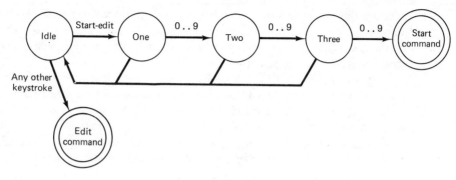

(a) *Command Recognizer States*

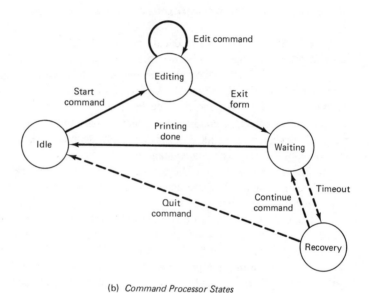

(b) *Command Processor States*

Figure 4.24 Event decoder finite state machine

therefore require several stages of recognition. The command processor FSM is required to ensure that editing of a new form does not begin until printing of the old one is done. Events causing state changes are receipt of a START__EDIT command, receipt of a NEXT__FIELD command when in the last field of a form, and receipt of a printing done notification. It might be thought that notification of a new page-line number range for printing should be a separate event. However, it is a direct consequence of a NEXT__FIELD keystroke, and so it is processed as part of that event. The dotted lines in the command processor FSM are discussed below.

One of the more irritating circumstances that can arise in an intelligent workstation is the keyboard going dead because a device has failed to respond. This is what could happen without the dotted lines in the command processor FSM, which provide for explicit rejection (instead of ignoring) of edit commands in the waiting state, and for exit from the waiting state if the printer does not respond. The lines are shown as dotted, because we did not include this possibility in the commands (a typical example of a specification error uncovered during design).

It is worth noting here that we have been able to define the major system modules and their interactions in considerable functional detail without making any commitment to whether the particular modules are packages or tasks, which module calls which other one, and how many calls are necessary to implement the data flow. Thus, the *data flow first* approach to design enables us to postpone commitment to these essentially administrative details. The commitments already made in Section 4.5.3 could easily have been postponed until the data flow picture was complete.

4.5.5 Structure for Background Printing

We are finally in a position to decide on the overall task interaction structure for background printing. Consider first the interaction between the keyboard interface task and the event decoder task. One approach would be to have the event decoder task call an entry GET__KEYSTROKE in the keyboard interrupt task to wait for a keystroke. This approach has the advantage that the keyboard interrupt task can never be held up by circumstances affecting another task which it has called. Another approach would be to have the keyboard interrupt task call the event decoder task to pass the keystroke when it does arrive. This has the advantage that the event decoder task will never miss other events because it is waiting for keystrokes. However, this is clearly one of those situations described in Chapter 3 where each task is too important to call the other. A transport task must be used between them.

The bidirectional data flow between the line printer task and the event decoder task can be handled easily by a unidirectional entry call from the line printer task to the event decoder task to wait for more lines to print. The call in itself, serves as notification that it has finished printing the previous set of lines. The page-line number range for a new set of lines to be printed can be returned as an output parameter of this call. Figure 4.25(a) shows the resulting structure.

As further reinforcement of the use of a transport task for keyboard events, consider the following scenario. If the event decoder called the keyboard interface directly, the following sequence of events could occur. While the line printer task is busy printing the first few lines of the form, editing operations managed by the event decoder task could succeed in freeing several more lines. The line range freed would be noted internally in the event decoder for release to the line printer on acceptance of the MORE__LINES call. At this point, suppose the operator pauses for thought while the event decoder task is waiting for another keystroke. Before the operator hits the next key, suppose the line printer task calls for more lines. Because the event decoder task is waiting elsewhere, the line printer task must also wait even though lines are available. The line printer task will not get its lines to print until the operator hits the next keystroke, freeing the event decoder task to process that keystroke and accept the MORE__LINES call. It is very unlikely that this small unnecessary delay in resuming printing would ever be important

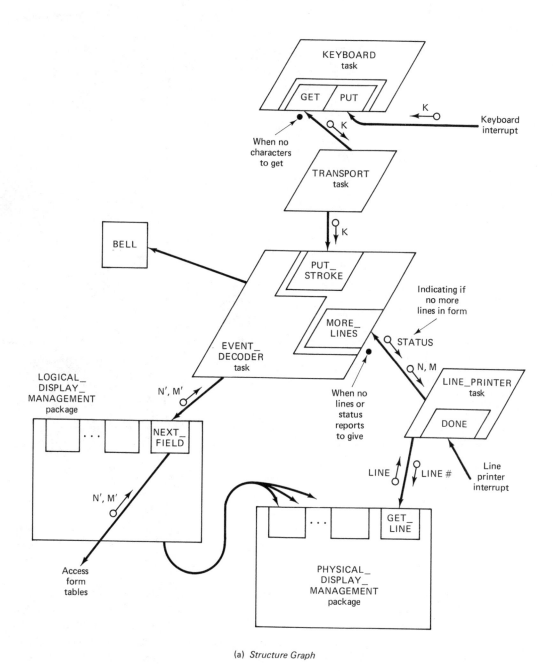

(a) *Structure Graph*

Figure 4.25 FORMS system high-level edit/print interactions

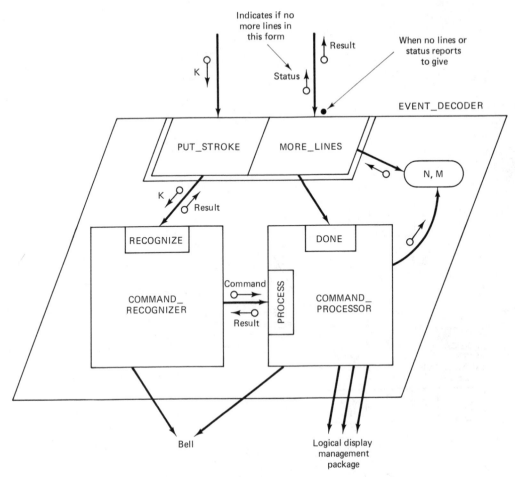

(b) *Internal Structure Graph of the Event Decoder Task*

Figure 4.25 (continued)

to the operator in this system. However, note that in rejecting it as unimportant, we are making assumptions about system timing which could be invalidated by subsequent changes to the requirements or to the system design. With a transport task between the keyboard and the event decoder, it is never possible for the printer to be held up unnecessarily when lines are available for printing because the event decoder task will never be waiting elsewhere when the printer task makes its call for more lines.

Note that Figure 4.25(a) does not show the complete system structure but only that involving the high-level edit/print interactions. The nature of the structure is obvious from the previous diagrams and discussions, and it would be a simple matter to draw on these to develop a complete structure diagram. However, note that it is often the case that complete structure diagrams are less informative than a number of partial diagrams

```
task EVENT__DECODER is
    entry PUT__STROKE (K : in KEYSTROKE);
    --ALWAYS ACCEPTED
    entry MORE__LINES (N,M : out LINE__NUMBER; STATUS: out STATUS__TYPE);
    --USED TO SIGNAL DONE AND TO GET MORE LINES
    --ACCEPTED ONLY WHEN LINES TO GIVE
    --SPECIAL CASE END OF FORM SIGNALLED BY STATUS
end EVENT__DECODER;

task body EVENT__DECODER is
    type STATUS__TYPE is (MORE, NO__MORE, DONE);
    RESULT: STATUS__TYPE : = DONE;
    STATUS: STATUS__TYPE : = DONE;
      N.M:     . . .
    --INTERNAL PACKAGE DECLARATIONS GO HERE
  loop
    select
      accept PUT__STROKE (K : in . . .)
      do RECOGNIZER.RECOGNIZE (K, RESULT); end;

    or

      when RESULT/ = DONE = >
      accept MORE__LINES (N,M : out . . .; STATUS : OUT . . .);
      do STATUS : = RESULT;
        N : = . . .;
        M : = . . .;
        if RESULT = NO__MORE then
        PROCESSOR.DONE;
        RESULT : = DONE; end if;
      end;
    end select;
  end loop;
end EVENT__DECODER;
```

(c) *Ada Program Skeleton*

Figure 4.25   (continued)

showing how parts of the system interact for particular purposes. Often one wants to focus on a particular package or task together with all of its interactions with other packages or tasks without regard to their interactions with each other.

We now turn to the internals of the Event Decoder task. Figure 4.25(b) provides one possible structure, employing nested packages to implement the command recognizer and processor modules. The controller is the main loop of the task.

An Ada program skeleton for the task is given in Figure 4.25(c).

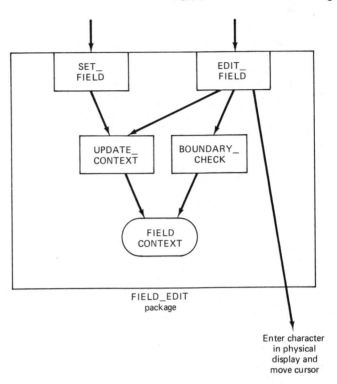

Figure 4.26 Alternative approach to the field edit package

4.5.6 Design Evaluation

A simpler interaction of the field edit package with the external world would result if a field context were maintained inside the package. *Field context* means the physical position and dimensions of the field on the screen together with all field attributes. Figure 4.26 illustrates this approach. It offers the attractive possibility of extensibility to include complete field editing functions similar to those associated with page oriented word processing.

However, before jumping on the bandwagon for this approach, consider Figure 4.27, which shows an approach to cursor control typical of that employed in many word processors but different from what we have assumed here. In this approach the cursor may be moved physically anywhere on the screen independently of the current logical context; it is up to the logical display management package to determine whether operations associated with the new cursor position are legal. It is difficult to reconcile this approach with that of maintaining all logical field operations, including cursor movements within the field, under the control of the field edit package, as suggested by Figure 4.26.

Of particular concern for designs which involve operator interactions is the extensibility of the design to cover possible new forms of interaction without major modifications. If changes are required, the important considerations are:

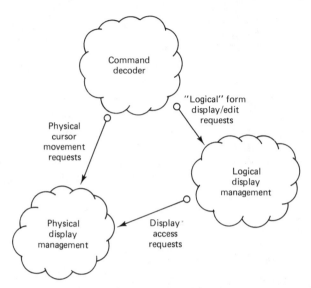

Figure 4.27 Data-flow graph showing mixed logical and physical cursor movements

- Can the changes be restricted to tables?
- Can the changes be restricted to code and tables in one module?
- Are changes required to the interactions between modules as well as to the modules themselves?

Changes in the FORMS system might be required due to deficiencies of the present system with respect to the following points:

- lack of provision for multiple keystroke commands or command echoing
- lack of a proper insertion facility in a field
- lack of operator control of printing
- inability to return to a field once the next field keystroke has been entered except by redoing the entire form
- lack of provision for form table storage or secondary memory

We must now ask ourselves if these deficiencies can be easily rectified within the framework of this design.

There is no problem with multiple keystroke commands. These could be handled by adding a keystroke sequence recognizer in the event decoder, which would include character sequences in commands as well as sequences of commands. Nor would there be any problem with echoing, because the system has been designed to accommodate effects on the screen of individual keystrokes.

Changes to provide for automatic movement of text in the field to the right or left on insertion or deletion would be confined to the internal logic of the Field Edit package and so could be accommodated fairly easily. The interface to this package would not even have to be changed provided that insertion or deletion requests were passed as character code parameters of the ENTER__CHAR procedure.

Operator control of printing and arbitrary ordering of field visits by the operator could be very easily handled at the sacrifice of concurrent editing and printing on the same form. The logic of this particular design is based on the requirement that lines at the top of the page can be printed while fields at the bottom are still being edited. To accommodate arbitrary ordering of field visits by the operators, the ability to simultaneously edit and print a single form in this manner would have to be sacrificed. However, the structure of the system is such that this is easily done. Simply modify the form table for each form so that only the bottom right hand corner field releases all of the lines for printing. A special small print-enable field could even be created just for this purpose. As for the arbitrary field ordering, the NEXT__FIELD command would have to be redefined to include a field number parameter, and the NEXT__FIELD procedure in the logical display management package would have to take account of this parameter. Otherwise the system would be unchanged.

An alternate approach to handling separate printing which would require some modification to the system is to add a print command. This print command would now have to be recognized by the event decoder, and printing would now take place on recognition of this command instead of on recognition of exit from the print-enable field in the form. With reference to Figure 4.25, the event decoder task would no longer retrieve the page-line number range as a parameter of the next field call. However, no change would have to be made to the way in which the line printer task interacts with the event decoder task. On receipt of the print command (which could have page-line number range as a parameter), the event decoder task would simply hand the page-line number range as a parameter to the line printer task as before.

Note that there is never any possibility of conflict between editing and printing in either the original system or any of these variations, because the event decoder prevents it. Therefore the decision to make physical display management a passive package is justified, and the decision to pass line numbers instead of whole lines to the printer is also justified. However note the possible lack of safety if additional tasks are added to the system.

Accommodating forms tables stored on secondary storage would also be quite easy. The NEW__FORM procedure in the logical display management package would have to be modified to access the file system to get the form table instead of simply going directly to the form tables already stored in memory. The rest of the edit part of the system would be unaffected.

4.6 THIRD DESIGN EXAMPLE: DIALOGUE

4.6.1 Introduction

As a final design example in this chapter, consider the interaction of human operators at geographically separate physical sites using the video screens of their workstations to prepare messages for remote operators and to receive messages from remote operators.

The interesting new problem introduced by this example is that of contention on an equal-partner basis for a resource (the screen) rather than on a master/slave basis as with the FORMS system. In the FORMS system, contention for the resource (the video memory) was between a master foreground task and a slave background task whose activities were explicitly initiated by the foreground task. A new feature of the DIALOGUE system is that the local and remote human operators interact on an equal partner basis. In a single workstation at a particular site, the local human operator and the remote human operator will each have a task acting on his or her behalf inside that workstation and, accordingly, these tasks must also interact on an equal-partner basis. This equal-partner contention introduces some new design issues.

Figure 4.28 provides a high-level view of the DIALOGUE system. The human operator at either end can enter command and data keystrokes via the keyboard. Keystrokes include three special function keys, namely, RESERVE, RELEASE, and SEND. The RESERVE function key reserves the screen for message preparation. The RELEASE function key releases the screen and clears it when the operator decides either to abandon preparing an incomplete message without sending it, or to release the screen after reading a message which has been sent from the remote operator. The SEND function key is used to send the message displayed on the screen to the remote operator and then to release and clear the screen. Keystrokes also include any alphanumeric key.

We shall not be concerned in this example with details of screen formatting or command echoing but only with sequences of interactions. Neither shall we be concerned with details of the communications network link. We assume that either a physical connection exists between the two terminals or that a connection can be established

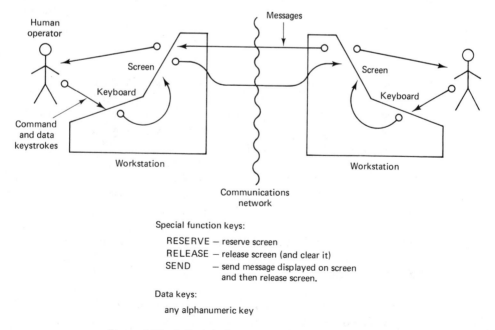

Figure 4.28 A final design example—DIALOGUE system

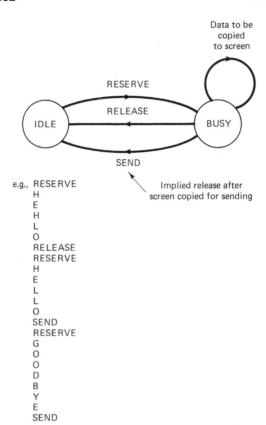

Figure 4.29 Finite state machine showing legal DIALOGUE system keystroke sequences

somehow through a public data network. We assume that a facility exists to send text messages to the current remotely connected terminal and to receive text messages from it. The design of such a message system is treated in Chapter 6.

Our main concern in this example is with sequencing. We want to avoid sequencing errors such as a locally prepared message being overwritten by a remotely arriving message before the local one has been sent.

It is quite easy to develop a finite state machine showing proper sequencing of local reserving, releasing and sending the screen. Figure 4.29 provides a finite state machine for these activities and gives an example of a legal sequence of keystrokes. Note the assumption implicit in this FSM that messages are passed from the screen to the messaging system as complete units. However, correct sequencing will also depend on remote events; before including them in a finite state machine, we must examine data flow.

4.6.2 Data Flow

Figure 4.30 provides a start on developing an edges-in data flow graph for this system. Within each workstation there must be a keyboard interface, a screen interface, and a message system interface. Moving inward from these edges, we recognize the need for

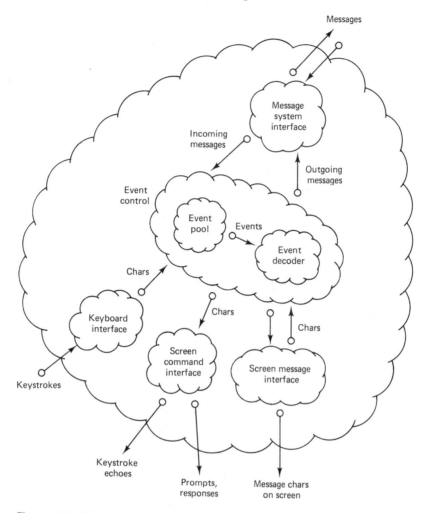

Figure 4.30 Edges-in data-flow graph development for the DIALOGUE system

an event control module which will provide the proper mediation between all of these activities. Inside this module we can identify the possible need for an event pool which serializes the keystrokes and incoming messages into a single stream of events and an event decoder which decodes these events and performs appropriate actions. The need for this serialization of the event stream arises, because remote events arrive at unpredictable times completely outside the control of either the human operator or the keyboard interface.

Given the idea of an event stream, we can now define an expanded finite state machine showing legal event sequences, as shown in Figure 4.31. In this finite state machine the former BUSY state has been renamed BUSY-LOCAL and a new state BUSY-REMOTE has been added. The BUSY-REMOTE state can only be entered from the idle state, thus, avoiding the possibility of overwriting the message on the screen.

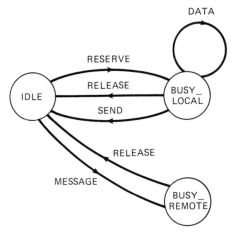

States:

IDLE: SCREEN_FREE
BUSY_LOCAL: SCREEN RESERVED FOR LOCAL MESSAGE
BUSY_REMOTE: SCREEN RESERVED FOR REMOTE MESSAGE

Figure 4.31 Expanded finite state machine showing legal DIALOGUE system event sequences

4.6.3 Structure

Given the data flow graph of Figure 4.30 and the event stream sequencing finite state machine of Figure 4.31, we can proceed to develop a structure graph for this system.

Figure 4.32 shows both structure and Ada code of a first attempt. Motivated by the discussion of the FORMS system design in Section 4.5.5, it includes two transport tasks, one for each type of event, to avoid any problems with unnecessarily delayed recognition of events. These transport tasks call PUT__STROKE and PUT__MESSAGE entries in the event decoder task.

The PUT__STROKE entry is accepted unconditionally. The PUT__MESSAGE message entry is only accepted when the FSM is in the idle state. Because there is only one transport task for each of these entries, it is not possible for the entry queues to contain more than one keystroke or more than one message so that if multiple keystrokes and multiple messages can arrive while the transport tasks are waiting for acceptance by the event decoder, they must be queued in the keyboard interrupt task or in the message system interface. In the keyboard interrupt task, this can be accomplished by providing a type-ahead buffer as shown. We are not concerned here with the internal details of the message system. However, whether or not the message system provides such buffering internally is irrelevant to the operation of Figure 4.32.

As shown by Figure 4.32(b), the finite state machine must be explicitly coded in the accept statements of the event decoder task. If it is desirable, for modularity, to provide a table-driven finite state machine, then the event sequence should be available internally in the event decoder task. This implies removal of the type-ahead buffer from the keyboard interrupt task, replacement of the PUT__STROKE and PUT__MESSAGE entries by a single PUT_EVENT entry, and addition of an event pool data structure internally in the event decoder task.

The result (structure graph only) is shown in Figure 4.33. Now, because the finite state machine operates directly on the event sequence, it can be completely table-driven. The *event pool* is defined as an internal package of the event decoder task with separate interface procedures to put and get keystrokes, messages, or the next event of either kind.

4.6.4 Design Evaluation

Lest the design decisions up to now have appeared somewhat too easy, let us examine another approach which appears at first sight to be very natural but which is logically more complex. This approach allows open competition for the screen between the keyboard decoder and the communications system. Missing is the intervening event stream

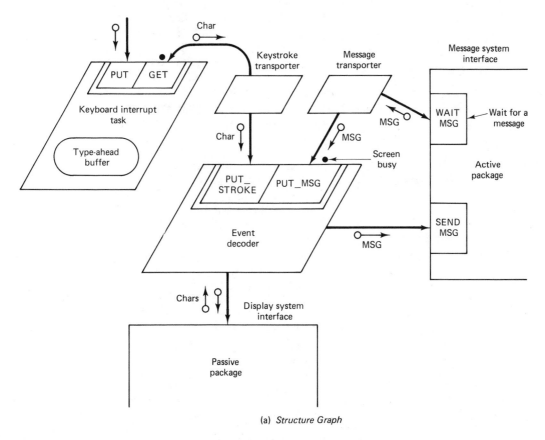

(a) *Structure Graph*

Figure 4.32 Event pool implemented implicitly by entry queues of event decoder task

```
task EVENT__DECODER is
  entry PUT__STROKE (K : in . . .);
  --ACCEPTED ANYTIME
  entry PUT__MSG (M : in . . .);
  --ACCEPTED ONLY IN IDLE STATE
end EVENT__DECODER;

task body EVENT__DECODER is
S : STATE : = IDLE;
. . .
loop
  select
    accept PUT__STROKE (K : . . .);
    do
      case S is
      when IDLE = >
        if K = RESERVE then S : = BUSY__LOCAL;
        else RING__BELL; end if;
      when BUSY__LOCAL = >
        case K is
        when RELEASE = >    S : = IDLE;
                            SCREEN.CLEAR;
        when SEND = >       S : = IDLE;
                            MESS.SEND ( . . . );
                            SCREEN.CLEAR;
        when in LEGAL__CHAR = >
                            SCREEN.WRITE (K);
        when OTHERS = >
                            RING__BELL;
        end case;
      when BUSY__REMOTE = >
        if K = RELEASE then
          S : = IDLE;
          SCREEN.CLEAR;
        else RING__BELL; end if;
      end case;
    end;
  or
    when S = IDLE = >
    accept PUT__MSG (M: . . .);
    do S: = BUSY__REMOTE;
      SCREEN.DISPLAY (M);
    end;
  end select;
end loop;
end EVENT__DECODER;
```

(b) *Ada Program Skeleton*

Figure 4.32   (continued)

136

serializer which characterized the previous design. This alternative approach is illustrated in Figure 4.34. In this approach a screen scheduler controls access to the screen without knowing anything about the purpose for which the screen is being requested. Because of the unpredictable timing of arrivals of requests, any competitor for the screen (keyboard decoder or communications system) may have to wait before screen access is granted. The problem with this approach is that the screen is used asymmetrically by the two competitors. The communications system only asks for the screen to display incoming messages but is not able itself to release the screen; this can only be done by the keyboard decoder when the screen is released by the operator. This results in an unpleasant asymmetry in the handling of keyboard and message events, which is entirely missing from the previous approach. This asymmetry adds complexity.

There is a general principle at work here. When multiple activities generated by human operators and system components can compete for resources, coordination of these activities should be centralized rather than distributed. Otherwise, complex interactions between the activities may be required, and modularity of the human interface subsystem is compromised.

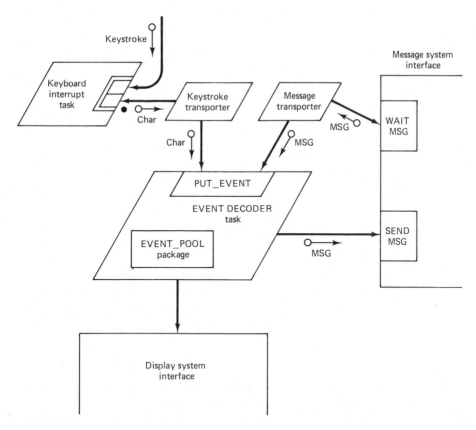

Figure 4.33 Event pool implemented by body of event decoder task

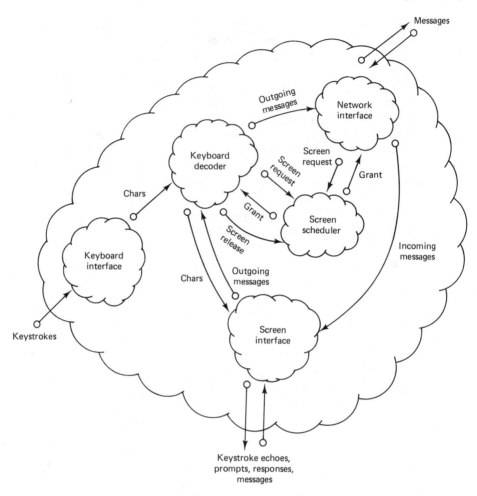

Figure 4.34   DIALOGUE system data flow—a more complex approach

In this design we have blithely ignored issues associated with message buffering and the network interface. These issues will be treated in Chapter 6.

4.7 CONCLUSIONS

This chapter has attempted to illustrate, using examples, design strategies and methodologies, the design process, and technical issues in design.

We are now ready for Part C, which explores the major issues raised in Part B in more detail.

Part C

Exploring Logical Design

This part begins by taking a more detailed look at some features of Ada that affect design, using both examples from Part B and new examples. It then tackles questions of modularity, reliability, and structure, through the design of a communications subsystem called COMM, for use with the DIALOGUE system. Finally, it tackles issues in the design of layered, concurrent systems in general, through the design of a system to implement the X.25 packet switching protocol.

Chapter 5

More Issues
About Ada

5.1 INTRODUCTION

In this chapter we explore some further Ada issues touched on only lightly, if at all, in previous chapters. We are primarily concerned here with the organization and interaction of *active modules,* that is, tasks or active packages.

Our approach in this chapter is to discuss what a designer may wish to express and then to discuss how it may be expressed in Ada.

Section 5.2 explores some important questions associated with task identifiers, task pools, and the dynamic access and creation of tasks, using the BANK example of Chapter 3 to illustrate many of the points. In passing, the identifier *aliasing* problem is treated.

Section 5.3 treats some important questions associated with task interaction structures. Linear and nonlinear interaction structures are defined and their properties examined using as examples flow-control, *readers-writers* scheduling, and task pool allocation problems. In passing, problems of *starvation* of tasks and of *races* between tasks are illustrated and solved.

Section 5.4 expands our view of event reporting to include exceptions. It shows how exceptions alter our view of system structure and argues that they should be used sparingly.

Section 5.5 treats the detection and controlling of aberrant behavior from a number of viewpoints. Can test-bed software be constructed to detect aberrant behavior, particularly in tasks and active packages? When should intertask protocols be used to provide protection from aberrant behavior in other tasks? How should the possibility of distributed target environments with potentially unreliable links and nodes be treated?

Section 5.6 considers system building issues. Ada has been characterized as a language for *structured system building* because of its support for module concepts. However, what about dynamic installation of new modules or reconfiguration of old ones? How should the designer view packages and tasks from a system building perspective instead of simply from a structured design perspective? It is in this section that we confront some major limitations of Ada.

5.2 ISSUES IN THE DYNAMIC ACCESS AND CREATION OF TASKS

5.2.1 Introduction

This section explores some important questions associated with dynamic interaction and creation of tasks. How may task identifiers be assigned and made known dynamically to all who need them (for example, to allow customer tasks to call otherwise anonymous members of task pools, or to allow secretary tasks to make calls back to previously anonymous customer tasks)? Hitherto, we have assumed all tasks were well-known so that their identifiers could be explicitly coded in call statements. A related question is: How may active packages implementing task pools protect themselves from misuse of dynamically assigned identifiers? A further related question is: How may members of task pools be dynamically created as needed?

Ada provides a template mechanism for identical tasks by allowing tasks to be defined as types. This allows us, for example, to define a single TELLER__TYPE task for the BANK example of Chapter 3. Instances of this single TELLER__TYPE may be created in a variety of ways, the simplest of which is to declare an appropriate number of tasks to be of type TELLER__TYPE. The names of these tasks may then be used in entry call statements. This is a much less cumbersome approach than that (used in Chapter 3) of defining each teller task individually with its own specification and body. However, it introduces identity problems, as we shall see.

5.2.2 Indirect Access to Anonymous Members of Task Pools

Direct use of the names of otherwise anonymous instances of task types is not necessarily the best way of identifying them in applications. In particular, it is often appropriate to identify members of task pools by application-dependent identifiers. Examples include the wicket numbers of the BANK example, connection identifiers in communications protocols, and device identifiers in I/O handlers. This approach enables rendezvous to be made with tasks hidden inside active packages.

Consider the BANK example again, retaining the wicket number mechanism but this time using a single task type for tellers. The wicket number mechanism creates an identity problem. The task body definition obviously can't include static initialization of the wicket number, as before. Each teller must therefore somehow acquire its wicket number dynamically. Two possibilities exist: either the dispatcher calls the teller or the teller calls the dispatcher.

The first possibility is illustrated in Figure 5.1(a). In this figure the teller tasks are components of an array. During initialization the dispatcher calls each task in the array, using the array name and index as a qualifier in the call statement, and passes the array index to the task to use as its wicket number. Later, the REQUEST_SERVICE procedure uses the wicket number passed to it by the customer in a similar fashion to call the correct teller.

The second possibility, of the teller calling the dispatcher, is more difficult to realize. As shown in Figure 5.1(b), the teller initially calls the dispatcher to GET its wicket number. Thereafter, whenever it is free, it calls a single READY entry in the dispatcher to pass on its wicket number. But how can the REQUEST_SERVICE procedure then contact the correct task using this wicket number? Under the circumstances, it can only call tellers successively until it finds the correct one. The problem could be solved, somewhat awkwardly, by providing a separate READY entry for each teller in the dispatcher, allowing the dispatcher to set up a correspondence table between wicket numbers and tellers which could be used by the REQUEST_SERVICE procedure to identify the correct teller.

Alternatively, the teller could pass both its name and wicket number to the dispatcher. But now we have come full circle: How does the teller know its own name? This question is addressed in Sections 5.2.3 and 5.2.4.

5.2.3 Direct Dynamic Connection Between Tasks

What if, instead of rendezvousing with unknown tasks through interface procedures of active packages, direct contact between tasks is desired? Then identifying values, useable directly in entry call statements, must be passed between tasks. This approach might be required to enable customers of the bank to call tellers directly. It might also be required to enable tellers to call customers directly, for example, if a transaction involved a lengthy background activity by the bank during which the teller could service other customers.

The ability to call another task directly using a dynamically-supplied value identifying the task will be referred to as *dynamic connection* or *dynamic access,* to contrast it with the *static access* characterizing all previous examples. A structure graph notation for dynamic access is shown in Figure 5.2. Task A gets a value identifying task B from somewhere and then calls an entry in task B using this value as a qualifier in the entry call. There is no intermediate procedure which knows the name of the task, given an application-assigned identifier, as there was in Section 5.2.2. The calling task does not need to know the value identifying the called task at the time the code is written, but it must know the called task's type so that it may know the entry names and parameters.

From the designer's viewpoint, such dynamic connections might be desirable between any module types; however, as illustrated in the figure, such connections between procedures or packages are illegal in Ada.

Let us now reexamine the BANK example, considering how dynamic connections may be made by customers to tellers and by tellers to customers. The former case may

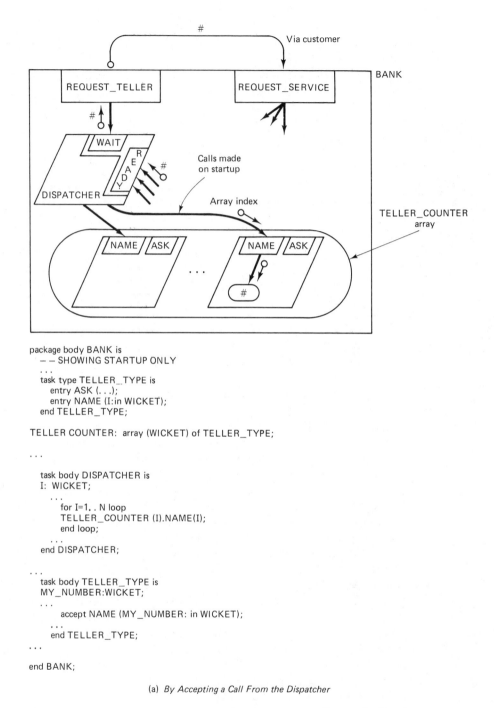

```
package body BANK is
   - - SHOWING STARTUP ONLY
   . . .
   task type TELLER_TYPE is
      entry ASK ( . . .);
      entry NAME (I:in WICKET);
   end TELLER_TYPE;

TELLER COUNTER:  array (WICKET) of TELLER_TYPE;


   . . .

   task body DISPATCHER is
   I:  WICKET;
      . . .
         for I=1. . N loop
         TELLER_COUNTER (I).NAME(I);
         end loop;
      . . .
   end DISPATCHER;

. . .
   task body TELLER_TYPE is
   MY_NUMBER:WICKET;
   . . .
      accept NAME (MY_NUMBER: in WICKET);
      . . .
      end TELLER_TYPE;
. . .

end BANK;
```

(a) *By Accepting a Call From the Dispatcher*

Figure 5.1 How a member of a task pool may discover its identity

144

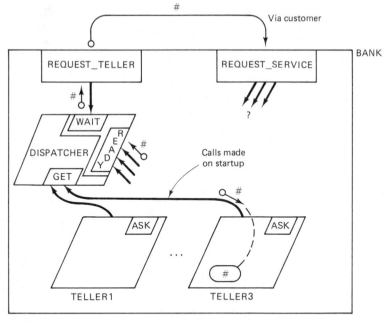

(b) *By Calling the Dispatcher*

Figure 5.1   (continued)

be characterized as dynamic connection in the forward direction of the customer/server relationship and the latter case as dynamic connection in the reverse direction of the customer/server relationship.

For reference purposes, Figure 5.3(a) depicts the original BANK example (with wicket numbers) as static connection in the forward direction.

Figure 5.3(b) depicts the BANK as providing dynamic connection in the forward direction, without wicket numbers. Here the dispatcher provides the customer a value

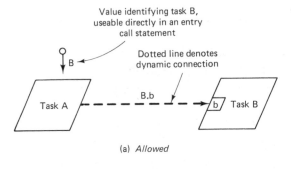

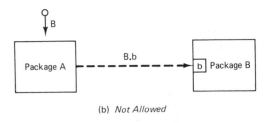

Value identifying task B,
useable directly in an entry
call statement

Dotted line denotes
dynamic connection

B

B.b

Task A — — — — — — b / Task B

(a) *Allowed*

B

B.b

Package A — — — — — — b Package B

(b) *Not Allowed*

Figure 5.2 Dynamic connections between modules

identifying the teller, and the customer uses this value directly in an entry call statement to the appropriate teller.

What values can be used to identify tellers in the absence of wicket numbers? How may the body of the teller task acquire the value which identifies a particular teller (namely, the teller executing the body at the time the value is needed)?

A simple (but, alas, incorrect) approach is to have the teller body pass the task type identifier to identify the task currently executing the body. The Ada Reference Manual encourages us to think this might work when it says that within a task body this identifier "denotes the task currently executing the body." This incorrect approach is illustrated in Figure 5.4.

A suitable approach is to use access variables. We defer discussion of access variables for tasks until Section 5.2.4. However, note that a task does not automatically know its own access variable. It must be given it explicitly via an initialization rendezvous, just as it had to be given its own wicket number in Figure 5.1(a).

Figure 5.5 illustrates dynamic connection in the reverse direction for the BANK example. Here customers identify themselves to the bank so that tellers may call them later. Even if this approach is not used for the first contact between the customer and the teller, it may be appropriate for the teller to report results to the customer some time after the initial rendezvous. Because it is unreasonable to expect server packages to know all customer names in advance, dynamic connection is the only logical approach for the reverse direction.

A simple (but also incorrect) approach is to have the customer body pass the task identifier to the bank. This incorrect approach is illustrated in Figure 5.6. Again, a suitable approach is to use access variables, as discussed in Section 5.2.4.

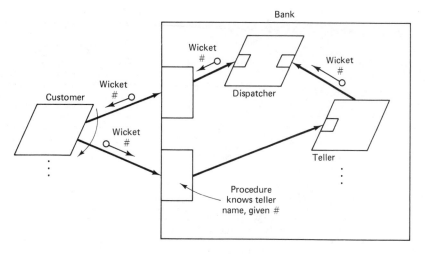

(a) *Case 1: Static Connection*

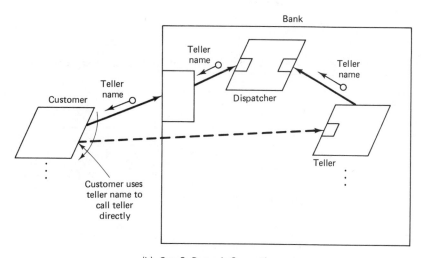

(b) *Case 2: Dynamic Connection*

Figure 5.3 The BANK example—connection in the forward direction (*notes:* Wicket_number is a program variable identifying a teller task indirectly. The procedure has all the teller calls explicitly coded in a case statement. Teller_name is a program variable identifying a teller task directly. It must not be a character string identifier of the task in the program text. An access variable is appropriate. No case statement is required.)

```
package BANK is
  ...
  task type TELLER_TYPE is
    entry ASK (TRANSACTION : in T_TYPE;
                     RESULT : out R_TYPE);
  end TELLER_TYPE;
  procedure REQUEST_TELLER (NAME: out TELLER_TYPE);
end BANK;

package body BANK is

  task body (TELLER_TYPE) is

    loop

      DISPATCHER.READY ( (TELLER_TYPE) );

      accept ASK ( . . .) do WORK; end;
      CLEAN_UP;
    end loop;
  end TELLER_TYPE;
  TELLER1, TELLER2, TELLER3 : TELLER_TYPE;
  task DISPATCHER is
      entry WAIT (NAME: out TELLER_TYPE);
      entry READY (NAME: in TELLER_TYPE);
  end DISPATCHER;
  task body DISPATCHER is separate;

procedure REQUEST_TELLER ( . . .) is
  begin DISPATCHER.WAIT (NAME);
  end;

end BANK;
```

> Task type identifier used in body as a self-identifying parameter to denote the task currently executing the body. Incorrect because only values of variables can be passed as parameters.

Figure 5.4 A simple but incorrect approach to task self-identification for the BANK example—Case 2

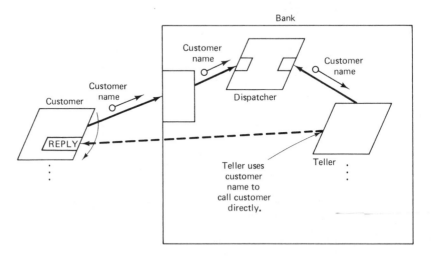

Figure 5.5 The BANK example—Case 3—Dynamic connection in the reverse direction (*note:* Customer_name is a program variable identifying a customer task directly. An access variable is appropriate.)

148

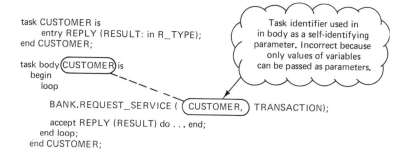

```
task CUSTOMER is
    entry REPLY (RESULT: in R_TYPE);
end CUSTOMER;

task body CUSTOMER is
    begin
       loop

       BANK.REQUEST_SERVICE ( CUSTOMER, TRANSACTION);

       accept REPLY (RESULT) do . . . end;
       end loop;
    end CUSTOMER;
```

Task identifier used in
in body as a self-identifying
parameter. Incorrect because
only values of variables
can be passed as parameters.

Figure 5.6 A simple but incorrect approach to task identification for the BANK example— Case 3

It is not only task pools such as the bank package which have naming problems. Consider the case of a MAILROOM package allowing tasks to send messages to other tasks by name and to receive messages for themselves by name. One approach would be for a customer task to pass its own name as a parameter of a RCVE call and then simply wait to return from that call until mail had arrived. Of course, if the customer task did not wish to wait personally, it could send a transport task for this purpose. The problem with this waiting approach is that it requires out-of-order scheduling. A customer will wait with other tasks in an internal entry queue in FIFO order but needs to be awakened only when its own mail arrives, not just when any mail arrives. As discussed in Chapter 3, out-of-order scheduling problems based on parameters of entry calls are awkward to handle in Ada. As suggested, a way around the difficulty is to provide each customer with its own internal entry in a task in the MAILROOM package. But this is obviously undesirable if the MAILROOM must serve many customers whose names are unknown a priori.

This is an example of a situation where reverse direction dynamic connection is desirable. Instead of waiting in an internal entry queue associated with the RCVE procedure, this procedure could simply be used to pass on the caller's identity to the MAILROOM package. If there is no mail immediately available for pick up, the caller may then go about its business and when it is ready to receive mail, invoke an accept statement for an entry which will be called by the MAILROOM package when mail arrives.

This approach is illustrated by Figure 5.7. The only thing to watch is that tasks in the mailroom package (which, of course, is an active package) are not held up waiting for customers to accept GIVE calls, thereby holding up other customers who want to receive or send mail.

One approach to ensuring that such holdup does not happen is for customers to promise to be ready to accept GIVE calls immediately after placing RCVE calls to the mailroom package. In this case, calling the RCVE procedure is good only for one mail receipt.

Another approach is to use the RCVE call to register customers with the mailroom package for multiple mail receipts and for the mailroom package to have a pool of transport tasks which give mail to customers as required. If a sufficiently large pool is maintained

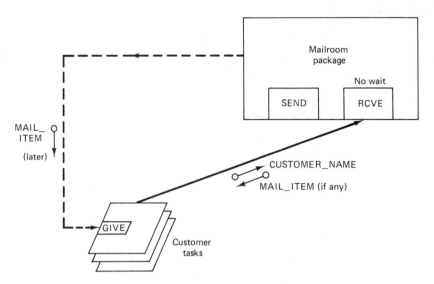

Figure 5.7 A reverse-direction, dynamic interconnection approach to a mail reception problem

to handle all customers or if members of the pool are dynamically created as required, then problems of waiting are avoided.

Without dynamic interconnection the only recourse is to introduce mailboxes. These are like the wickets in the bank example, except that they may be used for multiple interactions with the mailroom package. The externals of this approach are illustrated in Figure 5.8. Customers may rent and release mailboxes and may use the mailbox identifiers to send and receive messages. Internally in the mailroom package, mailbox identifiers could be used to index members of an entry family. Thus, each customer owning a mailbox could wait in its own entry queue for its own mail. Details of code for the MAILROOM example are left to the reader.

5.2.4 Dynamic Creation of Tasks

Because tasks may be defined as types, instances of tasks have many of the properties of variables. In particular, instances of tasks may be created dynamically in the same way that memory space for variables may be created dynamically:

- by declaring instances of task types in a dynamic context, for example locally in a procedure;
- by defining access variables (pointers) to task types and creating instances of these types using a "new" statement.

Task pools such as the teller pool in the BANK example are an obvious application of dynamic creation.

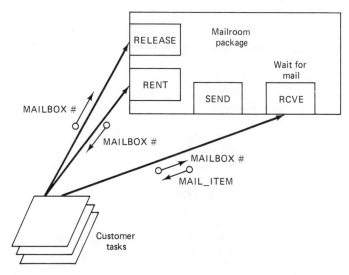

Figure 5.8 A forward-direction, static interconnection approach to a mail reception problem

Why not create instances of tellers only when customers need service and save the space taken up by task descriptor tables and stacks at other times? The issue is primarily one of implementation efficiency and, as such, is at a different logical level than the primarily design-oriented issues associated with dynamic connection.

An example of dynamic creation of tasks as they are required is given in Figure 5.9 for the BANK example. Note that the body of the TELLER__TYPE task contains no loop, so that each task instance terminates as soon as it has done its work. For simplicity, no limit on the number of tellers created is imposed in this example.

More significant from a design viewpoint is the requirement stated previously that access variables for tasks be used for dynamic connection. This requires dynamic creation, but not necessarily of the *as required* kind illustrated in Figure 5.9.

For example, in the BANK system tellers could be created by the dispatcher during initialization and then passed their own access variables for later use in self-identification. This approach is logically very similar to the wicket number approach of Figure 5.1(a), with access variables replacing wicket numbers.

5.2.5 Aliasing of Identifiers

A possible problem with all of these approaches is the aliasing of task identifiers. The term *aliasing* implies the existence of multiple copies of identifiers (whether application-assigned numbers or access variables). The aliasing problem arises if identifiers are not explicitly deallocated by their supplier when their use is no longer appropriate. For example, customers of the BANK package should not continue to use old wicket numbers or teller task access variables after the interaction with the teller is completed.

```
package BANK is
  procedure REQUEST__TELLER (NAME: out TELLER);

  task type TELLER__TYPE is
    entry ASK ( . . . );
  end TELLER__TYPE;
  type TELLER is access TELLER__TYPE;
end BANK;

package body BANK is
  task body TELLER__TYPE is
    accept ASK ( . . . ) do WORK end;
    CLEAN__UP;
  end TELLER__TYPE;

  task DISPATCHER is
    entry WAIT (NAME : out TELLER);
  end DISPATCHER;

  procedure REQUEST__TELLER ( . . . ) is
    begin DISPATCHER.WAIT (NAME);
    end;

  --DISPATCHER CREATES UNLIMITED NUMBERS OF TELLERS
  task body DISPATCHER is
  NAME : TELLER;
  begin
    loop
      accept WAIT (NAME : out TELLER)
        do NAME : = new TELLER__TYPE; end;
      end LOOP;
  end DISPATCHER;

  end BANK;
```

Figure 5.9 BANK example with tellers dynamically created as required

One approach to guard against aliasing in the BANK package is to make teller identifiers *in/out* parameters of the procedure call requesting teller service and to assign an invalid identifier on return from this procedure. Identifiers are checked for validity on all calls to the procedure. This, of course, requires that identifiers be limited private types of the BANK package.

This approach is illustrated for wicket number identifiers in Figure 5.10. It can be used to guard against simple aliasing problems of the kind described here. However, more general aliasing problems are not so easy to guard against, as we shall see in Chapter 6.

```
package BANK is
. . .
type WICKET, VALID__WICKET is limited private;
procedure REQUEST__TELLER (NAME: out VALID__WICKET);
procedure REQUEST__SERVICE (NAME: inout WICKET; RESULT: . . . );
private
   type WICKET is range 0 . . 3; --0 TO DEALLOCATE
   subtype VALID__WICKET is WICKET range 1 . . 3;
   end BANK;

package body BANK is
. . .
TELLER__COUNTER: array (VALID__WICKET) of TELLER__TYPE;
. . .

procedure REQUEST__SERVICE (NAME: inout WICKET; RESULT: . . . );
begin
   TELLER__COUNTER (NAME).TELLER__TYPE.ASK (TRANSACTION, RESULT);
   NAME : = 0;
exception
   when CONSTRAINT__ERROR = > RESULT : = INVALID__WICKET;
end REQUEST__SERVICE;
end BANK;
```

Figure 5.10   Protecting against wicket number aliasing in the BANK example

Just how far one should go in guarding against this type of misuse is debatable. In the BANK package as designed, we already rely on customers to call tellers after they have been allocated, otherwise tellers will wait forever. If the BANK is willing to trust customers to this extent, then it should be willing to trust them not to reuse old identifiers. Of course, failure on the customer's part to make the call can also be guarded against by redesigning the BANK package. One possibility is to specify that one interface procedure both waits for a teller and asks service of the teller. Another possibility is to require tellers to time-out on waiting for customer calls.

5.3 MORE TASK INTERACTION STRUCTURES

5.3.1 Introduction

A task will be said to have a *linear interaction structure* with respect to other tasks if there is no nesting of entry acceptances or entry calls within the critical sections of its accept statements.

All the task examples so far in this book have displayed linear interaction structures. However, cases arise in practice where it may appear at first glance, particularly to the experienced programmer, to be difficult or inappropriate to use such structures. The purpose of this section is to argue for the desirability of linear interaction structures, to show by example how they may be developed, and to introduce a new structure graph notation for the rare cases where they are unsuitable.

In passing we treat issues associated with appropriate representation of finite state machines, with *starvation* of tasks and with *races* between tasks.

Linear interaction structures are desirable for a number of reasons.

- The designer can clearly and unambiguously identify all waiting conditions, in terms of guards on entries, at the level of the task interface.
- The process of translating the designer's intentions into Ada code can be made relatively mechanical, thus minimizing the possibility of errors (and offering the enticing prospect of automated translation).
- The internal logic of each task follows a simple pattern of rendezvous-process-wait, which makes the overall system organization easy to understand.

Three examples illustrating the key issues are treated here.

- a task exercising flow control on data items sent to it (Section 5.3.2)
- a task implementing a finite state machine with a difficult out-of-order-scheduling aspect (Section 5.3.3)
- a task pool in which tasks are explicitly reserved and released by customers of the pool (Section 5.3.4)

Our emphasis throughout the exploration of these examples is not just on solving the technical problems but on developing solutions which have easy to understand task interface properties.

5.3.2 Flow Control Example

How a task may exercise flow control on data items sent to it was discussed briefly in Chapter 3. The solutions there all used linear interaction structures.

Consider now a possible nonlinear interaction structure to solve this problem, suggested by the linear structure of Figure 5.11(a). In this figure, A never waits for credit but only gets it if available at the time of the SEND call to B. However, a designer might wish to specify a different arrangement, for which we have, as yet, no structure graph notation, as follows. Suppose B grants credit to A by an *out* parameter of the SEND entry and that A waits for credit after its SEND call has been accepted, if credit is not immediately available (assuming it has indicated a willingness to wait by an appropriate value of the opcode parameter). If A calls B.SEND and, in doing so, exhausts its credit, then the SEND call will be accepted, but the rendezvous will not be terminated until credit is available. This credit will presumably be made available when another task calls B.RCVE to pick up an item. The only way of arranging the internal logic of B to satisfy

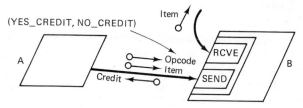

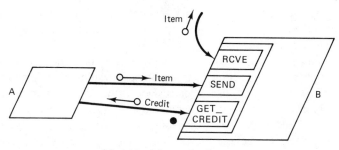

(a) *A Structure Graph Suggesting the Possibility of a Nonlinear Interaction Structure*

(b) *A Linear Interaction Structure*

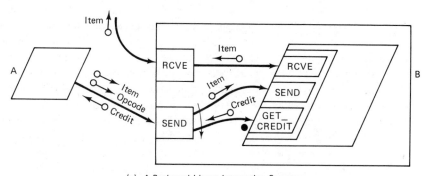

(c) *A Packaged Linear Interaction Structure*

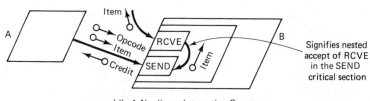

(d) *A Nonlinear Interaction Structure*

Figure 5.11   Linear and non-linear interaction structure for a flow-control problem

these external requirements is for the RCVE entry to be accepted within the critical section of the SEND entry, thus violating linearity.

We argue that, in general, nonlinear approaches may be complex, both from an interface viewpoint and from an internal logic viewpoint. Therefore, before introducing a new structure graph notation which can reflect a designer's requirement for a nonlinear interaction structure, we first consider why this approach may be complex and then show how the problem may be solved without resorting to nonlinear structures.

From an interface viewpoint, the nonlinear interaction structure is complex because it is more difficult to describe than a linear structure in which the call is either always accepted and then processed to completion immediately, or guarded and thereby not accepted until it can be processed to completion. The simple dot notation on an entry in a structure graph to indicate guarded conditional waiting is no longer sufficient to indicate the nature of the interface, because conditional waiting for the *out* parameter of the call may occur even when a guard is not present. Furthermore, the caller can no longer take the simple defensive action against prolonged waiting of making a timed entry call. Once the SEND is accepted, the caller is stuck at the acceptor's pleasure.

From an internal logic viewpoint, the nonlinear interaction structure is more complex because of the higher level of explicit coupling required between the code fragments which process the various entries. For example, what if the accepting task has a large number of entries in a single selective accept clause? Accepting one of them and then waiting for a call on another one before terminating the first rendezvous effectively closes all the other entries. If they shouldn't all be closed, then a nested, selective accept clause may be needed, and such a nested clause may be needed for all entries which trigger nested accepts. The resulting code will be complex. With linear interaction structures, coupling between entries is restricted to the setting and clearing of guards and the inspection and updating of local variables, all of which are straightforward operations.

Figure 5.11(b) shows the appropriate structure graph notation for a linear interaction structure which includes the possibility of waiting for credit after sending. Figure 5.11(c) shows how a user might see this approach if task B were hidden inside an active package, as it might be in practice. The approach of Figure 5.11(c) offers the twin advantages of the simplicity of single user call and the clarity of a linear task interaction structure.

If, in spite of these considerations, a designer wishes to specify a nonlinear interaction structure, then Figure 5.11(d) provides a new structure graph notation allowing him to do it. This notation indicates that termination of the SEND rendezvous may be delayed (depending on the value of the opcode parameter and the availability of credit) by accepting the RCVE entry in the critical section of the accept clause for the SEND entry. The SEND rendezvous will thus not be terminated until the RCVE rendezvous is completed, presumably thereby releasing credit.

The nonlinear structure of Figure 5.11(d) solves the problem and on the face of it is not particularly complex from an interface viewpoint. However, the complexity arises in general from the fact that entries involved in nested accepts may also be accepted directly as separate select alternatives, perhaps even guarded ones. It is even possible to visualize nested accepts of the same entry occurring in several different select alternatives and of this being true for several entries. We shall return to this complexity question in our treatment of the next two examples.

5.3.3 A Readers/Writers Example, Using Finite State Machines

Finite state machines are ubiquitous in many types of embedded systems. Accordingly, their explicit, consistent, and uniform representation in the Ada program text seems desirable, both for verifiability and readability. The use of linear interaction structures can accomplish this purpose.

We saw in Chapter 4 several examples of how finite state machine modules naturally arise in system design. In particular, the DIALOGUE example showed how a finite state machine could be implemented in a task using a linear interaction structure with entry calls to announce events and guards on the entries to defer processing of events until appropriate states. This approach was straightforward for the DIALOGUE example. However, an apparent problem can occur with out-of-order scheduling in more complex cases. This problem is illustrated and solved below using a readers/writers example.

The approach of this section is to work through a number of progressively more general versions of this example, using both linear and nonlinear interaction structures, culminating in a final version (Figure 5.16), which is both linear and general. Along the way, a number of issues are raised and resolved.

A problem which arises often in concurrent programming and which has been solved by many methods in the literature is the *readers/writers* problem. The essentials of this problem are that a data structure in primary or secondary memory is accessed by a number of tasks, some of which only need to read its contents and others to update it. In general, reading and writing can occur at any time, although only one task at a time should be allowed to write. While it is writing, all other writing and reading tasks must be denied access. However, when no one is writing, any number of reading tasks may be allowed access. The rules can be refined, as we shall see, but first consider the solution for this simple statement of the problem.

An obvious approach to this problem is to use a scheduler task to control access. Figure 5.12 illustrates the approach, assuming there are several readers but only one writer. The resource scheduler task has REQUEST__READ, REQUEST__WRITE, and FIN entries. Readers calling REQUEST__READ are held up in the entry queue if writing is taking place until the writer is finished. The writer calling REQUEST__WRITE is held up in the entry queue until all readers are finished. Return from either the RE-QUEST__ READ or the REQUEST__WRITE call denotes permission to proceed with reading or writing. Both readers and writers call FIN when they are finished. The problem as stated is a sequencing problem which is amenable to finite state machine solution along the lines of that employed in the DIALOGUE example of Chapter 4. Figure 5.13 illustrates both an appropriate finite state machine and the Ada code to implement it in the resource scheduler task. The linear interaction structure displayed by this particular Ada solution is attractive because of its explicit representation of the finite state machine, making it

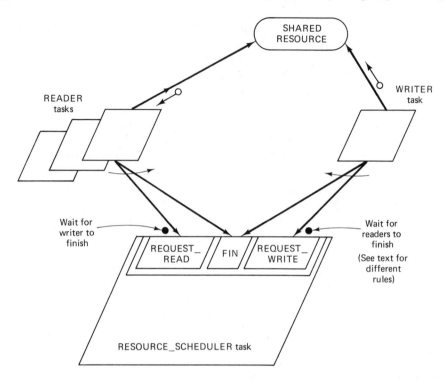

Figure 5.12   Readers/writers example—external view

straightforward to program, easy to verify against the state transition diagram, and easy to read.

However, the statement of the problem leading to this solution is faulty. A number of busy readers can lock out the writer indefinitely. This form of lockout exemplifies a system problem called *starvation*. It is not deadlock, because as soon as the readers cease to be busy, the writer may proceed. It is a milder system problem than deadlock but, nevertheless, undesirable. A proper statement of the problem should require that a writer be allowed to proceed as soon as all current readers have finished. This refinement introduces an aspect of out-of-order scheduling into the problem which makes the Ada implementation of the finite state machine in the form of Figure 5.13 less straightforward.

The tricky problem arising now is how to recognize (but not immediately accept) a REQUEST__WRITE call in the READING state as an event which should trigger a change to a new state. In this new state, new REQUEST__READ calls would not be accepted, and only when all pending FIN calls from current readers were accepted, would the REQUEST__WRITE call be accepted and the WRITING state be entered. The natural approach, following previous examples, would be to accept the REQUEST__WRITE call in the READING state and then to trigger an appropriate state change. However, also following previous examples, the next step would be to terminate the REQUEST__WRITE

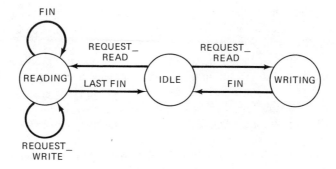

(a) *Finite State Machine*

```
task body RESOURCE_SCHEDULER is
type STATETYPE is (IDLE, READING, WRITING);
STATE : STATETYPE : = IDLE;
READERS : integer : = 0;
  loop
    select
      when STATE = IDLE = > accept REQUEST_WRITE
        do STATE : = WRITING; end;
    or
      when STATE ≠ WRITING = >
        accept REQUEST_READ
        do case STATE is
          when IDLE = > STATE : = READING; READERS : = READERS + 1;
          when READING = > READERS : = READERS + 1;
          end case;
        end;
    or
      when STATE ≠ IDLE = >
        accept FIN
        do case STATE is
          when READING = > READERS : = READERS − 1;
                           if READERS = 0 then
                               STATE : = IDLE; end if;
          when WRITING = > STATE : = IDLE;
        end;
    end select;
  end loop;
end RESOURCE_SCHEDULER;
```

(b) *Ada Program*

Figure 5.13   Readers/writers example—solution 1

rendezvous and reenter the selective accept clause with new guards appropriate to the new state. But this would incorrectly give writing permission to the caller of REQUEST __WRITE.

An approach using nested rendezvous to solve this problem is given in Figure 5.14. Although this solves the programming problem, it does not fulfil the aim of explicitly representing the finite state machine in a linear interaction structure in the program text. There is an implicit reading-waiting-to-write state in this program. Furthermore, the structure graph illustrating the intent at the interface is awkward, because FIN is accepted in two places, one nested and one not.

An explicit finite state machine representation is, however, easily obtained by noting that nothing can be done in the READING state for the prospective writer until the next FIN call arrives. Therefore, at the time of accepting the next FIN call, the REQUEST __WRITE entry queue can be checked and appropriate state changes made. This will protect the writer against ultimate starvation but may allow some additional readers to slip in before the next FIN call. We can restrict this to at most one reader by cross-checking the REQUEST_WRITE entry queue at the time of accepting the next REQUEST__READ call. We can increase our chances of not letting even one reader slip in by periodically cross-checking the REQUEST__WRITE entry queue in a delay alternative, instead of waiting for external calls. The finite state machine representation of this approach is given in Figure 5.15(a), and an appropriate Ada program directly expressing this finite state machine is given in Figure 5.15(b).

The essential idea of the solution of Figure 5.15 is the treatment of the REQUEST__WRITE entry queue count attribute as an auxiliary variable affecting state transitions which are triggered in the first instance by the acceptance of other entries or by timeouts. If, however, there is a requirement which explicitly forbids the acceptance of even one REQUEST__READ after a REQUEST__WRITE has arrived, then the solution of Figure 5.15 is no longer valid. That solution allowed for possible acceptance of a single REQUEST__READ while in the READING state but after a REQUEST__ WRITE call had occurred and before a FIN call had occurred.

A linear interaction structure to solve this problem can be realized by providing separate entries for the writer to post a request (POST__WRITE) and to wait for the request to be honored if it can't be honored immediately due to readers being active (WAIT__WRITE). If there is only one writer, then the posting entry is unguarded and the waiting entry is guarded. Otherwise, the posting entry must also be guarded, to avoid races among multiple writers between POST__WRITE and WAIT__WRITE. The same user interface can be maintained by nesting the scheduler task in an active package. This approach is illustrated in Figure 5.16. The finite state machine logic follows that of Figure 5.15 except that the transition from the READING to the READ__FINISH state is triggered by acceptance of POST__WRITE, and the transition from the WRITE__READY to the WRITING state is triggered by acceptance of WAIT__WRITE. To ensure that multiple writers are given priority over readers in the IDLE state, the priority mechanism of Figure 3.16 could be employed. The Ada code for the body of the task is left as an exercise for the reader.

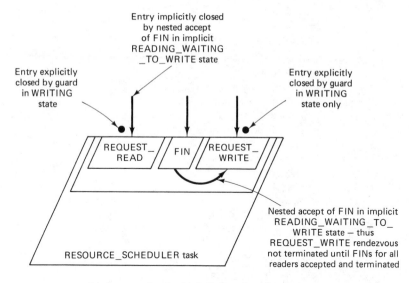

Entry implicitly closed
by nested accept
of FIN in implicit
READING_WAITING
_TO_WRITE state

Entry explicitly
closed by guard
in WRITING
state

Entry explicitly
closed by guard
in WRITING
state only

REQUEST_
READ

FIN

REQUEST_
WRITE

RESOURCE_SCHEDULER task

Nested accept of FIN in implicit
READING_WAITING_TO_
WRITE state — thus
REQUEST_WRITE rendezvous
not terminated until FINs for all
readers accepted and terminated

(a) *Structure Graph with Both Nested and Guarded
Accepts (Nonlinear Interaction Structure)*

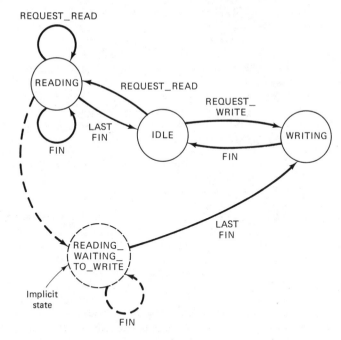

REQUEST_READ

READING

REQUEST_READ

LAST
FIN

FIN

IDLE

REQUEST_
WRITE

FIN

WRITING

LAST
FIN

READING_
WAITING_
TO_WRITE

Implicit
state

FIN

(b) *Finite State Machine with Implicit State*

Figure 5.14 Readers/writers example—solution 2 (nonlinear)

```
select
  when STATE ≠ WRITING = >
    accept REQUEST_WRITE
    do case STATE is
      when IDLE = > STATE : = WRITING;
      when READING = > loop
      accept FIN;
      READERS : = READERS − 1;
      if READERS = 0 then
        STATE : = WRITING;
        exit;
      end if;
      end loop
      end case;
    end;
or
  when STATE ≠ WRITING = >
    accept REQUEST_READ
    do case STATE is
      when IDLE = > STATE : = READING; READERS : = READERS + 1;
      when READING = > READERS : = READERS + 1;
      end case;
    end;
or
  when STATE ≠ IDLE = >
    accept FIN
      do case STATE is
      when READING = > READERS : = READERS − 1;
                       if READERS = 0 then STATE : = IDLE; end if;
      when WRITING = > STATE : = IDLE;
      end case;
  end;
end select;
```

(c) *Program Fragment Showing Nonlinear Interaction Structure*

Figure 5.14   (continued)

5.3.4 A Task Pool Example: AGENT_POOL

Here we treat an AGENT_POOL example, which is more general than the BANK example. Multiple agent tasks in a pool are allocated and deallocated at explicit customer request. Between allocation and deallocation, an agent is available for multiple interactions with the customer to whom it is allocated. Presumably these interactions generate a need for autonomous activity by the agents; otherwise, why use tasks? Some interesting and important task interaction issues arise in considering the interactions between the pool dispatcher, the customers, and the agents. Figure 5.17 illustrates the points.

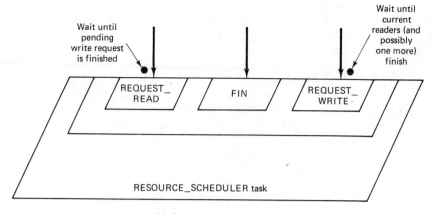

(a) *Structure Graph*

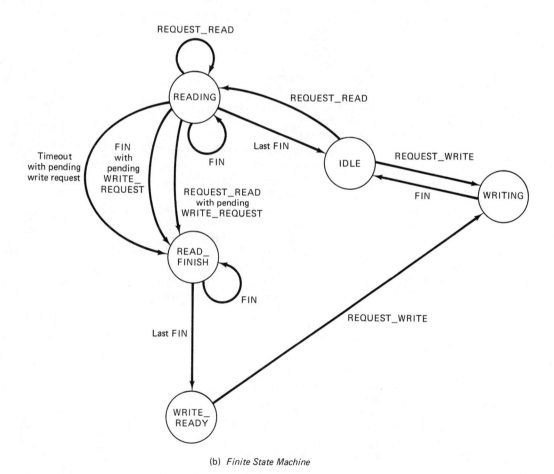

(b) *Finite State Machine*

Figure 5.15 Readers/writers example—solution 3

```
task body RESOURCE__SCHEDULER is
type STATETYPE is (IDLE, READING, WRITING, READ__FINISH);
STATE : STATETYPE : = IDLE;
READER : integer : = 0;
  loop
    select
      when STATE = IDLE or STATE = WRITE__READY = >
        accept REQUEST__WRITE
          do STATE : = WRITING; end;
    or
      when STATE = IDLE or STATE = READING = >
        accept REQUEST__READ
          do case STATE is
            when IDLE = >      STATE : = READING;
                               READERS : = READERS + 1;
            when READING = >
                               READERS : = READERS + 1;
                               if REQUEST__WRITE' COUNT>0)
                                 then STATE : = READ__FINISH;
                               end if;
          end case;
        end;
    or
      when STATE ≠ IDLE or STATE ≠ WRITE__READY = >
        accept FIN
          do case STATE is
            when WRITING = > STATE : = IDLE;
            when READ__FINISH = >
                    READERS : = READERS - 1;
                    if READERS = 0
                      then STATE : = WRITE__READY; end if;
            when READING = >
                    READERS : = READERS - 1;
                    if READERS = 0
                      then STATE : = IDLE;
                    else if REQUEST__WRITE' COUNT>0
                      then STATE : = READ__FINISH;
                    end if;
          end case;
        end;
    or
      delay TIMEOUT__PERIOD;
      if REQUEST__WRITE'COUNT>0
        then STATE : = READ__FINISH;
      end if;
    end select;
  end loop;
end RESOURCE__SCHEDULER;
```

(c) *Ada Program With a Linear Interaction Structure*

Figure 5.15   (continued)

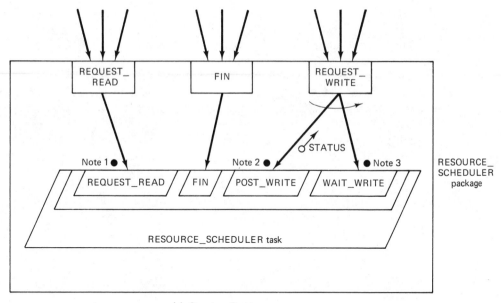

(a) *Structure Graph*

1. Closed while writers pending/active; 2. Closed while writers pending/active;
3. Closed while readers active

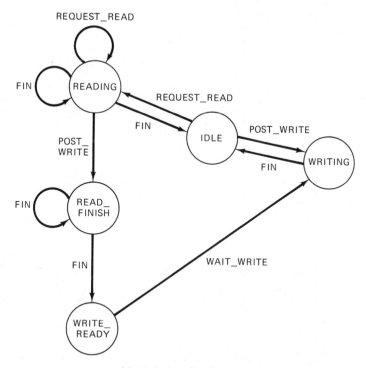

(b) *Finite State Machine*

1. All transitions are triggered by entry acceptance; 2. State values are used as guards

Figure 5.16 Readers/writers example—solution 4—packaged linear interaction structure

The basic idea is illustrated by Figure 5.17(a). Similarities to the bank example are obvious: the use of an integer (#) to identify an agent, the calling of DISPATCHER.FREE by a free agent, and the customer interactions on RESERVE (like WAIT in the bank example) and ASK. A new feature is the availability of an explicit CANCEL entry in the agent. The agent calls FREE to give the dispatcher its number after accepting a CANCEL call.

Solutions may involve agents waiting at the dispatcher or not waiting. Consider these possibilities in turn.

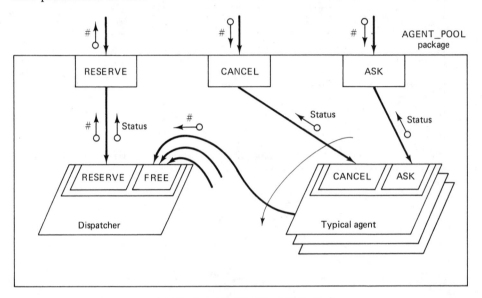

(a) *The Basic Idea (Omitting Initialization)*

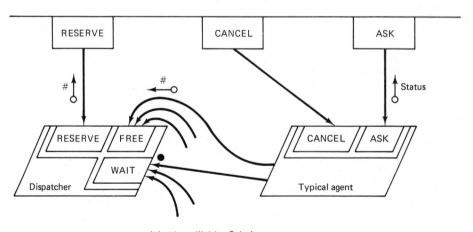

(b) *Linear Waiting Solution*

Figure 5.17 Interaction structures for the AGENT-POOL example (*note:* Agent #'s assumed fixed at startup.)

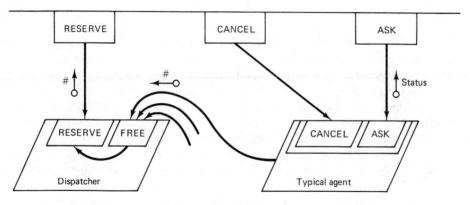

(c) *Nonlinear Waiting Solution*

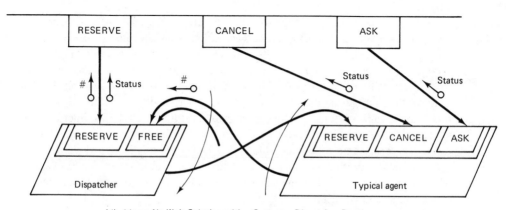

(d) *Linear No-Wait Solution with a Customer-Dispatcher Race*

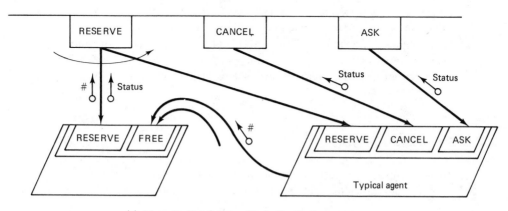

(e) *Linear No-Wait Solution Eliminating the Race*

Figure 5.17 (continued)

A linear waiting solution is shown in Figure 5.17(b). Here, the agent calls the unguarded FREE entry and then calls the guarded WAIT entry in the dispatcher. The idea is that the dispatcher gets free numbers via FREE, which can be handed over to customers via RESERVE, following which allocated tasks can be released by accepting WAIT. There is no guarantee in such a structure that calls on FREE and WAIT will be made in the same order by agents. Races between agents may result in a different order and, ultimately, in the customer receiving an invalid agent number.

This race problem may be solved by making WAIT in Figure 5.17(b) an entry family indexed by the agent number. This preserves the linearity of the solution.

Alternatively, this race problem may be solved by using a nonlinear nested accept approach, as illustrated in Figure 5.17(c). This avoids races between agents and ensures the correct numbers will be handed over to customers. However, this approach is potentially complex if the dispatcher has more entries, as will be the case in an example in Chapter 7.

A linear no-wait solution is shown in Figure 5.17(d). The new RESERVE entry in the agent is required to tell the agent when it has been allocated so that it can return an appropriate STATUS parameter to its callers to indicate whether or not it is able to provide service. The approach shown in Figure 5.17(d), in which the dispatcher makes the RESERVE call, opens the possibility of a race between a customer and the dispatcher to make the first call on the agent. If the dispatcher's call on RESERVE is not accepted first, then a valid customer's request via ASK will be rejected. The interface procedure of the pool package could take care of this problem by placing a second call on behalf of the customer again after a suitable delay. However, this is an awkward solution.

A better solution is to have the RESERVE procedure of the package call the RESERVE entry to tell the agent it has been allocated, before returning control to the customer, as shown in Figure 5.17(e).

5.3.5 Conclusions

Linear interaction structures are desirable for the reasons enunciated in Section 5.3.1. They can be arranged by structuring waiting conditions appropriately, as illustrated by the examples of Sections 5.3.2 to 5.3.4. With linear interaction structures, care must be taken to avoid race conditions, as illustrated in Section 5.3.4. If nonlinear interaction structures are desired, appropriate structure graph notation may be found in Sections 5.3.2 and 5.3.4.

5.4 EVENT NOTIFICATION

Another important aspect of module interactions is event notification.

Event notification may be classified as synchronous or asynchronous as follows:

- *Synchronous event notification* occurs from a called module to the calling module at the time of the call (procedure or entry). It may be performed using out-parameters of the call or by exceptions propagated to the calling module while processing the call.

- *Asynchronous event notifications* may occur at any time. They may be in response to previous calls but occur separately from these calls.

Our main concern in this section is with synchronous event notification. Asynchronous notification may be handled by any appropriate intertask communication mechanism. However, before proceeding to synchronous notification, we should ask the question, is there any other mechanism for propagating asynchronous events between tasks other than by conventional intertask communication using the rendezvous mechanism? The answer is no, except in unusual circumstances involving task termination. Exceptions raised during processing of accept statements may be propagated to the calling task at the point of the entry call; however, this is synchronous rather than asynchronous event notification because of the nature of the rendezvous.

We now turn our attention exclusively to synchronous event notification. An out-parameter of a procedure or entry call is a perfectly acceptable way of propagating a synchronous event notification back to a calling module and is in fact the only method used in examples of previous chapters. Therefore, why bother with exceptions?

Before answering this question, consider the nature of Ada exceptions. At its simplest, the ADA exception mechanism provides a way in which an error discovered during the processing of a call can be propagated back to an exception handler in the calling module as an abnormal return from the call.

Thus, the exception mechanism simply provides a way for separating error handling code from the code associated with normal operation. This is convenient for the programmer, but it can be argued that it is bad software engineering practice—normal operation and error handling should not be separated during design.

One very significant feature of the Ada exception mechanism is that not all exceptions need to be programmer-defined; some exceptions are defined in the language and are raised by code generated by the compiler when an error occurs. Whether the exception is raised by programmer-generated or compiler-generated code, the handling mechanism is the same. Thus, the program can handle errors which in other languages would cause it to abort. This is a powerful motivation for using exceptions.

Unfortunately, there is considerable motivation for not using them, because the rules for using exceptions in Ada are complex and inconsistent.

On balance, it seems that there will be occasions when the designer will wish to specify the use of exceptions. Accordingly, we need a structure graph notation for them. No such notation was provided in Chapter 3.

Given a rule that all exceptions are declared in the specification of the called module and handled in the body of the calling one, exception propagation is, from a structure graph viewpoint, somewhat like a reverse direction procedure call, as illustrated by Figure 5.18(a). The externally visible exception X in the right-hand module B triggers an invisible handler internal in the left-hand module A. Exception X is declared in module B in a manner visible to module A, so that module A knows a handler is required. When exception X is raised in module B (during a call from A to B), it is propagated to a

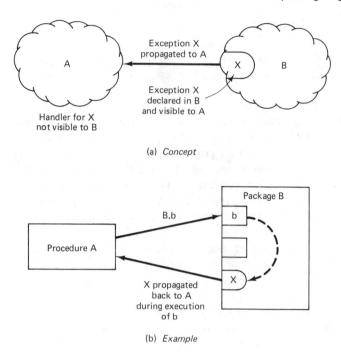

(a) *Concept*

(b) *Example*

Figure 5.18   Structure graph notation for exception propagation

handler in module A, invisible to module B. Figure 5.18(b) illustrates the concept for the case of an exception propagated from package B to procedure A. Procedure A calls procedure b in package B and during the execution of this procedure, exception X is raised. This exception is then propagated back to A at the point of the call. A handler for X must be present in A but is not visible to package B. For the exception X to be visible to the caller of B, it must be declared in B's specification, just as procedure b must be so declared.

Although exceptions may be propagated from B to A when A is a task or when both are tasks, there is no mechanism for declaring exceptions in task specifications. This and other complications make exceptions tricky in a tasking context.

When we view exceptions at a design level from a structure graph viewpoint, we can see that, far from simplifying the situation, exceptions complicate it by imposing an underlying *shadow* exception handling architecture behind and different from the architecture for normal operation. Why introduce this complication?

The author's strong bias is in favor of not using exceptions as a means of synchronous event notification between major system modules and instead to use them only internally within modules for special purposes, particularly where standard errors found by compiler-generated code need to be handled.

Notwithstanding these arguments, some designers may wish to opt for the use of exceptions for the more general case. An illustration of their use in this manner for the stack example of Chapter 2 is provided in Figure 5.19.

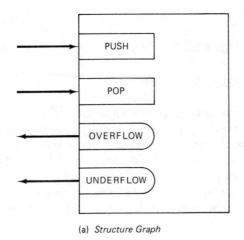

(a) *Structure Graph*

```
package STACK is
  procedure PUSH (E : in ELEM);
  procedure POP   (E : out ELEM);
  OVERFLOW, UNDERFLOW : exception;
end STACK;

package body STACK is

  SPACE : array (1 . . SIZE) of ELEM;
  INDEX : INTEGER range 0 . . SIZE : = 0;

  procedure PUSH(E : in ELEM) is
  begin
    if INDEX = SIZE then
      raise OVERFLOW;
    end if;
    INDEX : = INDEX + 1;
    SPACE(INDEX) : = E;
  end PUSH;

  procedure POP(E : out ELEM) is
  begin
    if INDEX = 0 then
      raise UNDERFLOW;
    end if;
    E : = SPACE(INDEX);
    INDEX : = INDEX − 1;
  end POP;

end STACK;
```

(b) *Ada Code (following the Ada Reference Manual)*

Figure 5.19 Stack package with externally handled exceptions

5.5 DETECTING AND CONTROLLING ABERRANT BEHAVIOR

5.5.1 Testing

Bugs in modules can be guaranteed to exist during system testing and integration. They may also, hopefully infrequently, occur during system operation if testing has not managed to find them all. The designer needs to be able to specify methods for abnormal module communication to be used for detecting, recording, and isolating such bugs.

Our concern here is not with debugging per se, which will be supported to a greater or lesser extent by the Ada programming support environments of particular computer systems supporting Ada. Rather, our concern is with the design of *instrumented test beds* for complete systems in operational form.

For example, it might be desirable to specify special testing interfaces for modules bypassing the normal rules of module access (for instance, to access the internal variables of a package which are not visible in the normal package specification). The author has used this approach successfully in projects employing monitors, which are a special form of package used for protected intertask communication in some non-Ada systems. In these projects, test-bed software was allowed to bypass normal monitor interfaces to read internal variables of the monitor.

Unfortunately, in Ada there is no explicit mechanism for specifying different forms of package or task interfaces for different purposes. Each package and task has a single specification and access to it is possible only as defined in that specification. The only way around this is to include special interfaces in the specification and comment them out in the operational version.

Designers would also like to be able to specify that test-bed software components be conditional parts of a program; that is, a mechanism for conditional compilation is desirable. Unfortunately Ada does not have such a mechanism. Again, special components may be included and commented out in the operational version.

At the design level, it is also desirable to be able to specify some means of recognizing and stopping the execution of rogue tasks or active packages without stopping the execution of the entire program so that intermediate results can be examined and the source of problems diagnosed. The recognition problem can be solved by embedded test-bed instrumentation in the program. But what of stopping execution?

In particular, what about stopping tasks that are suspected to have failed at points in time other than during rendezvous interactions with them? One method is available. A task may simply abort another task. Structure diagram notation for this approach is depicted in Figure 5.20. Aborting a task is an immediate action which may occur in the middle of some processing action of the task, thus leaving data in an inconsistent state. However, if the task is suspected to be misbehaving, its data may already be inconsistent.

Although it is possible to visualize using this mechanism in normal operation of a system, its prime use will probably be in system testing. For example, suspected failed tasks may be aborted to permit diagnosis.

It may be possible to make deductions about which tasks have failed by examining external events. For example, if during testing, tasks are required to deposit heartbeat

Figure 5.20 Structure graph notation for task termination

counts in a *test log* accessible to the test-bed software, it may be possible to diagnose failure of a task by failure of its heartbeat to increment after a certain time period.

Taking into account these various capabilities of Ada, Figure 5.21 shows possible test-bed environments for Ada packages and tasks. A special test version of an Ada package or task would contain a special test recorder and possibly a special trigger interface which would cause the package or task to record internal variables in a test log external to it. The test log could be examined by the test bed at desired points in time possibly triggered by exceptions from the package. The package would include statements embedded in its normal operating code to invoke the test recorder package to record important

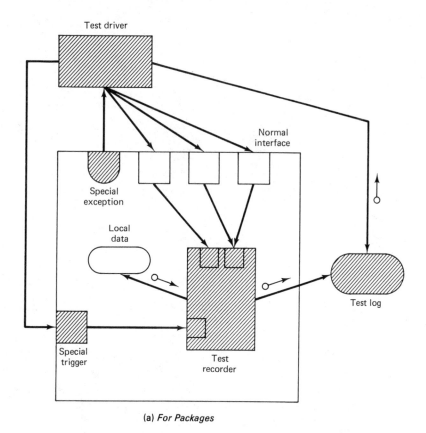

(a) *For Packages*

Figure 5.21 Possible Ada test-bed environments

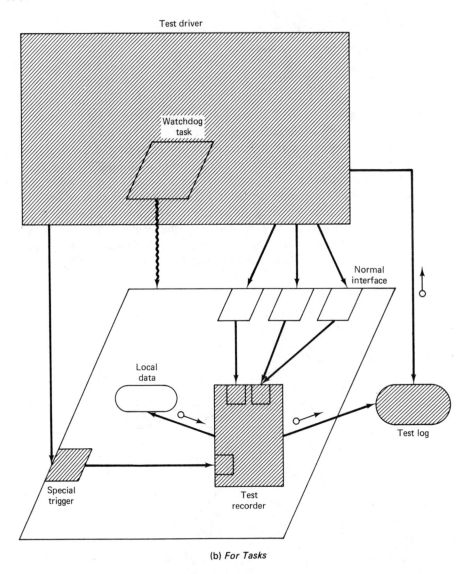

(b) *For Tasks*

Figure 5.21   (continued)

events such as passing a particular point in the program, violating a particular assertion, and so on.

As shown by Figure 5.21(b), the only extension to this mechanism required for tasks is the inclusion of one or more watchdog tasks in the test driver which would be capable of aborting suspected rogue tasks.

5.5.2 Self Protection by Intertask Protocols

Tasks are autonomous entities, and it may not always be possible to be sure that another task received a message intended for it. Consider Figure 5.22 depicting an intertask dialogue. Such a dialogue could occur, for example, between a customer and the MAIL-ROOM package discussed earlier. Suppose the sender of the message never receives a reply.

Possible reasons for this are as follows:

- The message never reached the target task.
- The target task has "died" (perhaps it is on another processor which has "crashed").
- Although sender and target are both willing to make a rendezvous, some underlying system problem is making it impossible (perhaps the two tasks are on different processors which are communicating via a failed link).
- There is a bug in the target task.

All of these except the first are possible reasons for the failure. The first is not possible because of the nature of the rendezvous mechanism; return from the SEND call implies receipt of the message.

In this sense the rendezvous mechanism is more reliable than one relying, for example, on messages deposited in a mailbox in shared memory. In the latter case, a rational response on the sender's part to a failure to receive a reply might be to try resending the message. However, this raises the possibility of the target getting multiple copies of messages. This further requires that the sender and the target agree on some mechanism for distinguishing copies of messages. In fact, a protocol is required between sender and target.

A *protocol* is a formalized dialogue between autonomous entities for purposes of reliable communication in the face of possible failures of either the entities or the communications medium between them but not failure of the protocol. Protocols are usually thought of as occurring between separate computers in a computer network but can also occur between tasks in an Ada program.

Although the rendezvous mechanism appears to eliminate the need for a protocol

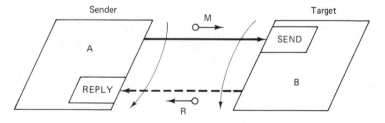

Figure 5.22 Intertask messaging—simple case

with respect to messages never getting from a sender to a target, this is partly an illusion. Recall from Chapters 3 and 4 that there is often a need to introduce a third-party task between sender and target to act either as a transporter of messages or a repository for messages. Even though all rendezvous associated with intercommunications between the two original tasks and the third-party task are completely reliable, messages may still fail to get from sender to target.

Should we worry about protocols at the Ada program level? The answer depends on the nature of the target environment for Ada programs.

If the target environment is a single processor, then it is probably best to assume that failure of a message to reach another task is a fatal error caused either by a hardware or a software fault, which renders all software running on that processor suspect. Intertask protocols are obviously not of concern in this context.

If the target environment consists of multiple processors connected either to common memory or to a common communications environment, then the possibility exists of processors or shared resources failing. If complete transparency is required in mapping single Ada programs onto the target environment, so that any task could run on any processor, then all intertask communication is potentially suspect. In these circumstances, it would be complex, inefficient and, ultimately, impossible to provide recovery mechanisms at its Ada program level for all possible failures; the target environment would have to provide the recovery mechanisms.

However, tasks will often fall naturally into sets such that intraset communication will be *close* and interset communication will be *loose* given some appropriate definition of the terms *close* and *loose*. If we require that such sets be allocated as units to individual target processors, then our recovery problem is much less complex. All tasks in such units have reliable communication among them as long as the unit is functioning. If the unit fails, all its tasks are potentially suspect, but the unit can be isolated from other units.

Therefore, such units must take account only of the possible failure of other such units and of the communication paths between them. Associated with each such unit is a communication package which provides for reliable communication with other units. We shall call such units *reliability units*. The reliability unit concept may be supported at the Ada program level or at the target environment level.

The nature of the reliability unit concept at the Ada program level is illustrated by Figure 5.23, for the sender/target example of Figure 5.22, assuming the sender and target are in different reliability units. An active communication package in each reliability unit could support entry call forwarding to tasks in other reliability units. The sender would use this package to forward a call to the target's SEND entry. The communications package in the target's reliability unit would make the required call (perhaps via a created *partner* task). Then it would return an acknowledgement of completion of the rendezvous. Until this acknowledgement arrived, the sender would be blocked. The REPLY call would be forwarded in the reverse direction in a similar fashion. Other approaches to inter-reliability unit communication are also possible. In any case, the existence of the reliability units is visible to the communicating tasks.

Support of the reliability unit concept at the target system level, would enable

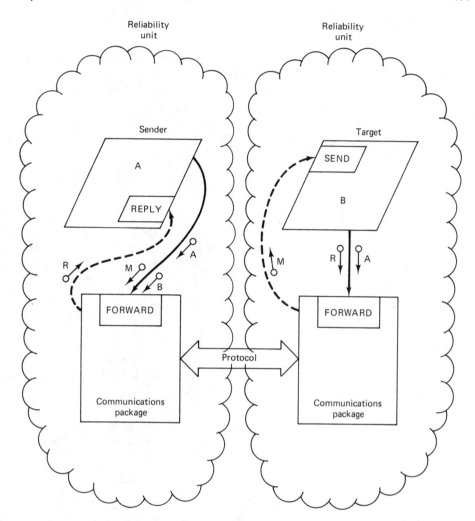

Figure 5.23 Entry call forwarding between reliability units

reliability units to be transparent to the communicating tasks. Then entry calls could be made at the Ada program level directly between tasks in different reliability units.

However, it seems unlikely, given the amount of work that remains to be done to make Ada and its application support environment available in uniprocessor and shared memory multiprocessor environments, that such distributed target system support will be available in the near future.

The reliability unit approach will be useful for the indefinite future, whether or not Ada support for distributed systems become available. Its only disadvantage is that a single Ada program cannot be developed for the target distributed environment, independent of any concern about how software is to be distributed over that environment.

5.6 SYSTEM BUILDING

Ada has been characterized in this book and elsewhere as a language for *structured system building*. We have attempted to show how structured designs may be developed with the aid of Ada. However, the actual business of structured system building involves more than just design. It also involves development, installation, and reconfiguration. Here we consider some concerns of the designer in this area and show how they relate to Ada.

A very natural design requirement is to make provision for the loading and running under Ada program control of Ada program modules whose nature is unknown a priori by the loading program. There is no provision for this in Ada. Thus Ada cannot be used to design and write conventional operating systems which run *a priori* unknown user programs.

A point which has arisen several times in our discussions is the conceptual uniformity which results in system design from similar-appearing interfaces to packages and tasks. The implication is that packages and tasks are modules at a similar logical level. One might conclude that packages and tasks should also be treated uniformly at the system building level. However, this is not the case. In Ada, packages can only be created at programming time. At most, copies of generic packages may be made by instantiation at compile time. Packages may be compilation units, and, thus, they represent implementation- and installation-level modules.

Tasks, on the other hand, may not be compilation units except as stubs. Tasks are types and instances of task types may be created dynamically at run time.

Why do these differences between packages and tasks exist when, from a design point of view, it appears desirable to view them as similar logical entities? The designers of Ada obviously visualize packages as the macroscopic units of system construction, static and few in number in comparison to tasks. In our design examples this viewpoint is seen in the appearance of active packages containing numbers of tasks. However, we have also seen instances of tasks containing packages. For system development purposes, such tasks must be nested in a context which can be a compilation unit, namely a procedure or a package.

The design-level logical similaritiy of packages and tasks, together with the comments in Chapter 3 about the ability to convert packages into tasks and vice versa, depending on the application requirements, suggest that a desirable feature of the language might be to postpone commitment to a particular module being a package or task until load time. Such an approach would allow a system to be tailored as a concurrent or sequential one for particular circumstances. However, there are no such features in Ada.

Chapter 6

Modularity, Reliability, and Structure: A Communications Subsystem Example

6.1 INTRODUCTION

This chapter focuses on issues in modularity, reliability, and structure through the particular example of a communications subsystem called COMM for the DIALOGUE system of Chapter 4.

Communications systems in general provide excellent examples illustrating the principles of modularity and reliability. This is because modularity is crucial if suppliers and customers are to be able to mix and match communication packages and services to enable computer systems of different types and capabilities to communicate with each other for different purposes. Reliability is a fundamental issue because of the possibility of failure or incorrect operation of both links and nodes in a communication network.

The communications example of this chapter is a particularly simple one in order to allow illustration of the principles of modularity, reliability, and structure without obscuring the discussion by details of complex communication protocols. A key principle on which we rely and which we attempt to demonstrate in this chapter is that the structure of a well-designed system implementing a protocol is not greatly dependent on the complexity of the protocol. Stated another way, we rely on being able to hide the complex details of protocols in modules whose interfaces are not greatly affected by the complexity. In what follows, we take advantage of this principle by designing the system without detailed knowledge of the protocol. Thus, the chapter serves also as an introduction to the subject of more complex, multilayered communications protocols. In so doing, it paves the way for further discussions of this subject in Chapter 7.

This chapter proceeds by first introducing the requirements of the COMM subsystem example in Section 6.2. Then major issues in modularity and reliability are discussed in

Sections 6.3 and 6.4 respectively, with particular reference to the COMM subsystem. A structure for the COMM subsystem is designed in Section 6.5. Section 6.6 conducts a design post mortem. Finally, Section 6.7 gives conclusions.

6.2 REQUIREMENTS OF THE COMM SUBSYSTEM EXAMPLE

Recall from Chapter 4 that the DIALOGUE system was assumed to have access to a message system interface (Figure 4.32), which was assumed to be an active package with interface procedures WAIT__MSG and SEND__MSG. WAIT__MSG required the calling task to wait for a text message arriving from the screen of the remote system. SEND__MSG provided for the transmission of a text message from the screen of the sending system. It was implicitly assumed in Chapter 4 that there was always enough memory available to store incoming and outgoing text messages. It was also implicitly assumed that an appropriate communications path existed between the two systems whose operators were sending messages to each other and that this communications path was either reliable or that any errors in it were hidden from callers of WAIT__MSG and SEND__MSG.

Our purpose in this chapter is to illustrate the principles of modularity and reliability by designing a COMM subsystem to provide this message system interface to calling tasks.

At the bottom end we shall assume that the COMM subsystem software accesses a hardware device which provides for interrupt driven, character-at-a-time, transmission and reception. Below that level, communications is assumed to be bit-serial. In this chapter we omit from the system design these lower bit-oriented levels. More sophisticated hardware devices are, of course, possible. Chips are available which provide for interrupt-driven, packet-at-a-time transmission and reception and which perform packet sequence checking as well. In fact, the design work of this chapter could be interpreted as the first step in the design of such a chip following the philosophy of software-driven system design espoused in Chapter 1. However, for the purposes of this chapter, we shall think of the COMM subsystem as software for driving character-oriented hardware.

We assume that the communications hardware connecting the two systems is installed and ready for communication when the two systems are turned on. That is, there is a dedicated physical link between the two systems. However, we do not assume that the link is necessarily reliable. Data transmitted over it may be corrupted by noise or completely lost (say due to a temporary break).

The COMM subsystem must be capable of detecting that data has been corrupted or lost.

We assume that the two systems at the ends of the link may be powered up or shut down completely independently of each other and that, therefore, there is a requirement for each to recognize that the other one is ready before attempting to send or resend data. That is, there is a requirement for formal link startup and shutdown protocols at the software level. For simplicity, we shall include only startup in our design.

There is also a requirement to take account of the possibility of remote system failure. For simplicity we shall assume such failures can be treated as if they were link failures. Thus we assume that each system either communicates correctly or does not communicate at all. A partial failure which results in continued operation of a malfunctioning communications protocol can cause unrecoverable errors at the level of protocol we are considering in this chapter.

For simplicity we shall not consider the possibility of other than short-term link failures which can be recovered from by appropriate retransmission of parts of messages. Longer-term failures would require higher-level recovery mechanisms.

We assume that memory capacity for communications buffers is limited, so that there is a need to exercise flow control on incoming and outgoing data. By *flow control,* we mean temporarily halting the flow of data.

The DIALOGUE systems allow both operators to send to each other simultaneously. This implies that the COMM subsystem should support simultaneous transmission and reception (that is, full duplex operation). Even if this were not a requirement of the DIALOGUE system, it would be a desirable general requirement of a communication subsystem.

We assume that messages are never longer than a full screen and that they are displayed from screen-sized message buffers.

6.3 MODULARITY

6.3.1 Introduction

The basic idea of modularity is to localize or isolate the effects of perturbations or changes. Depending on what types of perturbations or changes are being considered, there may be various types of modularity.

For example, we may characterize the type of modularity which arises when it is easy to respond to changes in system requirements as *flexibility*. This type of modularity arises when a system has been designed in such a manner that a single change in a requirement results in changes to as small a number of modules as possible, preferably only to one.

We may characterize the type of modularity which arises when modules of a system can be assigned to different persons for independent implementation with as little coordination as possible as *implementation modularity*.

The kind of modularity that arises when the effects of significant real time events such as operational errors are localized in a system may be called *event modularity*.

We may characterize the type of modularity which arises when system software does not need modification to adapt to changes in underlying hardware as *transparency*.

Finally, we make mention of *understandability modularity*. This is present when a system is partitioned into easily digestible parts with clear personalities. The need for this kind of modularity may suggest partitioning even when other critieria would not suggest it.

Other types of modularity may no doubt be defined, but these will suffice for our purposes.

We now proceed to discuss ways in which the degree of modularity of a system may be characterized and assessed before turning our attention to the COMM subsystem from a modularity viewpoint.

6.3.2 Degrees of Modularity

According to Myers, (see References) two criteria for assessing the degree of modularity are module strength and module coupling. Myers has provided categories for identifying the degree of modularity with respect to each of these criteria.

Myers' categories of module strength, in order of decreasing modularity, are as follows:

- Functional or informational strength exists when a module may be viewed as a collective single function or when it is based on a shared concept, shared data, or a shared resource.
- Communicational strength exists when there is a sequential relationship with respect to data among the functions of the module (for example, one function processes the output of another).
- Procedural strength exists when there is a sequential relationship among the functions of the module determined by external events (for example, one function must be exercised before another in time).
- Logical strength exists when there is a single access point for multiple functions.
- Coincidental modularity exists when the functions have no relationship to each other.

Myers' categories of module coupling, in order of decreasing modularity, are as follows:

- uncoupled
- data coupled via homogenous parameters
- stamp coupled via nonglobal structured data
- control coupled via external selection of an internal control path
- external coupled via homogenous global data
- common coupled via structured global data
- content coupled via internal access between functions of the module

These categories of module strength and coupling are provided here mainly to give the reader a mental check list of modularity criteria. Although they will not be used explicitly in any extensive way in what follows, their use is implicit in many of the choices to come between design alternatives.

Before turning to the COMM subsystem, consider the relationship between these categories of module strength and coupling and the previous design examples in Chapter 4.

The LIFE system of Chapter 4 lacks flexibility with respect to changes in operator commands, because such commands require modifications to two modules, namely, the line holder and the word string command decoder. These two modules each have high functional and informational strength and are weakly coupled by a small number of parameters. However, one of the parameters is a word code derived from a word dictionary in one module and used in another module to decode word strings. Both the word dictionary and the tables defining legal sequences of word strings would have to be modified for changed commands, and this involves modifying two modules. As was pointed out in Chapter 4, the way around this particular difficulty is to merge the two modules into a single character-string command decoder module. This module still possesses high functional and informational strength. Therefore, according to Meyer's criteria, the resulting system is more modular than the original one because of the elimination of the intermodule coupling component. There is of course a limit to increasing modularity by merging modules, and this limit is reached when the merged modules themselves lose functional or informational strength or when understandability is compromised.

An example of high event modularity is the DIALOGUE system of Chapter 4. All events associated with the human operator, including commands, notifications of results of commands, reporting of system errors, and so on, are funnelled through a single event decoder module. This module has high functional and informational strength and needs no coordination with other modules to handle events correctly.

6.3.3 The COMM Subsystem from a Modularity Viewpoint

Although we shall need to defer some design decisions until we have considered reliability issues in Section 6.4, we can take the first steps in designing the COMM subsystem based only on modularity issues.

There is a data hierarchy in the COMM subsystem which suggests a corresponding hierarchical or layered module structure. At the top level, the COMM subsystem deals with messages which are variable length character strings taken from the video screen memory of the workstation. At the bottom level, the COMM subsystem deals with characters sent to and received from the link hardware.

Using the *edges-in* design strategy of Chapter 4, a first pass produces a one-layer module structure, as shown in Figure 6.1(a). In this figure a single message management module M handles messages at its top level and characters at its bottom level.

However, for a variety of reasons, we can anticipate that it will be desirable to break messages into intermediate, fixed-length blocks. We shall call these blocks *frames*. We can anticipate that this will be particularly desirable for reliability purposes, because if communications failure occurs during transmission of a frame, only that frame need be retransmitted, instead of the whole message. Other reasons also are important:

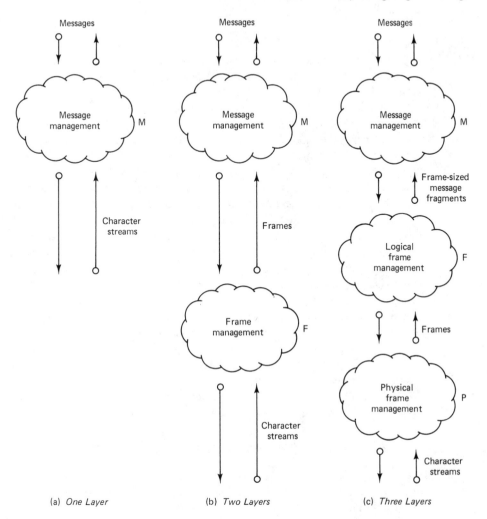

Figure 6.1   Possible layered organizations for COMM

- Allocation of communications buffers is easier to manage if it is in terms of fixed-size frames
- Synchronous transmission and reception are easier to manage in terms of fixed-size frames
- Hardware transparency is likely to be more easily achievable, because hardware devices tend to operate in terms of fixed-size frames

Frames introduce an intermediate level in the data hierarchy. Corresponding to the new data hierarchy is the two-layered module structure of Figure 6.1(b), in which a frame management module F is interposed between the message management module M and the hardware.

We can anticipate that the frame management module will have responsibilities not only for the correct physical structure of frames but also for logical issues associated with recovery if the frame should be lost during transmission. It will, accordingly, be natural to partition the frame management module into two layers, as shown in Figure 6.1(c)—a logical frame management module F, concerned only with correct sequencing and error recovery of frames, and a physical frame management module P concerned only with the actual transmission and reception.

From a modularity viewpoint, the structure of Figure 6.1(c) has a number of attractions.

- Each module should have (if correctly designed) high functional strength and low coupling.
- Understandability modularity is potentially high, because each module should have (if correctly designed) a clearly defined function and *personality*.
- Event modularity is likely to be high, because each module has its own set of events to manage, uniquely associated with its own function (the message management module is concerned with events associated with entire messages; the logical frame management module is associated only with correct sequencing of and failures associated with frames; the physical frame management module is concerned only with the physical arrival and departure of complete frames).
- We can hope for a high degree of hardware transparency because it should be possible to structure the lower level modules in such a way that they can easily be replaced by chips.

Assuming that our design choice will involve multiple layers, there are modularity issues associated with different approaches to layer coupling. Figure 6.2 provides a data flow view of three different approaches to layer coupling. Layers may be coupled directly, as shown in Figure 6.2(a). They may be coupled indirectly through interface modules, as shown in Figure 6.2(b). Alternatively, they may be coupled through a centralized system control module which manages all interfaces between all layers, as shown in Figure 6.2(c).

In general the layer modules of Figure 6.2 will be specified in Ada as passive or active packages. Because the timing of events in the upward and downward directions through the layers is in general unpredictable, we can anticipate that multiple tasks will be required in the layer modules of Figures 6.2(a) and 6.2(b); that is, these layer packages will be active ones. The approach of Figure 6.2(c) offers the possibility that a system controller package could perform all the sequencing and, therefore, that the layer packages themselves could be passive.

Now, what of system structure? Consider the structure graphs of Figures 6.3 to 6.5, depicting specific forms of coupling between layer packages, to implement the data flow views of Figure 6.2.

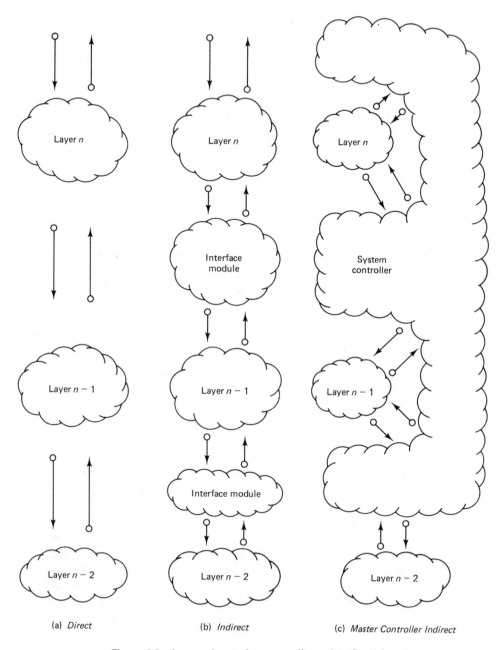

Figure 6.2 Approaches to layer coupling—data flow view

(a) *Direct*   (b) *Indirect*   (c) *Master Controller Indirect*

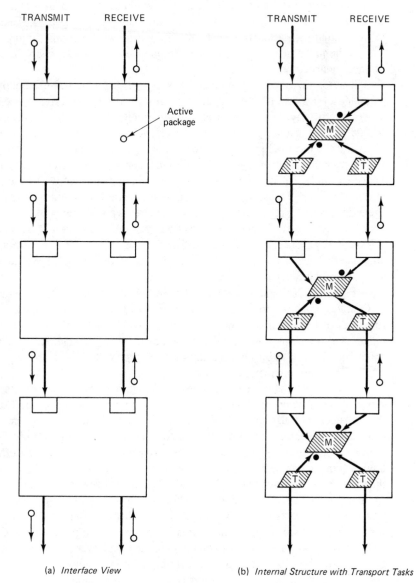

(a) *Interface View*   (b) *Internal Structure with Transport Tasks*

Legend:

T   Transport task
M   Main layer task

Figure 6.3   Direct, top-down layer coupling

In general, the direct coupled approach could have several different structural forms, including unidirectional calls in a downward direction (Figure 6.3) and mutual calls between adjacent packages in both the up and down directions (Figure 6.4). We shall refer to the latter two forms as having, respectively, top-down and symmetrical package interaction structures.

The top-down package interaction structure of Figure 6.3 is attractive because it is familiar and because it guards against deadlock arising from careless use of mutual calls between active layer packages. Because it is familiar, it is easy to understand for persons unused to concurrent systems. Each layer package may be characterized as an agent, following the terminology of Chapter 3. Each package receives calls from higher layers and places calls to lower layers. No calls are made in an upward direction between layers. Transmission of items downward is always initiated from above by calling a procedure of a lower layer. Transmission of items in an upward direction is always initiated from above by calling a procedure of a lower layer to wait for items to arrive from below.

The symmetrical package interaction structure of Figure 6.4 is, on the other hand, a less familiar one. It may therefore make the system harder to understand for the uninitiated. Furthermore, it harbors the danger of deadlock, depending on the internal structure of the layer packages.

Figures 6.3(b) and 6.4(b) and (c) show how the canonical task interaction structures of Chapter 3, shown in Figure 3.18, map onto the direct-coupled package interaction structures of Figures 6.3(a) and 6.4(a), respectively. The dual transport task approach of Figure 3.18(e) maps onto either the top-down or the symmetrical package interaction structures, while the buffer task approach of Figure 3.18(h) maps only onto the symmetrical package interaction structures.

The choice between the top-down interaction structure of Figure 6.3(a) and the symmetrical structure of Figure 6.3(b) thus depends not only on the external aspect of the packages, but also on tradeoffs between possible internal structures. As discussed in Chapter 3, the transport task approach to internal structuring is more flexible than the buffer task approach, but requires more tasks and may be somewhat less efficient (although both require the same number of rendezvous to transfer data). The number of tasks in the transport task approach could be reduced by adopting the single transport task approach for reception, following Figure 3.18(d), leaving it to the main layer tasks to make transmission calls. However, we can anticipate that the requirement for flow control will make this approach inappropriate. This is because of the possibility of the main layer task having to wait for transmission credit at the next lower layer, as suggested by Figure 3.19(b), thereby blocking it from accepting calls from above. Thus two transport tasks appear to be required if the transport task approach is adopted.

Figure 6.5 shows possible structures for the indirect coupled approach. In Figure 6.5(a) each layer is an active master package which accesses a separate interface package for each higher and lower layer. This structure is less modular than earlier ones. Because none of the layer packages has a defined procedural interface of its own, the purpose of each package is less clearly visible. The system also possesses a higher degree of coupling than those of Figures 6.3 or 6.4, simply because there are more modules and more

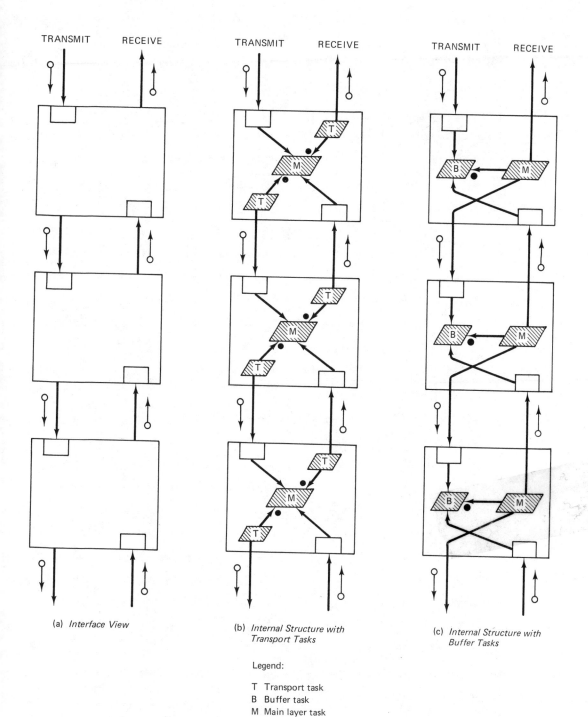

(a) *Interface View*

(b) *Internal Structure with Transport Tasks*

(c) *Internal Structure with Buffer Tasks*

Legend:

T Transport task
B Buffer task
M Main layer task

Figure 6.4 Direct, symmetrical layer coupling

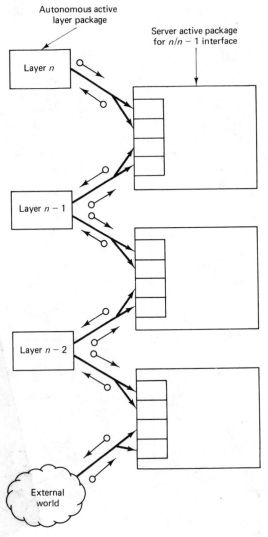

Figure 6.5 Approaches to indirect layer coupling

(a) *Master Layers with Server Coupling*

interfaces between modules for the same degree of overall functionality. Furthermore, the overall control structure is less clear.

Figure 6.5(b) shows another possible structure for the indirect coupled case; it has either active layer packages and no master controller or passive layer packages and a master controller. In either case the responsibility for transferring data between layers resides outside the layers themselves. This approach suffers from the fact that in the Ada specification the procedures of the layer package which are accessible from above and

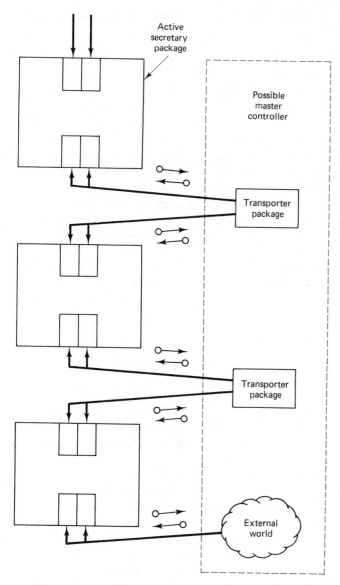

(b) *Server Layers with Transporter or Master Controller Coupling*   **Figure 6.5**   (continued)

below are lumped together in a single interface specification. Thus the procedures for use by the next lower layer are visible to the next higher layer as well, and vice versa. This structure also is less modular than those of Figures 6.3 or 6.4.

Based on all of the foregoing discussion of modularity, we make the following tentative design decisions for the COMM subsystem:

- adopt a three-layer structure as illustrated by Figure 6.1(c)
- use direct coupling between the layers, as suggested by Figure 6.2(a) and as illustrated by either Figure 6.3 or 6.4

As discussed earlier, the choice between Figures 6.3 and 6.4 is not clearcut. For illustrative purposes, we choose (somewhat arbitrarily) the top-down structure of Figure 6.3. We leave it as an exercise for the reader to develop the symmetrical structure of Figure 6.4 (noting that only Figure 6.4(c) represents a significantly different approach).

Having adopted a layered system organization, it behooves us to be careful with the terminology for describing data flow between layers. From an overall system viewpoint, data may be viewed as flowing downward for transmission and upward after reception. We may also view downward-going data as outgoing and upward-going data as incoming. To avoid confusion, the terms *transmission, reception, outgoing* and *incoming* should be used only in this system-wide sense and not to indicate direction of flow across individual layer boundaries. Only the terms *downward* and *upward* may be unambiguously used in both contexts. For example, incoming data may be said to flow into or out of a layer, implying that it flows into the layer from below or out of the layer in an upward direction.

6.4 RELIABILITY

6.4.1 Introduction

In this section we discuss reliability issues in the light of COMM subsystem requirements. As we shall see, our reliability concerns can be tackled mainly at the data flow level of design. Thus this section discusses issues which are mainly independent of the use of Ada as a design language.

Before addressing these concerns directly, consider the nature of faults, errors, and mechanisms for their detection and recovery. A fault is a system malfunction which causes an observable error in some aspect of system operation which may, in turn, result in total system failure, partial system failure, or no system failure, depending on the degree of error detection and recovery present in the system.

Faults may be the result of mistakes made in design and implementation, or they may arise unavoidably during system operation, from the following sources:

1. human error, including
   (a) bad commands and responses
   (b) bad data
2. communications failure, including
   (a) corrupted data
   (b) lost data
   (c) duplicated data

3. component failure, including
   (a) failed processor
   (b) failed communications link
   (c) failed device
   (d) failed reliability unit

Our treatment of faults and errors in this chapter will be based on the assumption that the combined DIALOGUE/COMM system is a single *reliability unit* (in the sense of Chapter 5). Thus our reliability concerns are confined to:

- internal logical correctness of the combined DIALOGUE/COMM system
- detection and/or recovery from external operational errors.

Because of the reliability unit assumption, we do not consider the possibility of internal operational errors in the COMM subsystem itself.

6.4.2 Internal Logical Correctness of the COMM Subsystem

The area having the most potential for design and implementation mistakes in the COMM subsystem is communications buffering.

Figure 6.6 shows a possible data flow graph for communications buffer flow. Shown in this figure are the event decoder module E and the M, F and P modules identified in Section 6.2. Also shown are separate screen message and frame buffer pool modules S and B, which have preallocated sets of fixed-size buffers for use by the various modules of the subsystem.

An assumption of Figure 6.6 is that data frames are held for periodic retransmission until they are acknowledged. This assumption follows naturally from the arguments which led to the introduction of frames in Section 6.2.

Consider Figure 6.6 from the viewpoint of frame buffer flow first. For transmission, empty buffers flow from the frame buffer pool B to the message management module M, where they are filled with appropriate data. They then flow to the logical frame management module F for transmission. F hands full buffers over to the physical frame management module P. When transmission is completed, control of the full buffers reverts to F, for possible retransmission later. Eventually, when transmitted frames are acknowledged, the empty frame buffers flow back to the buffer pool B from the logical frame management module F. For reception, empty buffers from the frame buffer pool B flow to the physical frame management module P, where they are filled with incoming data. Filled frame buffers flow upwards and eventually trickle back to the frame buffer pool B from higher-level modules.

Now consider message buffer flow. In Chapter 4, we implicitly assumed a single display buffer (which is just that part of memory containing the message displayed on the screen) and entirely ignored the question of message buffering. However, in general,

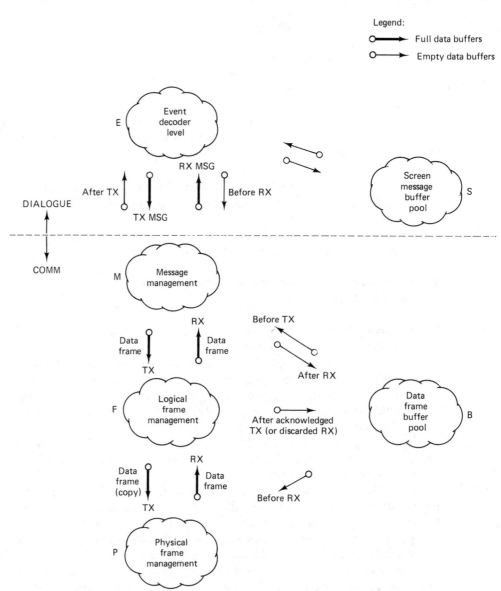

Figure 6.6   Data frame flow in the COMM subsystem with shared buffer pools

we may visualize a pool S of screen-sized message buffers, any one of which may be used for screen display on a software-selectable basis.

Figure 6.6 includes the flow of messages to and from such a pool of message buffers. E gets empty message buffers from the pool S for both transmission and reception. On transmission, a full message buffer from E is copied into frame buffers by M and then sent back to E. On reception, an empty message buffer from E is filled with data and then sent on to E.

Sources of potential design and implementation mistakes in this scheme include aliasing (the existence of multiple copies of an access variable for a buffer) and deadlock (due to competition for empty buffers and to intermodule flow control of full ones).

6.4.2.1 Aliasing   Aliasing was mentioned briefly in Chapter 5, and a method of deallocating identifiers was proposed to prevent it from occurring in a limited context. However, in the context of this chapter, aliasing is difficult to avoid.

With reference to Figure 6.5(a), aliasing may arise as follows. Suppose pointers (access variables) to frame buffers are passed between the various modules. It is obvious that in normal operation several modules may have copies of the same frame buffer pointer, although in correct operation only one module at any given time will have the right to use this pointer. A property of Ada and other similar languages is that the ability to use a pointer is not withdrawn when a copy is handed over to another module. Explicit use may be made of this property in system design by requiring that a module having temporary possession of a copy of a pointer discard it when it has finished using it. The original possessor of the pointer may then reuse it. For example, in Figure 6.5(a), the physical frame management module may discard its copy of a buffer pointer when it has transmitted it, if the logical frame management module F retains the original pointer.

A problem with allowing aliasing is that small mistakes in using it can have large and difficult-to-diagnose effects. For example, suppose that the COMM subsystem is being debugged from the bottom up in such a way that an incorrect logical frame management module is being tested with correct physical frame management and frame buffer pool modules. The possibility exists that the incorrect logical frame management module could use an old copy of a buffer pointer which is now in the hands of the physical frame management module in such a way as to cause this correct module to fail in an apparently mysterious manner. Given that aliasing is specified by the designer, the possibility of such problems is unavoidable.

6.4.2.2 Deadlock and Local Flow Control   We introduce the term *local* here to distinguish conditions occurring within a particular system connected to a communications facility from conditions occurring between different systems connected to the same communications facility.

Flow blockages of various kinds in Figure 6.6 can lead to deadlock. Flow blockages may occur as follows:

- at a pool due to the pool running out of empty buffers
- at any other module due to its inability to accept any more full buffers (the refusal to accept more full buffers is said to be *exercising local flow control*)

A module may exercise local flow control for strictly local reasons, such as hitting an arbitrary, implementation-dependent capacity limit, or it may exercise local flow control because it is required by a protocol between *peer* modules in separate systems connected via a communications facility, as discussed further in Section 6.4.2.

Flow blockages can result in deadlock if individual tasks in the various modules are themselves blocked while waiting for flow blockages to clear. Then the possibility of circular waiting and consequential deadlock rears its ugly head.

Prevention of deadlock due to blockages in frame data flow in Figure 6.6 requires that the following conditions be met at the frame mangement level.

- The pool B must contain at least enough empty frame buffers to satisfy the transmission capacity limit of the logical frame management module, with one left over for reception. Fewer buffers could result in deadlock if all of them end up waiting in the logical frame management module F for acknowledgements which can never come because there are no empty buffers to receive them in. Note that the minimum possible pool size is two buffers (corresponding to a transmission capacity limit of one buffer).

- The reception side of the physical frame management module P must always pass on a full buffer before it waits for an empty one. This will ensure that eventually at least one empty buffer will trickle back to the pool for use in reception, even if all the other buffers are tied up waiting for acknowledgments.

- The transmission side of the message management module M must stop trying to fill empty frame buffers with message fragments as soon as the logical frame management module F exercises transmission flow control on it (that is, when F's transmission capacity has been reached). This will ensure that the frame buffer pool B is not drained of empty buffers which have no immediate place to go and which may be needed for reception. Otherwise, incoming acknowledgements which would free buffers waiting in F could be blocked.

An assumption underlying these conditions is that the message management module M will never block permanently the flow of received frames, thereby preventing them from ever trickling back to the frame buffer pool B. Such a guarantee can be made if the screen message buffer pool S has a minimum of two buffers and if the message management module M always reserves at least one of them for reception. Then any unavailability of an empty message buffer for reception will always be temporary.

If these conditions are not met, deadlock can occur in various ways. One of the most dramatic is as follows. Suppose F has reached its transmission capacity while M is partway through copying a message buffer into frame buffers for transmission. Suppose E has filled up the remaining message buffers with operator messages for transmission; or suppose that there is only one message buffer in the entire system. Then the flow of received frames will eventually be blocked because the unavailability of a message buffer for reception blocks received frame buffers from trickling back to the pool. Thus incoming acknowledgements for tranmitted data frames are blocked. Permanent blockage of both transmitted and received frames is the result. The entire system is deadlocked! Even worse, the deadlock could embrace a pair of systems trying to send messages to each other simultaneously!

We have adopted a conservative approach to solving the deadlock problem. A less conservative approach is to allow unconstrained open competition, with protection provided by avoidance or recovery mechanisms. The reader is referred to any textbook on operating systems for further treatment of the deadlock problem.

6.4.2.3 Local Flow Control Mechanisms
As we have seen, in any multiple-module system data flow control may have to be exercised between communicating modules. Various approaches to intermodule flow control were discussed in Chapter 3, including the approach of issuing credit in advance. With the credit approach a sender will never send an item until it first obtains credit from the target to do so. This approach is attractive in a shared buffer pool context because it avoids tying up buffers which have no place to go.

A direct way of issuing credit in a shared buffer pool context is to issue the sender an empty buffer in which to put the data. This direct mechanism is the simplest when credit depends solely on buffer availability, as it does at DIALOGUE/COMM interface. At this interface, therefore, credit may appropriately be issued in the form of an empty message buffer.

A less direct credit mechanism requires that the sender get credit to send one or more data items before itself acquiring empty buffers in which to put the data items. This mechanism may be more suitable when credit depends on circumstances other than buffer availability, as it does at the interface betweeen the M and F modules of the COMM subsystem. For example, we have assumed that the F module has a finite capacity for holding unacknowledged data frames, independent of the availability of buffers. As we shall see in Section 6.4.3, this capacity is a parameter associated with the frame protocol between peer F modules in different systems. Indeed, transmission flow control could be exercised by the F module on the M module even when empty buffers are available in the frame buffer pool B.

So far we have spoken of credit only in terms of buffers of application data (in this case, screen messages or fragments thereof). Figure 6.6 shows only the flow of application data. However, as we shall see in Section 6.4.3, intermodule data flows may be mixed, including not only application data, but also nonapplication (or control) data associated with intersystem protocols. For example, at the F/P interface some frames may contain only protocol messages, associated with activities such as link startup or intersystem (global) flow control of data frames.

When intermodule data flow is mixed in this way in a layered system, lower layers must treat all components of the data flow equally, because they cannot tell the difference between them. Otherwise the layered modularity of the system would be violated. For example the P module must treat all frames flowing between the P and F modules equally, because it cannot (and should not) distinguish between data and control frames. Only the F module distinguishes different types of frames. This means that local flow control of mixed intermodule data flows cannot be applied selectively to the application data components of the flow.

As a consequence, the F module must have an internal mechanism to tell it when to stop trying to transmit new data frames. It cannot rely on the P module to do so. This mechanism is the data frame capacity limit mentioned earlier.

As another consequence, the F module cannot selectively stop the flow of upward-going data frames from the P module by local action at the F/P interface. Its only option for local reception flow control at this interface is to discard data frames after they have arrived.

As a final remark on local flow control mechanisms, we note that from a control structure point of view, credit for one item may be obtained implicitly by a sender by returning from a SEND call to a package or given implicitly to a sender by making a RECEIVE call to a package. The implication of this view of credit is that internal tasks of the packages must be designed to block callers of SEND, or to delay calling RECEIVE, until credit is available.

6.4.3 Detection and Recovery from External Operational Errors Using Protocols

6.4.3.1 Introduction   A protocol is a dialogue between *peer* modules at the same level in different systems, for the purpose of achieving reliable communication between the systems at that level. Overall reliable communication between systems may require protocols at several levels. Protocols require the exchange of protocol messages between peer modules. To distinguish these protocol messages from other forms of messages, we shall call them *protocol data units,* or PDUs; this terminology is consistent with that used by workers in protocol standardization.

We shall now consider requirements for protocols at the various levels of the COMM subsystem.

6.4.3.2 Protocols at the Message Management Level   The requirements of our example design do not take into account the possibility of other than temporary link failure.

Therefore, it will be sufficient to rely on the human operator to acknowledge entire messages (by sending replies), to save message copies, if desired, until acknowledgement, to retry messages, and to ignore duplicate messages resulting from retries. There is no need for the message management module to perform these functions. In other words, there is no requirement for a message level protocol.

All that is required of the message management module is the copying and delimiting of individual messages. Delimiting is required so that the end of an incoming message can be detected. Delimiting could be performed by inserting a message header containing a message number in the data part of each frame of the message, by inserting a frame count in the data part of the first frame of the message, or by inserting an end-of-message marker in the data part of the last frame of the message.

6.4.3.3 Protocols at the Logical Frame Management Level   As indicated by previous discussions, a protocol is required at this level. Protocol data units at this level may be either data frames containing fragments of application messages or control frames not containing user data but exchanged between peer logical frame management modules for some other purpose.

For sequence analysis and error checking purposes, data frames need to be sequence numbered and to contain redundant error check codes. It should be possible to send several data frames in sequence without waiting for individual acknowledgement of each one first because of the requirement for a full duplex operation.

To improve communication efficiency, we can piggyback acknowledgements of data frames on data frames going in the reverse direction instead of sending these acknowledgements separately. This may be done by associating two sequence numbers with each outgoing data frame: the send sequence number, which is the frame's own sequence number, and the receive sequence number, which is the sequence number of the next expected incoming data frame. The receive sequence number serves as implicit acknowledgement of all data frames with smaller sequence numbers. Based on pending acknowledgements, the sender may decide after a time interval to retransmit data frames. Therefore it must keep copies of data frames until they are acknowledged.

Flow control of data frames may be based on a maximum allowable range of outstanding sequence numbers, known as a *window*. This window defines the F module's capacity, referred to in previous discussions. When the number of sent but not acknowledged, or received but not picked up data frames exceeds this window, transmission or reception flow control, respectively, is exercised. This flow control may be exercised without control frames. On transmission the outgoing flow of data frames simply stops while the TX window is full except for retransmissions. On reception incoming data frames are simply discarded while the RX window is full. With this approach the exercise of flow control by a remote receiver is indistinguishable to the sender from link or remote node failure. While the flow control condition is in effect, the sender will not receive acknowledgements and may perform fruitless retransmissions.

The use of control frames by a receiver to inform senders when flow control of data frames has been imposed (RECEIVE_NOT_READY) and when it has been lifted (RECEIVE_READY) improves efficiency by forestalling fruitless retransmissions and possible erroneous conclusions about link failure while flow control is in effect. For simplicity we omit explicit consideration of flow control frames in our design.

Therefore, in our example, control frames are required only for link startup. The startup frames do not need to be sequence numbered. They will therefore require individual acknowledgement. Two frame types are required: a START frame and a START_ACK frame, to provide acknowledgement.

We may summarize the frame protocol requirements as follows:

- Data frames are fixed-size and contain two sequence numbers (send and receive), in addition to a message fragment.
- Sequence numbers of data frames are calculated modulo a predefined window size.
- Local flow control is exercised on either transmission or reception when the window is full.

- Data frames are acknowledged by the receive sequence number, which indicates the next expected incoming send sequence number (by implication acknowledging all previous ones); a null data frame can be used to provide acknowledgements when there is no data to send.

- Unnumbered control frames (START and START_ACK) are required for link startup.

- Two phases of operation are implied—startup and data transfer. During the startup phase only START and START_ACK frames are exchanged in order that both ends of the link may agree that they are up and the link is operational before sending data. During the data transfer phase, only data frames are exchanged.

- Frame check codes are used to provide redundant data for error checking purposes.

6.4.3.4 Overview of the COMM Subsystem Protocols   At this point we can either develop the details of the protocols first (PDU formats, sequencing rules, states, etc.) before proceeding with the design of the system, or proceed with the design of the system first and fill in the details of the protocols as and when they are required. We shall adopt the latter, stepwise refinement approach here and simply note in passing that in most practical protocol system design situations, the protocol is given in detail first and the system must be designed to fit it. However, at this point we have sufficient information to proceed with system design, without being overly concerned about the details of the protocol.

This situation is somewhat similar to that encountered in the event sequence problems of Chapter 4. There we developed the overall structure of the system based only on knowledge of the events which must be handled and not of the details of a finite state machine processing of the event sequences.

Consider the original data flow graph of Figure 6.6 from a broader perspective, including PDU flows between peer modules in different systems, as shown in Figure 6.7.

At a conceptual level the peer message management modules communicate directly with each other in terms of screen messages, and the peer logical frame management modules communicate directly with each other in terms of PDUs of the frame protocol. In physical fact each of these levels of communication between peers is handled by lower-level system modules.

At the message management module level we have identified only a need for local flow control and message delimiting. This can clearly be handled by a local interface in individual systems between the message management and logical frame management modules and need not involve an explicit protocol between peer message management modules in different systems.

We have identified a need for protocols between peer logical frame management modules for data transfer and for link startup. Only the data transfer protocol is directly concerned with data coming from or going to the message management module. The link startup protocol is not concerned at all with message data but rather has its own autonomous activities resulting in the creation and absorption of PDUs.

With this perspective we are now ready to proceed further with system design.

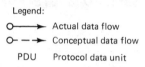

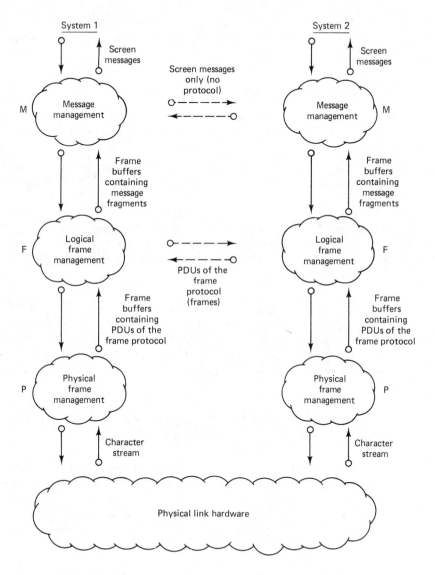

Figure 6.7 Peer communication between COMM subsystem modules at different nodes

6.5 COMM SUBSYSTEM DETAILED DESIGN

6.5.1 Introduction

This section develops details of the COMM subsystem design, based on the issues discussed and conclusions reached in Section 6.4. We begin with data flow in Section 6.5.2, and then proceed to structure and internal logic, in Section 6.5.3. Subsections of 6.5.2 and 6.5.3 discussing the same layer are identically numbered for easy cross-reference.

6.5.2 Data Flow

Figure 6.8 provides an overview, from a data flow viewpoint, of the basic design decisions (both explicit and implicit) made so far, as a starting point for more detailed design. The E, M, and F layers are in general accordance with the top down structure of Figure 6.3(b), with the exception that no tasks are needed in the M layer, because it only acts as a passive conduit. The P layer simply serves as an I/O driver and accordingly needs only an input and an output task.

Some elements of structure are already in place in Figure 6.8, namely the packages and tasks. However, we leave details of the control interactions to Section 6.5.3.

The only significant element missing from this figure is an explicit indication of how local credit is arranged at the M/F and F/P interfaces. We leave these details to Section 6.5.3.

6.5.2.1 The DIALOGUE/COMM Interface   Note how at the DIALOGUE/COMM Interface message buffers are assumed to be permanently allocated for transmission and reception, in accordance with the discussion in Section 6.4.2.2. Note also how credit for transmission and reception is assumed to be managed at the DIALOGUE/COMM interface by handing over empty message buffers, in accordance with the discussion in Section 6.4.2.3.

6.5.2.2 The Event Decoder Module   The message buffer flow control rules suggested by Figure 6.8 may be summarized as follows:

- E gives an empty message buffer to M for reception purposes on startup; after every reception and subsequent release of the screen by the operator, E returns this buffer to M.
- E gives a full message buffer to M for transmission when the operator strikes the SEND key; when M has copied this message buffer into frame buffers, M returns the buffer to E for reuse.

These rules are conservative but appropriate for the problem. On occasion they may slow up the system. For example, they do not allow an unused TX buffer to be

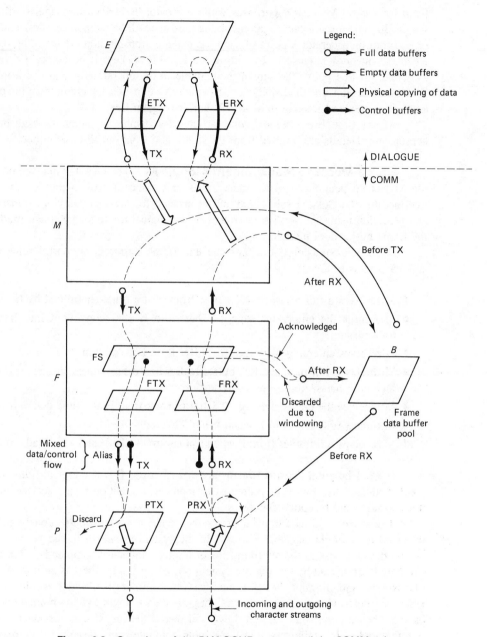

Figure 6.8 Overview of the DIALOGUE system and the COMM subsystem

freed for use by M for RX purposes while a previously arrived message is still on the screen. In these circumstances, an incoming message will be temporarily flow controlled.

From the operator's point of view, E extends transmission credit to the operator, when the operator requests it by hitting the RESERVE key, if an empty TX buffer is available. At this point, the screen is available to the operator for entry of a message. When the operator hits the SEND key, E withdraws transmission credit from the operator and will not extend it again until its TX buffer is again free.

At any time, we assume E may arrange for display of either message buffer as appropriate. Details are omitted from the figure and from our discussion here.

6.5.2.3 Message Management Module M   The message management module M has no peer protocol to manage. Its only concerns are to provide the service interface for the COMM subsystem and to arrange for message copying, transmission, and reception using the service interfaces of the logical frame management module and the frame buffer pool module.

From M's viewpoint, the message and frame buffer flow control rules may be summarized as follows:

- M receives a full message TX buffer from E at a time determined by E.
- M returns the empty message TX buffer to E after copying it into frames for transmission.
- M receives an empty message RX buffer from E on startup.
- M directs a full message RX buffer to E when it has copied the last frame of an incoming message into the buffer.
- M receives the empty message RX buffer back from E at a time determined by E.
- M directs full frames to F when it has TX credit from F.
- M receives full frames from F when frames are available and M is ready to receive.

6.5.2.4 Logical Frame Management Module F   The logical frame management module F has two peer protocols to manage in addition to the service interface, transmission, and reception functions.

The startup and data transfer protocols are never active simultaneously and so are managed by a single task, the FS task. In the system as specified, the human operator has no direct access to the startup protocol through keyboard commands. This protocol can only be triggered by turning the system on. Accordingly, there is an implicit system management module, not shown in the overview of Figure 6.8, which would be responsible for triggering the startup protocol. In general, we might like the human operator to have keyboard commands to shut down and restart the link if it is suspected that there is a temporary link failure or that the remote computer has crashed and perhaps might come back up. This functionality will not be included in this design example but could be easily added.

Note in Figure 6.8 that the FS task inserts control frame buffers into the outgoing stream and removes them from the incoming stream without any interactions with the layer above. An assumption of this figure is that empty frame buffers are not used for outgoing control frames. A supply of small buffers suitable for outgoing control frames is held by the logical frame management module and used in a cyclic fashion. A local credit mechanism between the F and P modules ensures that control buffers are not reused by F before P has finished with them.

6.5.2.5 Physical Frame Management Module   Because of aliasing of buffer pointers, the F module still retains control of buffers containing outgoing frames. Therefore, as soon as P has transmitted all of the characters of a full buffer, it simply forgets that it ever had the buffer.

Note that, on reception, empty frame data buffers may be cycled back to the reception function if the frame check code indicates an error.

6.5.3 Structure and Logic

6.5.3.1 Introduction   The data flow requirements on which the structures of this section are based are contained in correspondingly numbered parts of Section 6.5.2.

We use linear interaction structures throughout, as defined in Chapter 5.

6.5.3.2 New DIALOGUE/COMM Interface   The original DIALOGUE system event decoder of Figure 4.31 and 4.32 must be modified to take account of buffering and flow control conditions not previously considered. The new structure is shown in Figure 6.9. Because the SEND procedure of the M package imposes a potentially lengthy conditional wait on the caller until the entire message has been copied into frame buffers, a transmission transport task (ETX) is required between the event decoder and this procedure. The previous reception transport task has been renamed ERX.

The previous PUT_MSG entry in the event decoder (E) task has been renamed PUT. It provides for no-wait handover of incoming messages. Three new entries in the E task provide places where the transport tasks ETX and ERX can wait for an outgoing message (GET), report sending done and return the empty TX buffer (RETURN), and pickup an empty RX buffer (PICKUP).

The E task provides an empty buffer to M via PICKUP on startup and following release of a displayed RX buffer by the operator.

The ETX task cycles between calls to E.GET, to wait for a message to send, to M.SEND, to send the message, and to E.RETURN to report sending done and to return the empty buffer.

The ERX task cycles between calls to E.PICKUP, to wait for an empty buffer, to E.RCVE, to hand over the empty buffer and to wait for it to be filled by an incoming message, and to E.PUT to hand over the message.

6.5.3.3 New Dialogue System Event Decoder   Modified logic for the E task is given in Figure 6.10. Figure 6.10(a) shows the revised finite state machine controlling the operation of this task and Figure 6.10(b) shows the corresponding Ada code. New features of this finite state machine are the addition of two extra states

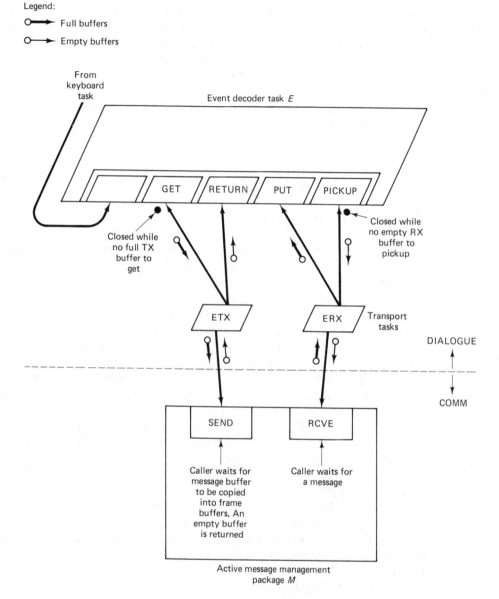

Legend:

O——► Full buffers

O——► Empty buffers

Figure 6.9 New DIALOGUE/COMM interface structure

(READY__TO__SEND and SENDING) and two new auxiliary variables (IN__MSG and __RX DONE). The READY__TO__SEND state provides a guard condition for the acceptance of the GET entry (open only in this state). The SENDING state provides a means of exercising TX flow control on the operator until the TX buffer is returned. (Until this occurs, there can be no return to the IDLE state, which is the only state in

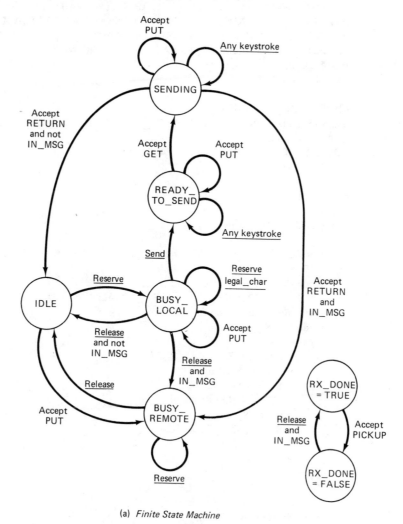

(a) *Finite State Machine*

Figure 6.10 New event decoder logic (*notes:* 1. Operator-triggered events (keystrokes) are underlined; 2. IN__MSG is a boolean indicating whether a RX message is ready for display or being displayed; 3. *Release* triggers return of a buffer to M in any state, if there is one to return.)

which the operator is not TX flow controlled.) The IN__MSG variable is used to record the presence of a message after a call on PUT. It is required because calls on PUT are accepted in any state but only cause state changes in the IDLE state; IN__MSG is used to record the occurrence of a PUT call so that appropriate state changes can be made when other events occur. Calls on PUT are accepted in any state, because reception credit is given by the E task to M by passing an empty buffer to M; therefore, there is no need to exercise RX flow control via a guard on PUT, as was done in the original DIALOGUE system design. The RX__DONE variable is used as a guard on the PICKUP entry. In

```
task EVENT__DECODER is
  entry PUT__STROKE (K : in . . . ); -- KEYSTROKE (NO WAIT)
  entry GET( . . . ); -- CONDITIONAL WAIT FOR AN OUTGOING MESSAGE
  entry PUT( . . . ); -- INCOMING MESSAGE (NO WAIT)
  entry RETURN( . . . ); -- EMPTY MESSAGE BUFFER (NO WAIT)
  entry PICKUP( . . . ); -- CONDITIONAL WAIT FOR AN EMPTY MESSAGE BUFFER
end EVENT__DECODER;

task body EVENT__DECODER is
type STATE is (IDLE, BUSY__LOCAL, BUSY_REMOTE, READY__TO__SEND, SENDING);
S : STATE : = IDLE;
IN__MSG, RX__DONE : BOOLEAN : = FALSE;
. . .
begin
loop
  select
    accept PUT__STROKE (K : . . . );
    do
      if K = RELEASE and IN__MSG then IN__MSG : = FALSE; SCREEN.SWITCH; end if;
      case S is
        when IDLE = >
          if K = RESERVE then S : = BUSY__LOCAL;
          else RING__BELL; end if;
        when BUSY__LOCAL = >
          case K is
            when RELEASE = >
              if not IN__MSG then
                S : = IDLE;
                SCREEN.CLEAR;
              elseif IN__MSG then
                S : = BUSY__REMOTE;
                SCREEN.SWITCH;
              end if;
            when SEND = >
              S : = READY__TO__SEND;
            when in LEGAL__CHAR = >
              SCREEN.WRITE (K);
            when OTHERS = >
              RING__BELL;
          end case;
        when BUSY__REMOTE = >
        if K = RELEASE then
              S : = IDLE;
              SCREEN.CLEAR;
              RX__DONE : = TRUE;
          else RING__BELL; end if;
    end case;
  end;
```

(b) *Ada Program Skeleton*

Figure 6.10   (continued)

```
   or
     accept PUT(M : . . . );
       do
         IN__MSG : = TRUE;
         if S = IDLE or S = SENDING then
             SCREEN.SWITCH; end if;
          if S = IDLE then S : = BUSY__REMOTE; end if;
       end;

   or
     when RX__DONE = >
     accept PICKUP ( . . . );
       do
         GIVE__EMPTY__BUFFER;
         IN__MSG : = FALSE;
         RX__DONE : = FALSE;
       end;
   or
     when S = SENDING = >
     accept RETURN (M : . . . );
       do
         if not IN__MSG then S : = IDLE;
         elseif IN__MSG then
         S : = BUSY__REMOTE;
       end if;
     end;
   end select;
  end loop;
 end EVENT__DECODER;
```

(b) *Ada Program Skeleton (continued)*

Figure 6.10   (continued)

any state, the RELEASE keystroke will open this entry by setting RX__DONE to true if IN__MSG is true. (Both variables will be set back to false when a call on the entry is accepted.)

6.5.3.4 Message Management Package   Because the M package does not need to be an active package, all the functions may be performed by its interface procedures M.SEND and M.RCVE, as shown in Figure 6.11. The ETX and ERX tasks wait for credit and/or frame buffers through these procedures.

The M.SEND procedure first waits on F.SEND for TX credit. When it has credit it calls B.PICKUP for an empty frame buffer, copies a message fragment into the buffer, and calls F.SEND to transmit it. Return from F.SEND normally grants transmission credit for another frame. The B.PICKUP/F.SEND cycle is repeated until there is nothing left of the message. On the last call to F.SEND, a parameter set by M.SEND indicates it is not willing to wait for credit. After return from this last call to F.SEND, the M.SEND

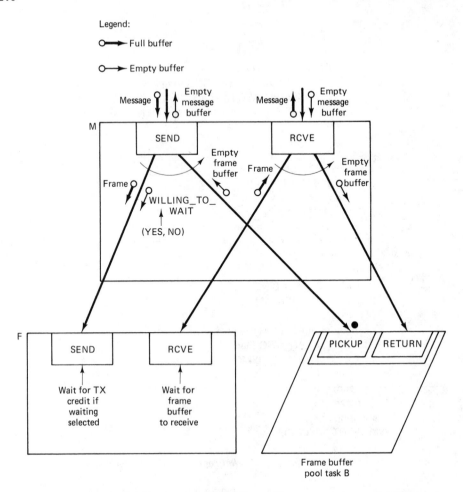

Figure 6.11 Passive message management packet structure (assuming single-message-buffered TX and RX and no message protocol)

returns the now-empty message buffer to its caller. Note that no explicit TX credit parameter needs to pass from the F package to the M package because the M package in our example cannot send multiple frames in a single F.SEND call. Credit to send one frame is implicitly given by return from F.SEND (provided the parameter is set indicating willingness to wait for credit).

The M.RCVE procedure waits first on F.RCVE for an incoming data frame. When such a frame arrives the procedure copies it into the empty message buffer and then returns the frame buffer to the pool via B.RETURN. When it detects the end of the message (by examining the data part of the frame buffer), it returns the now-full message buffer to its caller. At this point, RX flow control is exercised on the frame level, because F.RCVE will not be called again until M.RCVE is called again.

6.5.3.5 Logical Frame Management Package   An appropriate structure for the necessarily active logical frame management package F is shown in Figure 6.12. The main new external features of this package, compared to the M package, are the use of the external timer package and the presence of the START procedure. The START procedure is not shown as being used by any higher-level module, because we have not specified how the COMM subsystem interacts with the local system management modules which handle system startup. The main new internal feature of this package, compared to the M package, is the frame service task FS. The FTX and FRX tasks are needed only because of the FS task. The F package manages a full-duplex protocol involving sequences of frames arriving autonomously from above and below. The sequences are not independent becaue of acknowledgement requirements, and the package itself may add frames to the sequences or remove them. The FS task controls all of this activity. The FTX and FRX tasks are transport tasks which interact with the physical frame management package P for the FS task so that it can continue with its other duties.

The FS task has entries, called from above, to SEND outgoing frame buffers containing message fragments and to RCVE incoming ones. Other entries, called from below, are used to GET outgoing frames and to PUT incoming ones. A START entry triggers the startup protocol. A PICKUP entry gives TX credit to the next higher user, as described below. A delay alternative provides for timeout on failure to receive acknowledgements.

The SEND entry of the FS task returns a credit parameter on every call; if the credit parameter is zero and the caller has indicated a willingness to wait, the SEND procedure calls PICKUP to wait for credit.

The FTX task cycles between calls to P.SEND and FS.GET, transferring a frame on each cycle. Return from P.SEND implies credit to send the next frame. Note that this credit mechanism is strictly local between the F and P packages and does not distinguish between data and control frames. On startup, credit is assumed to be available, so the FTX task calls FS.GET first to wait for a frame.

The FRX task cycles between calls to P.RCVE and FS.PUT, transferring a frame on each cycle. On startup, the FRX task calls P.RCVE first to wait for a frame. The job of discarding data frames when the RX window is full is left to the FS task.

How should the internal logic of the FS task be organized to manage all this activity? For modularity, separation is desirable between the peer protocol logic and the local-system-dependent logic for handling local flow control, frame buffer manipulation, and queueing. A possible approach which satisfies this requirement is illustrated in Figure 6.13. The F__PROTOCOL package encapsulates all the logic of the peer protocol, including that for startup and data transfer. The various entries of the FS task interpret entry calls and parameters as events of the peer protocol. Event identifiers are passed to the PROCESS procedure of the F__PROTOCOL package, which returns action identifiers for consequent actions. The action identifiers are examined and acted on by the entry routine which called PROCESS in the first place. Actions include preparing and enqueueing data and control frames for transmission, and arranging for proper disposition of received data and control frames. The actions are performed using the services of the F__QUEUE and F__MANIPULATE packages.

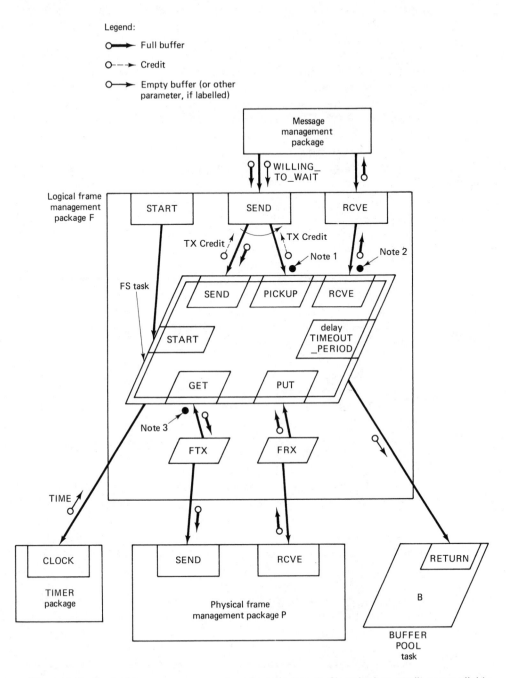

Figure 6.12 Logical frame management package (*notes:* 1. Closed when credit not available in data transfer phase; 2. Closed when no data frames to pick up in data transfer phase; 3. Closed when no frames to transmit.)

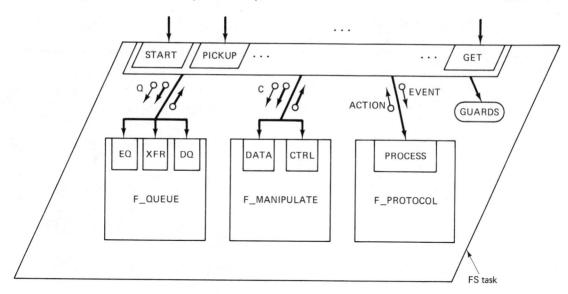

Legend:

○———▶   Frame buffers

EQ   Enqueue

XFR   Transfer (between queues)

DQ   Dequeue

Q   Queue identifier(s)

C   Operation Code

Figure 6.13   Internal packages of the FS task

With care using the package approach, it should be possible to structure the internal logic of a task such as the FS task so that its internal peer protocol package is portable between different types of implementations (for example, between implementations requiring callers to wait for items to pick up, as in this example, and implementations without this requirement, which simply return status parameters indicating nothing to pick up, or between implementations employing transport tasks, as in this example, and implementations employing the buffer task approach of Figure 6.4(c)).

The F__PROTOCOL package's prime function is to manage the finite state machines and auxiliary variables controlling the startup and data transfer phases of operation. For our simple protocol there is one finite state machine and two auxiliary variables. The finite state machine controls the peer-to-peer protocol sequences which result in the peers agreeing that communication has been established and it is safe to send data frames. The auxiliary variables are the current send and receive sequence numbers for outgoing data frames.

A simple finite state machine is illustrated in Figure 6.14(a). For simplicity, the basic assumptions of this figure are somewhat unrealistic, as follows:

- Systems may start up independently at any time, but once they are up, they stay up. Therefore, START frames arriving in the UP state do not signify an attempt to restart after a crash during the data transfer phase of operation. Rather, they only occur during link startup, as a result of timeout in the COMING-UP state.
- The only actions required in the UP state are maintaining the current send and receive sequence numbers. These sequence numbers will both be set to zero on initial entry to the UP state; because of assumption 1, they do not need to be reset

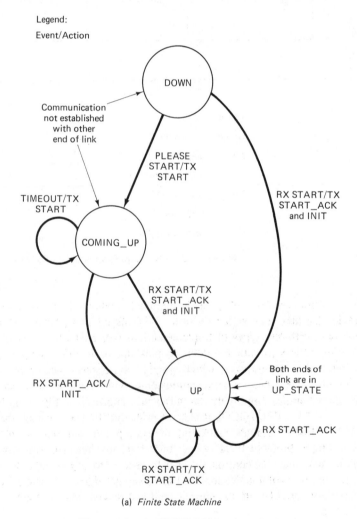

Legend:
Event/Action

DOWN

Communication not established with other end of link

PLEASE START/TX START

RX START/TX START_ACK and INIT

TIMEOUT/TX START

COMING_UP

RX START/TX START_ACK and INIT

RX START_ACK/ INIT

UP

Both ends of link are in UP_STATE

RX START_ACK

RX START/TX START_ACK

(a) *Finite State Machine*

Figure 6.14   F_PROTOCOL package logic

```
package F_PROTOCOL is
  type EVENT_TYPE is (PLEASE_START,
                      TIMEOUT,
                      RX_START,
                      RX_START_ACK,
                      RX_DATA,
                      REQUEST_TX_DATA,
                      TX_DATA);

  type STATUS-TYPE is (OK, NOT_OK);
  type WINDOW is range 0 .. MAX;
  type EVENT (INDICATOR:EVENT_TYPE) is
    record
      case INDICATOR is
        when RX_DATA = >
          SEND_COUNT, RCVE_COUNT:WINDOW;
        when others = >;
      end case;
    end record;
  type ACTION_TYPE is (TX_START,
                       TX_START_ACK,
                       Q_REQUEST_TX_DATA,
                       TX_DATA,
                       CLEAR_ACKED_FRAMES,
                       SEND_UNACKED_FRAMES,
                       DISCARD_RX_DATA,
                       NIL);

  type ACTION (INDICATOR:ACTION_TYPE) is
    record
      TIMEOUT_PERIOD:TIME;
      case INDICATOR is
        when Q_REQUEST_TX_DATA = >
          SEND_COUNT, TX_CREDIT:WINDOW;
        when TX_DATA = >
          RCVE_COUNT:WINDOW;
        when CLEAR_ACKED_FRAMES = >
          FIRST_FRAME, LAST_FRAME, TX_CREDIT:WINDOW;
        when SEND_UNACKED_FRAMES = >
          FIRST_FRAME, LAST_FRAME:WINDOW;
        when others = >;
      end case;
    end record;
  procedure PROCESS (E:in EVENT; A:out ACTION);
end F_PROTOCOL;
```

(b) *Ada Specification*

Figure 6.14   (continued)

to zero when START frames arrive in the UP state. There are no other data transfer states besides the UP state.

To give the flavor of the approach, a specification of a possible F__PROTOCOL package is given in Figure 6.14(b). The package determines the acceptability of events and indicates the consequential actions. It performs no processing of control and data frames itself. The event and action parameters are variant records, enabling send and receive sequence counts to be passed in and out when required.

Send and receive sequence counts from received data frames are passed in to the package. The received value of the send sequence count is internally incremented and stored for use as the receive sequence count in the next transmitted data frame. The received value of the receive sequence count is used to determine whether any previous transmitted data frames have been acknowledged.

A pair of send sequence counts is passed out from the package if an acknowledgement or timeout has occurred, to identify the sequence range of previously transmitted frames which may be returned to the pool, or which must be retransmitted.

A send sequence count is passed out from the package when a data buffer arrives from above for transmission (for inclusion in the data buffer as the send sequence count of the frame).

A receive sequence count is passed out from the package when a data buffer is about to be passed downward for transmission (for inclusion in the data buffer as the receive sequence count of the frame).

The body of the F__PROTOCOL package is easily implemented using tables for the finite state machine, following the approach taken for the LIFE system command decoder in Chapter 4. The details are left as an exercise for the reader.

Given this view of the F-PROTOCOL package, it is easy to see how it can be used by the various entries of the FS task to help manage the flow of frames.

Figure 6.15 indicates the nature of the internal frame data flow in the FS task. The internal queues shown are assumed to be accessed via the F-QUEUE package of Figure 6.13. Manipulations of frames are assumed to be performed by the F-MANIPULATE package of Figure 6.13. Examples of manipulations are adding headers to data frames on transmission and stripping them on reception, preparing control frames, and updating frame headers with appropriate count values before sending them.

The retransmit queue contains copies of the transmitted but not yet acknowledged frames. The capacity of this queue is determined by the flow control window for transmission. Frame copies are deleted from this queue only when they have been acknowledged; their buffers can then be returned to the pool. Frame copies in this queue are transferred to the transmit queue when they have timed out without acknowledgement. The delay time will be reset on every invocation of the F-PROTOCOL package, to ensure wakeup at a time no later than the oldest time in the retransmit queue, plus the acknowledgement timeout period.

The transmit queue holds outgoing data and control frames for pickup by GET. Both types of frames are queued together, without distinguishing them, in FIFO order.

The receive queue holds incoming data frames not yet picked up via RCVE. Its

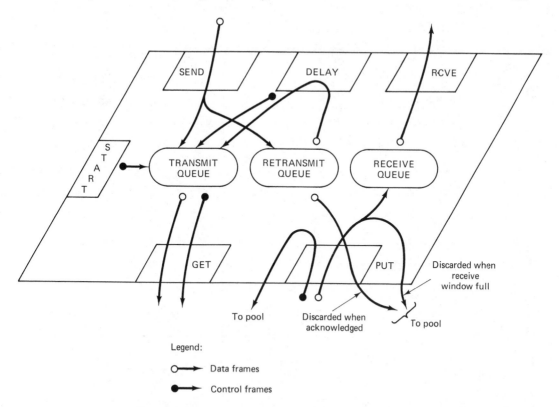

Figure 6.15 Further internal logic of the FS task—frame data flow

capacity is determined by the flow control window for reception. If there are no empty places in this queue, as determined by the F-PROTOCOL package, the PUT entry will discard data frames.

We leave it as an exercise for the reader to develop further details of the interactions among the various entries and internal packages of the FS task to manage the data flow of Figure 6.15.

6.5.3.6 Physical Frame Management Package The physical frame management package P needs only two tasks, as shown in Figure 6.16. The PTX and PRX tasks are the interrupt service routines which transmit and receive characters from the character-oriented communications hardware assumed at the start of this chapter. On the hardware side, interrupt entries transfer characters. On the system side, the SEND entry of the PTX task transfers frames downwards and TX credit upwards; the PICKUP entry of the PTX task is used to wait for credit if it is exhausted by the SEND call; and the RCVE entry of the PRX task transfers frames upwards and empty buffers downwards.

The use of P.RCVE to transfer empty buffers downwards frees the PRX task from having to call the buffer pool B itself; thus it decreases the probability of the PRX task

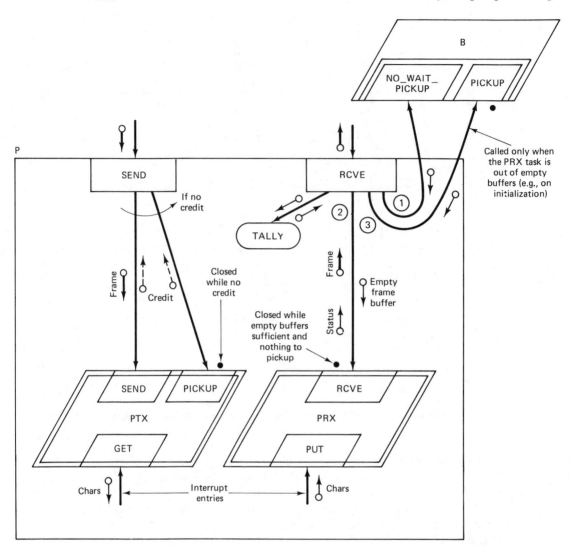

Figure 6.16   Physical frame management package structure

missing characters. The PRX task is initialized in this manner with an appropriate number (at least two) of empty frame buffers from the pool.

During the normal operation, the P.RCVE procedure calls a NO__WAIT__PICKUP entry of the buffer pool task B when TALLY is greater than zero. TALLY is used to maintain a running record of the difference between the number of frames passed upwards and the number of empty buffers passed downwards. The PICKUP entry is used only when the PRX task indicates it has run out of empty buffers, as described below.

The buffer pool task is required to have a NO__WAIT__PICKUP entry so that the caller of P.RCVE does not have to choose between waiting in two conflicting places (at B for empty buffers and at PRX for full ones). Thus any possibility of deadlock is avoided.

When the PRX task has received a full frame, it clears the guard on RCVE (if it is set) and is immediately ready to start filling the next empty buffer. When the RCVE entry is accepted, a frame is handed over to the caller, and the guard on RCVE is reset if the PRX task has at least one empty buffer but no more frames. If the PRX task has neither frames nor empty buffers, then it indicates this condition to the caller of RCVE by returning an appropriate value of a status parameter. While the PRX task has at least one empty buffer but no frames, the RCVE entry is closed.

The PTX task has internal queue space for an appropriate number (at least two) of frame copies (probably represented by access variables). When it has transmitted a copy, it immediately frees that space in the queue (thus effectively discarding the copy) and starts work on the next frame copy in the queue. While there are no free spaces in the queue, the PICKUP entry is closed by a guard.

The interrupt entries transfer frames one character at a time between the program and the hardware, adding or deleting framing characters as appropriate. This is a consequence of the assumption made at the beginning of this chapter that the hardware is character-oriented. With such hardware, performance could be a problem. Due to the rendezvous overhead, characters could be lost during high-speed, synchronous operation. A way of avoiding such problems is to write the actual interrupt service routines in assembly language and to use a timed delay to force the PRX task (for example) periodically to check for and pick up incoming characters from the assembly language interrupt service routine's input buffer. Alternatively, better hardware could be specified.

6.6 DESIGN POST-MORTEM

6.6.1 Introduction

Many system details have been omitted from this design discussion. The actual mechanisms for handling the creation of buffer space and the allocation of pointers have not been considered. Nor have any details been provided for internal queueing structures in various modules in which data can accumulate. Package and task specifications have not been given in detail and parameter type declarations are missing.

The system logic has been developed for the most part in pictures and words. Only a few program fragments have been given to illustrate key, new points. Thus, program fragments are given only for the event decoder task and a simple version of the F-PROTOCOL package specification. However, no program fragments are given for the message management package, or the physical frame management package, because no new issues are involved.

A more general F-PROTOCOL package might be internally complex in detail, depending on the complexity of the more general protocol, but the nature of its interfaces to the local system for sending, receiving, and flow-controlling frames would be essentially as given in the COMM subsystem design independent of its level of internal complexity.

The variant records defining events and action would, of course, require additional components, to take account of additional types of frames in the protocol.

The COMM subsystem design as given is at an appropriate logical level for the first attempt at defining the major features of the system architecture. The material as given is appropriate for a design walkthrough. Following this walkthrough, complete interface specifications for all packages and tasks would be developed and a start made on defining the omitted details.

We now examine the COMM subsystem design from two viewpoints:

- In Section 6.6.2, we consider extensions, for greater functionality.
- In Section 6.6.3, we consider the possibility of different fundamental design decisions leading to different system structures.

6.6.2 Design Extensions

The design is relatively independent of the details of the frame protocol. Therefore, it should be relatively easy to include frame-level protocol features such as explicit end-to-end link flow control, link shutdown and restart control, and link failure notification. These affect primarily the frame protocol package.

It should be possible to include end-to-end frame data flow control in the frame protocol package without affecting the mechanisms already existing for local flow control within the logical frame management package.

An approach to reporting link failure, shown in Figure 6.17, would be to have a special CHECKER task wait on a special entry in the frame service task which would be accepted after link failure. This task would then report back to other concerned packages and tasks. Of course, appropriate procedures and entries would have to be provided and the internal logic of the various modules appropriately modified.

An active message management package would be required for multibuffered transmission and reception of messages (assuming more than two message buffers were available). It would also be required to support a message level protocol which could automatically recover from link or remote system shutdown and restart without losing or duplicating messages. A possible structure, having the same external interfaces as before, is shown in Figure 6.18. The logic is similar to that of the F package, with differences to account for the use of actual buffers to give credit and the fact that buffers must therefore be returned.

6.6.3 Different Fundamental Design Decisions

The COMM subsystem used shared buffer pools. Such shared pools may be undesirable for at least two reasons:

- Complexity—open competition for shared buffers and aliasing of buffer pointers may increase logical complexity and therefore increase the possibility of design or implementation mistakes.

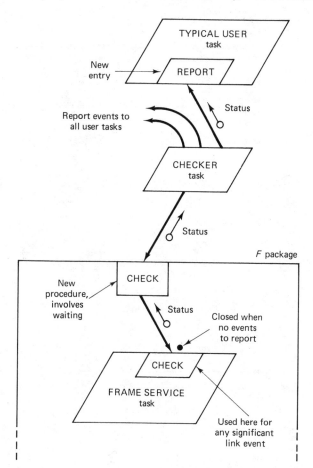

Figure 6.17 Reporting significant frame level events to higher levels (*note:* Not all procedures and entries shown.)

- Transparency—the need for shared memory makes it impossible to allocate different modules to different processors which do not share memory.

    Note that competition for shared buffers was not used at the higher levels of the system. The message buffer pool was placed under sole control of the event decoder task. What about applying the same approach to frame buffering? Frame buffers would be under the sole control of the logical frame management package. Instead of empty frame buffers being separately acquired, they would be exchanged for full buffers at each appropriate interaction. On transmission empty buffers going up would be exchanged for full buffers coming down; on reception the reverse would be true.

    Even though this approach eliminates direct competition for frame buffers, it still requires a shared pool. Empty and full buffers are exchanged, implying that buffers from a shared pool are passed by reference. Thus aliasing is still a problem and transparency is still compromised.

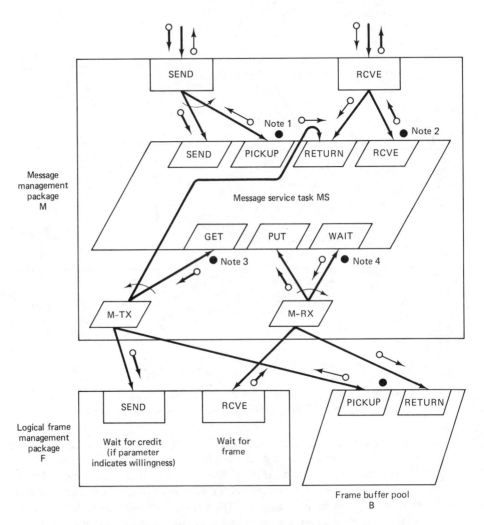

Figure 6.18 Possible active message management package structure (*notes:* 1. RCVE is closed while there is no message to pick up; 2. PICKUP is closed while sending is in progress; 3. GET is closed if nothing to transmit; 4. WAIT is closed if there is no empty RX message buffer.)

222

If the system design is required to be transparent to a possible absence of shared memory, then intermodule data flows must be by value, as shown in Figure 6.19. Each module must now have buffer space to accommodate copying buffers from one module to another. When copying is used, it is meaningless to speak of credit being given in the form of actual empty buffers; instead, it must be given in the form of counts of units of data.

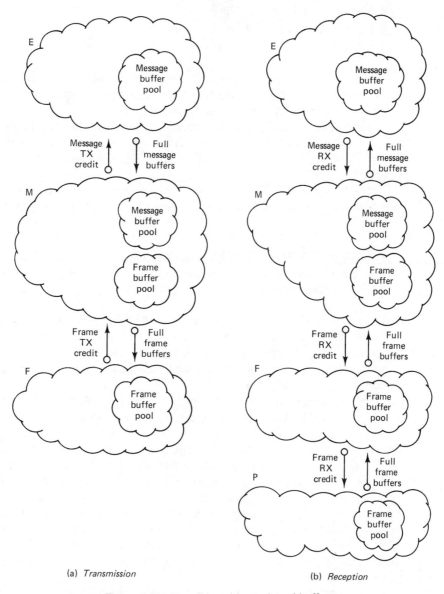

(a) *Transmission*   (b) *Reception*

Figure 6.19 Data flow without shared buffers

The COMM subsystem emerged from the design process as a three-layer system with six tasks (Figure 6.8). Use of an active M package would increase this to nine tasks. The relatively large number of tasks was a particular result of the design decision that each active layer package would require callers to wait for transmission credit and for items to receive. Each layer, thus, has three places to wait:

- for calls from above;
- for transmission credit from below; and
- for items to receive from below.

In general, three tasks are required to wait in these three places. The only exceptions are the M layer, which is not active, and the P layer, which requires only two interrupt service tasks, one for transmission and one for reception.

The number of tasks could be reduced, if each layer package provided only no-wait calls which returned status parameters. Then, the need for transport tasks would vanish. However, the internal logic of the remaining tasks would be more complicated as a result.

The logical nature of the tradeoffs between designs with many and few tasks is easy to identify. Many tasks can result in simpler system and task logic for at least two reasons:

- There is no need for busy-checking for events.
- When an event occurs, the task processing the event is immediately aware of the context of the event.

On the other hand if there are few tasks, there will be less context switching and dispatching overhead. This is unlikely to be very important in higher system layers, where task switches are likely to occur relatively infrequently. However, it could be important in lower system layers. The quantitative tradeoffs are implementation-dependent and largely outside the scope of this book.

The combined DIALOGUE/COMM system was specified as a single reliability unit. Therefore, the COMM subsystem design guards against a wide variety of external failures, but not against internal failures in its own logic. Such failures could be handled by breaking the system down into smaller reliability units, each of which protects itself from failures in the others. In general, each module of a layered communication system could be a separate reliability unit interfaced to higher and lower modules by a possibly unreliable communications link. In this general case, protocols may not only be required *horizontally* between peer modules in separate nodes of a communication network but possibly also *vertically* between the different reliability units forming the vertically separated layers. This general possibility should be kept in mind, even though it will not be explored further here. Figure 6.19 could provide a starting point for the development of an appropriate system design.

However, no matter how the system is split into reliability units, there may be a possibility of a reliability unit developing a fault in its internal logic which causes it to behave in a disruptive manner without completely disabling it. Such a fault might be the result, for example, of a failed bit in a memory chip. If the fault is sufficiently pathological, it could cause the unit to behave in a way that appears rational but disrupts the system. For example, what if it continues to obey the syntactic rules of all protocols but not the semantic ones? It might then acknowledge protocol data units which others have sent but which it has not received causing loss of data.

Such problems are difficult to solve. One approach to solving them is to *kick them upstairs* by assuming that some higher-level unit will eventually notice the problem and initiate recovery action. However, we eventually run out of higher-level units, and the highest-level unit might be the one with the problem. Then the ultimate appeal must be to a human operator.

Another, expensive, approach is to specify physical redundancy of unreliable components. For example, one might specify that two complete links be available so that the active link could be switched if excessive retransmissions were occurring.

6.7 CONCLUSIONS

What is important in this chapter is not so much the structure of the final COMM subsystem (although it is a viable one) but the process of design which was used to arrive at this structure and the graphical notation which was used to describe it. The design decisions were depicted in pictorial form in a manner suitable for group discussion. Although the process is relatively informal, the pictures have formal meaning in Ada terms and can be used to develop Ada code in a relatively mechanical fashion.

Chapter 7

Logical Design of Layered Systems: An X.25 Protocol Example

7.1 INTRODUCTION

This chapter tackles the problem of designing layered systems, using layered protocols as examples. It uses the three-layer CCITT X.25 protocol as a specific example for concreteness, but its methods are intended to be generally applicable to layered systems of any kind. Of particular interest are layered systems to implement the seven-layer ISO model for Open System Interconnection (OSI).

Of the three layers of the X.25 protocol, this chapter will be concerned only with the top one (layer 3—the so-called *packet* layer). Layer 2 of X.25 (the so-called *link* layer) uses a more complex version of the logical frame management protocol of the COMM subsystem of Chapter 6. This link protocol is called HDLC (High-Level Data Link Control). The additional complexity of HDLC can be hidden in a link layer package with essentially the same specification as the logical frame management package of Chapter 6. The general internal structure of that package is still suitable, and only details need to be changed. This chapter will assume the existence of such a package without treating its design further.

Our main purpose in this chapter is to show, using X.25 as an example, how our design methodology may be used to develop appropriate layered system structures for realistically complex problems. It is not our purpose to provide either a detailed treatment of X.25 or a complete system design to implement it. Accordingly, at each stage of the design, we introduce only those aspects of X.25 necessary to make design decisions for that stage, and we stop the design process when a system structure has emerged which can be explained clearly and unambiguously in pictures and words. At this stage in an actual design project, a major design review would be performed before proceeding to fill in details and write programs. In accordance with the purpose of this chapter we give no program examples, relying on previous chapters to show how designs expressed in structure graph form can be converted into programs.

For readers unfamiliar with X.25, Section 7.2 provides a brief overview of it sufficient for the purposes of this chapter.

Section 7.3 develops a design for an X.25 packet layer package.

Section 7.4 provides a design postmortem.

Section 7.5 suggests approaches for more elaborate layered protocols, such as are required for the ISO Model for Open Systems Interconnection.

Section 7.6 concludes Chapter 7, Part C, and the book.

7.2 THE GENERAL NATURE OF THE X.25 PROTOCOL

The X.25 protocol enables its users to establish multiple *virtual circuits* with remote systems and to exchange data packets with these systems using the virtual circuits. A *virtual circuit* is a logical communications pathway which may be multiplexed with other virtual circuits over a single physical link to a public data network. For each such link there is a predefined set of virtual circuit numbers which are used by both the users and the network to identify the virtual circuits sharing that link. Both incoming and outgoing packets contain a virtual circuit number.

In practice the X.25 protocol will be managed by an X.25 protocol manager module in each system. However, it is not the purpose of the X.25 protocol specification to dictate the structure of this module. The specification is concerned only with what flows between the different communicating systems. Thus, it is concerned only with formatting, sequencing, and functionality of protocol data units (PDUs). In the case of X.25, the packet layer PDUs are known as packets and the link layer PDUs as frames.

Figure 7.1 illustrates the nature of the use of X.25. User modules establish virtual circuits connecting them with remote user modules via the services of the X.25 protocol managers.

The main purpose of the link and packet layers are as follows:

1. The link layer provides for error-free, correctly sequenced, flow-controlled communication of frames over a single link. As well it provides for link startup and shutdown.

2. The packet layer provides for error-free, correctly sequenced, flow-controlled communication of packets over each virtual circuit. It also provides for establishing and clearing virtual circuits. Although the concept of X.25 illustrated by Figure 7.1 is of user modules communicating over virtual circuits via the network, many of the X.25 interactions are with the local network interface; that is, they are not end-to-end between users. However, connection requests and responses and clear requests and responses are end-to-end, and hence, the complete connection is con-

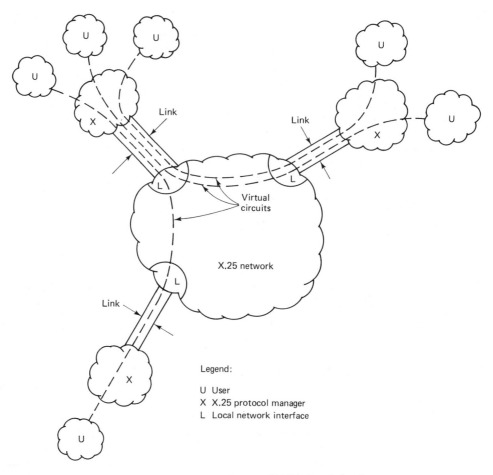

Figure 7.1   A logical view of X.25 virtual circuits

sidered to be end-to-end in nature. The system structure to implement X.25 itself is not affected by whether or not certain of its interactions are end-to-end. However, higher layers may be affected.

Management of a single virtual circuit at the packet level is logically very similar to the management of a single link at the link level. Virtual circuits and links are both communication *connections* which can be opened and closed at will. Therefore, the experience gained in Chapter 6 in designing the logical frame management package for a single link will be applicable to the design of managers for each virtual circuit of the packet layer. The main new features of the packet layer which will concern us in this chapter are as follows:

- multiplicity of virtual circuits to be managed;
- dynamic nature of the virtual circuits (at any time, a variable number may be active); and
- multiplexing of the active virtual circuits over a single lower level connection.

User data and packet layer control information are contained in packets of typically 128 or 256 bytes. Packet control information, such as the virtual circuit number, type of packet, packet number (on that virtual circuit), etc., is contained in a packet header. Link control information, such as the frame send and receive sequence numbers and the error check code, is added to form the frame header and trailer.

The X.25 packet level specification gives the following kind of information:

- types and formats of the packets;
- possible states of virtual circuits (e.g., cleared, call setup, data transfer, and clearing);
- changes in state required upon receipt of a packet, occurrence of a timeout, etc.;
- packets to be issued as a result of the state changes.

This kind of information is complicated in detail but familiar in nature from previous examples in Chapters 4, 5 and 6. It leads to the design of modules which provide control of event sequencing via finite state machines. Only the details of the finite state machines are affected by the details of the X.25 specification if the design is modular.

For our purposes it will be sufficient to identify the types of user packets and their uses. This information is given in Table 7.1 for a subset of X.25.

TABLE 7.1 USER PACKET TYPES AND USES FOR A SUBSET OF X.25

Packet name	TX or RX	Use
Data	TX	User data
Call-request	TX	Request call on a particular VC to a given address
Clear-request	TX	Clear call in a particular VC
Call-accept	TX	Reply to an incoming-call packet
Clear-confirm	TX	Reply to a clear-indication packet
Data	RX	User data
Incoming-call	RX	Indicate call on a particular VC from a given address
Clear-indication	RX	Indicate call on a particular VC should be cleared
Call-connected	RX	Confirm a call-request
Clear-confirm	RX	Confirm a clear-request

7.3 X.25: STUDY IN LAYERED SYSTEM DESIGN

7.3.1 Introduction

Following common sense and the lead of Chapter 6, it is natural to divide the overall X.25 protocol manager into layers corresponding to the layers of the protocol with each layer as an active package, as shown in Figure 7.2. Parameters and waiting conditions for this figure will be given in Section 7.3.3, following the development of the internal data flow design of the packet layer in Section 7.3.2.

7.3.2 Packet Layer Internal Data Flow Design

Given the background of the BANK example of Chapters 3 and 5, the AGENT__POOL example of Chapter 5, and the COMM example of Chapter 6, we can begin the data flow design phase with a head start. Identification of the main internal tasks can be performed immediately based on these examples. The main data flow issues are then concerned with the routing and flow control of packets between tasks.

Figure 7.3 identifies the tasks of the packet layer package and shows the data flow between them. Many of the design decisions implicit in this figure will be familiar from previous examples. In particular the use of multiple virtual circuit managers (VCM) tasks and a single dispatcher task follows naturally from the BANK and AGENT__POOL examples. Here for the first time, we see a significant practical application of this type of structure. As in previous examples each task in the pool has a permanently assigned

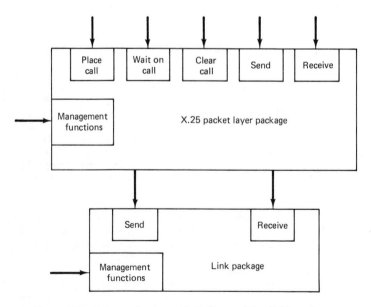

Figure 7.2   Nature of external interfaces of the X.25 packages

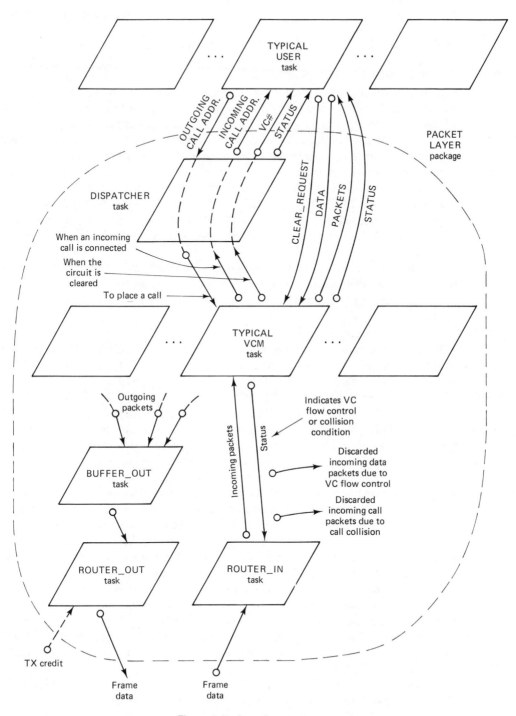

Figure 7.3 Data flow in the packet layer

number to identify it. In this case the number identifies the virtual circuit managed by the task.

The dispatcher in Figure 7.3 has slightly more to do than previous dispatchers, because requests for virtual circuits may originate not only from local users but also from the network. The dispatcher keeps track of the status (free or busy) of VCM tasks and allocates them to users in response to incoming or outgoing call requests.

The VCM tasks manage all packet flows for their respective virtual circuits for both call control (clearing and establishment) and data transfer. They interact with the dispatcher to report incoming calls, to report themselves free after circuit clearing, and to receive addresses for outgoing calls. Otherwise they interact with users, with the ROUTER_IN task, and with the BUFFER_OUT task. Each VCM task has a permanently assigned virtual circuit number, which it keeps in a local variable and which is passed around to the dispatcher and to users as required. Possession of this number enables the possessor to contact the VCM task.

A key design decision implicit in Figure 7.3 is that VCM tasks are able to interact with other tasks while their circuits are cleared. This enables them to handle incoming-call packets directly. As a consequence the data flow patterns are very clear and direct in Figure 7.3.

A single reception transport task is identified in Figure 7.3. This task is called ROUTER_IN because it routes incoming packets to the correct VCM tasks. Only one such task is needed for many VCM tasks because there is only one place to wait for incoming packets: the RCVE procedure of the link layer package.

Incoming packets are routed to the appropriate VCM task by the ROUTER_IN task. Control of packets which cannot be accepted by the VCM task reverts immediately to the ROUTER_IN task, which simply discards them. Flow control is not the only cause of the VCM task's inability to accept incoming packets. Another cause is *call collision,* defined as the same virtual circuit number appearing simultaneously in an outgoing call-request packet and an incoming-call packet. The rule in X.25 is that the outgoing call takes precedence, and the network clears the incoming call. Accordingly, the ROUTER_IN task simply discards incoming-call packets when call collision occurs.

In X.25, the term *call collision* refers to packets actually received and sent. An attempt by a user to connect an outgoing call using a VCM task which has already accepted an incoming call is not call collision in the X.25 sense, because no call-request packet has been sent. Therefore the outgoing call will not be placed.

Further incoming packets destined for a flow-controlled virtual circuit might still be *in the pipe* in the link layer package at the time of the discard. If the flow-control condition is lifted before they are picked up by the ROUTER_IN task, they will (apparently unfairly) be passed on to the correct VCM task. However, the rules of X.25 will cause them to be discarded at this point because of the gap in the packet number sequence caused by the first discard.

A single transmission transport task called ROUTER_OUT is identified in Figure 7.3. Only one such task is needed for many VCM tasks, provided there is an intermediate BUFFER_OUT task, as shown in the figure, where all outgoing packets from all VCM tasks are buffered for pickup. Outgoing packets are sent to the link by the ROUTER_

OUT task when it has frame TX credit. While frame TX credit is not available, outgoing packets pile up in the BUFFER_OUT task up to the limit of its buffer capacity. If its buffer capacity is the sum of all the transmission flow control windows of all the VCM tasks, then the VCM tasks will never need to worry about local TX credit.

The above mechanism is consistent with the way the logical frame management package of Chapter 6 gives credit. However, it violates the original justification for a credit mechanism given in earlier chapters. Recall that the justification was to avoid allocating buffers to send transactions which could not be immediately completed. This violation did not occur in Chapter 6, because multiple logical connections were not being multiplexed over a single link as they are here. This violation cannot be avoided here, because frame TX credit cannot be preallocated fairly among individual virtual ciruits.

7.3.3 Packet Layer Internal Structure Design

The internal tasks and data flows of the packet layer have already been identified, so our main concern here is with interaction structures and functionality. Most of the issues have already been discussed in previous chapters.

The internal structure will be partially determined by the interface details omitted from Figure 7.2. A more complete interface structure graph is provided in Figure 7.4.

The main points to note about the Packet Layer procedures of Figure 7.4 are as follows:

- The WAIT_FOR_CALL procedure returns the number of an already connected virtual circuit. If the call is not wanted (as indicated by the address parameter), the appropriate response is to use the CLEAR procedure immediately.

- For simplicity, the SEND procedure is identified as a no-wait procedure (implying there are no guards on the corresponding entries of internal tasks).

- There is no credit parameter associated with the SEND procedure. A flow control condition is reported via a status parameter after an attempt to SEND has been made.

- For simplicity, no timeout parameters are included in any of the procedures.

The reader should be careful not to confuse the two possible meanings of the word *call*, as exemplified in the phrase: A user *calls* the WAIT_FOR_CALL procedure to wait for a *call*. As with overloading in Ada, the intended meaning will be evident from the context.

Sufficient Ada interface specifications have been presented previously for structure diagrams such as Figure 7.4 that at this point the translation of this figure into such a specification can be left to the reader.

The internal structure graph of Figure 7.5 follows naturally from the interface structure of Figure 7.4, from the data flow graph of Figure 7.3, from a commitment to linear interaction structures between tasks, from the discussion of the AGENT_POOL example, and from the fundamental design decision that free VCM tasks do not wait at

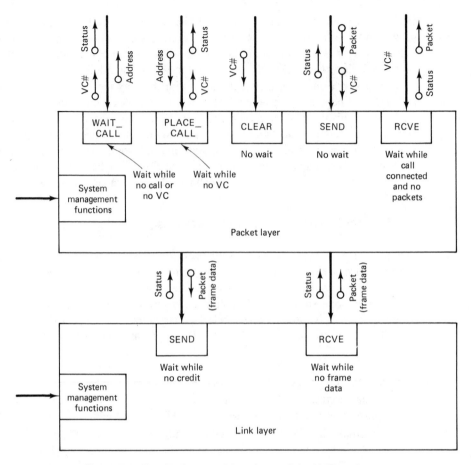

Figure 7.4 Detailed external interfaces of the X.25 packages

the dispatcher to be allocated but rather just declare themselves FREE and then return to wait for calls on their own entries. *Virtual circuit numbers (VC#)* identify both virtual circuits and their manager tasks.

We leave it to the reader to define Ada interface specifications as required for the various tasks of Figure 7.5. There is nothing new in doing so at this stage.

We now briefly describe the functionality of each of the tasks and the interactions between them.

7.3.3.1 DISPATCHER Task The dispatcher allocates free VCM tasks to users as follows:

- for incoming calls, by returning an allocated VC# as a parameter of the WAIT__ FOR__CALL entry following a REPORT call from a VCM task which has connected

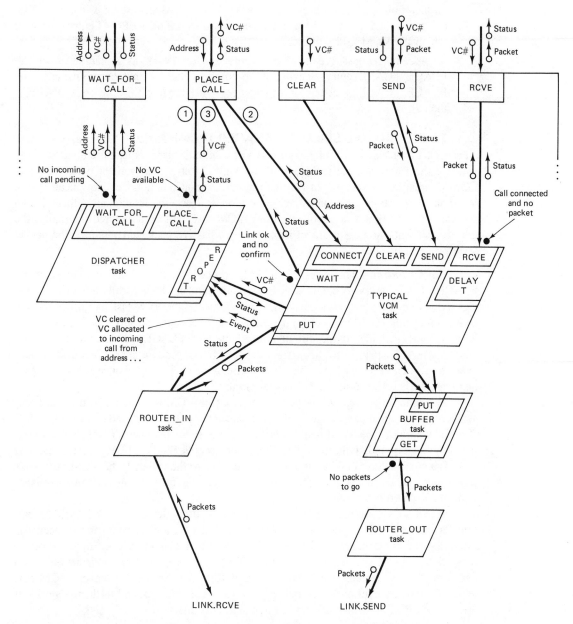

Figure 7.5 Packet-layer package internal structure

235

an incoming call (if no user is at WAIT__FOR__CALL, a status value indicating
this is returned to the VCM task as an out parameter of the REPORT entry following
which the VCM task will clear the call)

- for locally requested calls, by returning a free VC# as a parameter of the
  PLACE__CALL entry, leaving it up to the caller of that entry (namely, the
  PLACE__CALL procedure of the package) to ask the free VCM task to CONNECT
  the call

7.3.3.2 VIRTUAL CIRCUIT MANAGER (VCM) Tasks

VCM tasks manage
all aspects of virtual circuit interactions. A virtual circuit manager task is similar in many
ways to the frame service (FS) task of the logical frame management package of the
COMM subsystem example. In fact the only significantly new issues introduced by the
VCM tasks are associated with their allocation and access. Individually, their design
presents no new issues or problems. Each VCM task will be structured internally like
the FS task with the peer protocol managed by a passive package containing the packet
level protocol FSMs.

Call Control   The PLACE__CALL procedure first calls the dispatcher's
PLACE__CALL entry to obtain a virtual circuit number. It then calls the VCM task's
CONNECT entry and passes it the destination address. If the VCM task has just connected
an incoming call, the CONNECT entry will return a status parameter indicating the circuit
is no longer available. If the circuit is available, the PLACE__CALL procedure then
calls the WAIT entry; in the meantime the VCM task sends a connect-request packet.
When a call-connected packet arrives on that circuit via PUT, the call on WAIT is accepted
and the user is released to use the virtual circuit.

When an incoming-call packet arrives at a free VCM task via PUT, the VCM task
sends a call-accepted packet and notifies the dispatcher of the connected call via REPORT.
If there is no user, the VCM task is notified via the status parameter of REPORT so that
it may clear the call. Otherwise the dispatcher accepts WAIT__FOR__CALL, passing
the originator's address and a virtual circuit number to the caller. If the VCM task is not
free at the time of arrival of an incoming-call packet, the packet is ignored in accordance
with the X.25 collision rules.

When a CLEAR request is made by the local user, the VCM task leaves the data
transfer phase, sends a clear-request packet and waits for a clear-confirmation packet in
return before declaring itself FREE. When a clear-indication packet arises from the
network, the VCM task leaves the data transfer phase, sends a clear-confirmation packet
and immediately declares itself free via REPORT. In either case when the VCM task
leaves the data transfer phase, all data packet queues are cleared, and further data packets
arriving via PUT are discarded until a new call is connected.

Data Transfer   All of the logic and data structures concerning data packet transmission, reception, acknowledgement, and retransmission are internal to the VCM task.
The outstanding data packets are stored in two queues, a retransmit queue containing
data packets sent but not acknowledged and a receive queue, containing data packets
received but not picked up. The primary controlling factors in the task are the state of

the task, which includes the state of the virtual circuit, the size of retransmit and receive queues, and the time in the system of the oldest unacknowledged packet. The logic will be similar to that required for the logical frame management service task of the COMM subsystem.

In the data transfer state, the VCM task always accepts the SEND, PUT, and CLEAR entries but only accepts RCVE if the receive queue is not empty. Upon each acceptance of an entry, the VCM task takes the appropriate action, updating queues and sending packets, then returns to the selective accept clause to wait for the next call. If the retransmit or receive queues are full (their capacity is determined by the virtual circuit flow control window), then flow control will be exercised on transmission from above or reception from below, as the case may be. Transmission flow control is exercised by a VCM task by terminating a SEND rendezvous without accepting the data packet; the flow control condition is indicated to the caller by a returned STATUS parameter. Reception flow control is exercised in a similar fashion by terminating a PUT rendezvous without accepting a data packet (control packets are always accepted, however).

Retransmission of packets is handled in the fashion of the COMM subsystem. Each packet is stamped with the time of its last transmission. The head of the retransmit queue is the oldest, hence, it will require retransmission first. Before entering the selective accept clause, the VCM task determines how much time is left on the head of the queue of unacknowledged packets and sets up a delay parameter accordingly. Should no accept occur before the timer expires, the delay alternative is taken, and unacknowledged packets are retransmitted. If an entry is accepted, the delay is adjusted appropriately.

7.3.3.4 ROUTER_IN, ROUTER_OUT, and BUFFER Tasks   The ROU-
TER__IN task waits at the link package for incoming frame data, decodes the frame data as a packet for a particular virtual circuit, and calls the PUT entry of the appropriate VCM task to hand over the packet. Depending on the value of a STATUS parameter returned after the PUT rendezvous, it may have to discard the packet (return it to the frame buffer pool); this will be required if the VCM task is exercising reception flow control or if the VCM task is not free at the time of arrival of an incoming-call packet.

The ROUTER__OUT task is a simple transport task which moves one packet at a time from the BUFFER task to the LINK package while it has frame TX credit.

The BUFFER task simply accumulates outgoing packets for all virtual circuits.

7.4 DESIGN POST-MORTEM

7.4.1 Introduction

Many of the comments made in the COMM subsystem design post-mortem also apply here and will not be repeated.

The design presented in Figure 7.5 emerged after several frustrating attempts to simplify the awkward internal logic of a dispatcher task based on a slightly different system structure. This different structure had incoming call packets for unallocated VCM tasks flowing to the dispatcher instead of the VCM task. The three-way interaction (with the ROUTER__IN task, the designated VCM task and the user) proved awkward to describe clearly. No matter how it was approached, the internal logic of the dispatcher seemed excessively complex, considering the relative simplicity of the allocation problem. There is a rule that applies in writing and design which is helpful in such situations: When what one is trying to say seems difficult to say, perhaps one is trying to say the wrong thing. As soon as the system structure of Figure 7.5 was adopted, the problems with the internal logic of the dispatcher task disappeared. We were trying to say the wrong thing! From another viewpoint, the structure which was causing problems is clearly not as modular, by the criteria of Chapter 6, as that of Figure 7.5. Accordingly, we should have expected problems!

The awkwardness mentioned above arose primarily because of the fixed allocation of virtual circuit numbers to VCM tasks. The simplicity of the solution of Figure 7.5 is directly due to this fixed allocation. Dynamic allocation would require a different solution.

7.4.2 Design Extensions

In practice, timeout parameters would be needed for the interface procedures of the packet layer package which involve waiting; the requisite timeouts would be implemented by making timed entry calls from the interface procedures to the appropriate entries of internal tasks, as shown in Figure 7.6. Internal tasks would have to ensure that they were never stuck waiting for a timed-out call, resulting in deadlock. Recall that deadlock can occur

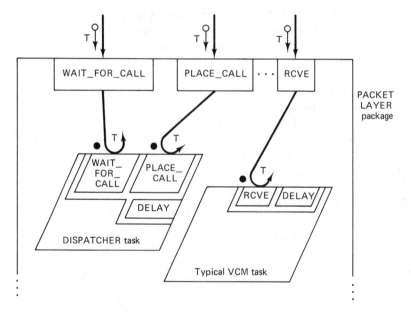

Figure 7.6 Packet-layer interface timeouts (*note:* Not all procedures and entries shown.)

when a task has accepted a timed call, based on the count attribute of an entry, only to find that the caller has timed out between the evaluation of the count attribute and the acceptance of the entry.

The question was not discussed in Section 7.3 of how to notify users of the lifting of packet transmission flow control. The implicit assumption was that a user who was flow controlled on transmission would simply keep calling SEND at suitable time intervals until the packet was accepted. However this solution is not very satisfactory. Too short a retry period may use up excessive processor time in busy waiting. Too long a retry period may reduce throughput unacceptably. In either case the logic is more complex than necessary because of the need to program retries explicitly.

A solution to this event notification problem which does not require retry is shown in Figure 7.7. A CHECKER task calls a new CHECK entry in the dispatcher to wait for

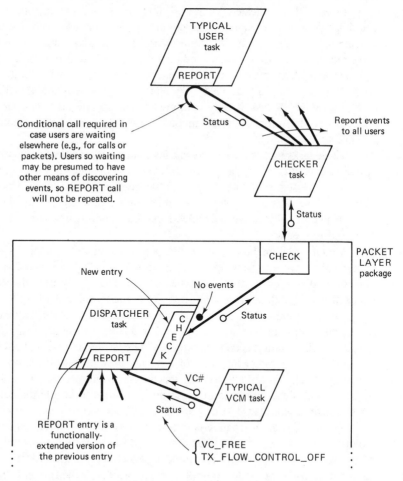

Figure 7.7 Reporting significant packet layer events to users (*note:* Not all procedures and entries shown.)

significant packet level events. The only significant event under consideration at the moment is the lifting of transmission flow control on a virtual circuit. However, others are possible. When an event occurs, the CHECKER reports it to users via conditional entry calls. These calls must be conditional in case the user is waiting elsewhere.

Another solution is to specify a credit mechanism between the user and the packet layer package.

7.4.3 Different Design Decisions

The X.25 packet layer package emerged from the design process with $N + 4$ tasks for N virtual circuits. Fewer tasks are also possible, as follows.

Instead of a dedicated VCM task for each virtual circuit, one or two main tasks could handle all packet layer virtual circuits. One main task could be used to manage all virtual circuits for the entire layer. Or a pair of main tasks could be used, one to manage call control for all virtual circuits and the other to manage data transfer. These tasks must maintain explicit state tables and data packet counters for each circuit. Still required are the ROUTER__IN and ROUTER__OUT tasks. No longer required is the DISPATCHER task. The BUFFER task is only required if two separate tasks manage call control and data transfer. Therefore the total number of tasks required by these approaches is at most five and at least three.

These tasks will require many entries so that they can accept entry calls for different virtual circuits differently, according to the different states of the circuits.

As discussed in Chapter 6, quantitative performance tradeoffs between designs with many and few tasks are implementation-dependent and largely outside the scope of the book. However, qualitative judgements can be made, as discussed in Chapter 6 and as discussed further below.

Modularity is on the side of the task-per-virtual-circuit approach. There is an inherent conceptual clarity in designing a system so that *form* follows *function*. If the system's function is displayed by the form which implements it, then the design is likely to be easier to understand and to implement. We argue that this is likely to be the case with the task-per-virtual-circuit approach. A virtual circuit is logically independent of and concurrent with other virtual circuits, and is therefore naturally managed by a task. An important consideration is that the program logic is simpler if virtual circuits are managed separately. For example, handling of timeouts is simpler with the one task-per-virtual-circuit approach. To follow a similar mechanism with fewer tasks requires that the tasks maintain extra data structures or more intricate logic to enable the delay alternative of the selective accept clause to find and time-out the correct packet or circuit.

Another design alternative is to take the task-per-virtual-circuit approach but allow the dispatcher to create the tasks as needed and permit them to exist only for the duration of the call. The user would be passed an identifier for the task managing his virtual circuit, following the philosophy of dynamic access in the forward direction discussed in Chapter 5.

The dynamic task approach offers the possible advantage of not tying up memory with context tables and stacks for idle tasks. In this dynamic task approach, to enable the ROUTER__IN task to access the VCM tasks, we require a look-up table maintained by the dispatcher and containing the access variables of the VCM tasks.

When a VCM task finishes, the dispatcher must know that the circuit is free and that it can create a new task to manage that circuit when it is next allocated; hence, the VCM tasks must still call DISPATCHER.FREE. Furthermore, we must adopt the previously rejected structure in which the ROUTER__IN task sends incoming-call packets to the dispatcher.

The ROUTER__IN task must be prevented from attempting to access a terminated VCM task. However, such a situation can arise due to a race between the ROUTER__IN task and a VCM task, as follows. ROUTER__IN could obtain the access variable to a VCM task in between the time the task declares its circuit clear to the DISPATCHER and terminates and the time when the dispatcher updates the table. This problem can be solved, but the solution adds complexity. Two possible approaches are:

- Design the VCM task so that after it declares its circuit free, it performs a selective wait on all of its entries together with a delay alternative. Any entry calls now issued on the manager will cause the manager to return a cleared status to the caller. After timeout, the task terminates.
- Include a local exception handler in each task rendezvousing with a VCM task to recover from this erroneous condition should it occur.

Clearly, the dynamic task approach is more complex.

Throughout Chapters 6 and 7, only top-down control structures have emerged from the design process; in these structures each layer calls the next lower one for all interactions. This approach was originally suggested for layered systems at the beginning of Chapter 6 because it is familiar and avoids deadlock due to careless use of bidirectional calls between layers. However, our intent is not to advocate top-down control structures as necessarily the best or only ones.

Symmetrical control structures are also possible. The differences between top-down and symmetrical control structures may be only a matter of cosmetic packaging, as illustrated by Figure 7.8 (which follows Figure 6.4(b)). If we draw the package boundaries differently between tasks in our top-down X.25 structures, the package interactions can be made two-way without changing the nature of the task interactions. All we have done in this figure is moved the ROUTER__IN task of Figure 7.5 into the link layer package and added a new interface procedure PUT to the packet layer package. The new PUT procedure now decodes frame data and directs packets to the correct internal task, whereas formerly the body of the ROUTER__IN task performed this function. Thus the ROUTER__IN task itself does not need to distinguish packets for different virtual circuits; it acts simply as a transport task for frame data.

An alternative symmetrical structure, using buffer tasks instead of transport tasks, might be based on Figure 6.4(c). We leave development of the details to the reader.

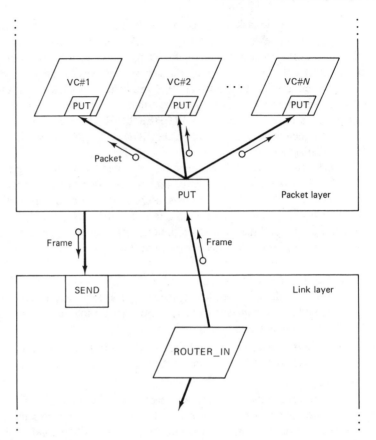

Figure 7.8 Nonhierarchical package structure derived from a hierarchical one by repackaging

7.5 EXTENDING THE DESIGN APPROACH TO THE SEVEN-LAYER OPEN SYSTEM INTERCONNECTION MODEL

This section discusses briefly how the design approach may be applied to the ISO's seven-layer model for Open System Interconnection (OSI).

The Open System Interconnection model is based on the concept of entities providing services to higher-level entities. To provide services, entities interact with remote peer entities by exchanging protocol data units via services provided by lower level entities.

Although entities may rely on lower-level entities to manage the physical exchange of protocol data units, each entity's protocol data units are logically private. To permit this logical privacy, the protocol data units of higher layers are nested in those of lower layers in exactly the way X.25 packet level protocol data units (packets) are nested in link protocol data units (frames).

Each entity is said to have a service access point (the identifier of the entity) and to manage connections (like X.25 virtual circuits). Services are provided via service primitives, which may have associated parameters. Service primitives may flow in two directions between entities.

Just as with X.25, protocol specifications for OSI define only the protocol data units to be exchanged, together with their sequences and effects, and not the system structure to implement the protocol.

In our designs the OSI entities are active packages. The service access points are the names of the packages. Primitives are implemented using visible procedures of packages.

Based on our design examples, guidelines for designing an OSI system with a top-down control structure following the pattern of Figure 6.3(b), are as follows:

- Make each OSI layer an active package.
- Make each entity within the layer a visible active package called from above.
- Define the service primitives in terms of visible procedures of the package, with appropriate parameters. Use separate procedures for primitives handled in different protocol states for clarity of structure.
- Provide a minimum of two tasks in each entity package, one to manage the service interface and one to transport upward-going interactions from the next lower layer (assuming interactions with lower layers are full duplex and may require waiting). Provide an additional transport task if downward-going interactions with the next lower layer may require conditional waiting.
- Provide at least one task for each connection managed by the layer to control the protocol associated with establishing, using, and clearing the connection.
- For multiple connections, provide a buffer task to accumulate downward-going interactions for pickup by the appropriate transport task, if there is one.

The X.25 design serves as an example of the application of these guidelines. Readers particularly concerned with OSI conventions should note, however, that a few details of this example are anomalous relative to OSI. In OSI, a WAIT__FOR__CALL procedure would not provide a connected call but only an indication of an incoming-call packet. A separate ACCEPT__CALL procedure would be needed to confirm acceptance of the call. Furthermore, in OSI, circuit identifiers would be dynamically assigned to circuit manager tasks in certain cases (for example, in the transport layer).

Similar guidelines for designing an OSI system with a symmetrical control structure, following the pattern of Figure 6.4(c), could also be developed. We leave this as a project for the reader.

The previous discussion tantalizingly reveals only the tip of the OSI iceberg. Many other important issues associated with system design and implementation for OSI are being investigated in the author's laboratory.

7.6 *CONCLUSIONS*

This section concludes Chapter 7, Part C, and the book.

Part C has served to illustrate how, during system design, interactions and tradeoffs between a large number of issues in modularity, reliability, and structure can be explored and resolved using a graphical notation and methodology based on Ada. The graphical notation and methodology provide a suitable basis for group discussion. The process of developing a design using this graphical notation and methodology can be relatively informal. However, its end product, namely, a well-annotated set of structure graphs, has formal meaning in Ada terms and can be used to develop Ada code in a relatively mechanical fashion.

A key feature of all the designs developed in Part C (and elsewhere in this book) is the definition of different procedures and entries of packages and tasks for different services provided by the packages and tasks. For tasks, we have shown how separate entries should be provided for different interactions, to provide so-called *linear interaction structures,* which have no nested rendezvous. This approach enables structure graphs to display the different nature of the processing of the different calls in a very clear and explicit fashion. For tasks, this ensures the waiting structure is explicit at the task interface. Thus it enables design to be performed in detail at the structure graph level, and it makes explanation of the final design possible without resort to code.

In general we have shown how single and multiple tasks can be advantageously hidden inside packages for modularity.

As appropriate for the design-oriented aims of the book, the role of Ada in Part C has been primarily to provide the inspiration for and the semantics of the graphical notation. Therefore, actual examples of Ada programs do not occupy a large amount of space in Part C.

The design examples chosen in Part C to illustrate the approach are interesting in themselves. Many design issues relating to protocol systems have been discussed and resolved. The power of the approach is illustrated by its ability to deal with such issues in a compact and understandable fashion.

Chapter 8

References

The list below includes only works explicitly referenced in the text.

BOOCH, G., *Describing Software Design in Ada*. September, 1981, ACM SIGPLAN Notices, pp 42–47.

BOWEN, B. A. and R. J. A. BUHR, *The Logical Design of Multiple Microprocessor Systems*. Englewood Cliffs, NJ, Prentice-Hall, Inc., 1980.

CCITT Recommendation X.25.

HANSEN, PER BRINCH, *The Architecture of Concurrent Programming*. Englewood Cliffs, NJ, Prentice-Hall, Inc., 1977.

IAPX-432 Object Primer. Intel Corporation, January 1981.

MYERS, G. J., "Reliable Software Through Composite Design," New York, Petrocelli/Charter, 1975.

PYLE, I. C., *The Ada Programming Language*. Englewood Cliffs, NJ, Prentice-Hall, Inc., 1981.

Reference Manual for the Ada Programming Language. Draft revised MIL-STD 1815, United States Department of Defense, July 1982 and ANSI/MIL-STD-1815A, United States Department of Defense, January 1983 (both references were used at different times).

WEGNER, P., *Programming with Ada: An Introduction by Means of Graduated Examples*. Englewood Cliffs, NJ, Prentice-Hall, Inc., 1980.

YOURDON, E. and L. CONSTANTINE, *Structured Design*. Englewood Cliffs, NJ, Prentice-Hall, Inc., 1979.

Chapter 9

Questions for Self-Study

CHAPTER 2

2.1 Redesign the stack package of Figure 2.3, using a single interface procedure as suggested by the Pascal approach of Figure 2.5(b). Rewrite the body of the package (Figure 2.4) in Ada. Comment on the differences between the new package and the old one from the point of view of understandability, modularity and functionality.

2.2 Write a Pascal program for a stack package following Figure 2.5(b). Enumerate the significant differences between the Pascal program and the corresponding Ada program. Consider both the appearance of the program text and the run-time behavior of the program. What is the significance of the package concept at run-time in Ada, relative to the corresponding Pascal program?

2.3 Design and program in Ada a new version of the buffer task of Figures 2.7 and 2.8 for use as a line buffer. The new task will have entries to WRITE characters and to READ lines. As before, the WRITE entry will be closed when the task's buffers are full. The READ entry will be closed when a complete line is not yet available. Assume that lines are variable length strings of fixed maximum size, terminated by a special character.

2.4 Suppose that a programmer needing a passive buffer package for use by a single task decides, as a matter of convenience, to use an available buffer task instead. Strictly speaking, this is not the correct use of a buffer task. In correct use, the READ and WRITE entries are called by different tasks. In the programmer's intended use, these entries would be called by the same task. Which versions of the buffer tasks of Figures 2.7 and 2.8 and of Question 2.3 could be used successfully in this way? Which could not? Explain.

2.5 Design and program in Ada a passive buffer package for use in the application of Question 2.4. Following Question 2.3, this buffer package will have procedures to WRITE characters and to READ lines. However, the line-available condition will have to be handled differently.

2.6 For the buffer task example of Figure 2.7, implemented as in Figure 2.8(d), give the minimum/maximum number of context switches required to transfer a character from producer to the consumer, assuming that the three tasks are the only ones in the system. Explain.

2.7 Rewrite the stack package example of Figure 2.4, defining the PUSH and POP procedures as stubs, following Figure 2.12. (The approach of Figure 2.12 can be applied not only to nested packages but also to procedures of a package.)

2.8 Investigate different ways of handling interrupts in different multi-tasking systems and contrast them in detail with the Ada approach illustrated by Figure 2.15.

2.9 (a) Write the specification and body of an Ada task to implement the functional equivalent of a general counting semaphore. Semaphores are used for signalling between tasks in such a way that signals are never lost. A general counting semaphore has two indivisible primitives called WAIT and SIGNAL, an internal counter to keep track of the excess of signals over waits, and a FIFO wait-queue where tasks may wait for signals. A task calling WAIT is blocked in the wait-queue if there have been more past calls on WAIT than on SIGNAL; otherwise, it is allowed to proceed. The task at the top of the wait-queue is allowed to proceed when the next SIGNAL occurs.
(b) The intent of SIGNAL is that its callers always be allowed to proceed without blocking (except possibly for the case where, in a prioritized, uniprocessor system, the task at the head of the wait-queue is of higher priority than the signalling task). WAIT should be similarly non-blocking if there have been sufficient past SIGNAL calls. Explain how this intent is violated by your Ada program; describe two ways in which this violation could affect the temporal behavior of the tasks calling the semaphore.

CHAPTER 3

3.1 Draw structure graphs for the buffer task examples of Chapter 2 using the full graphical notation of Figures 3.2 and 3.3.

3.2 For the buffer task examples of Chapter 2, give specific instances of structural delays, congestion delays and latency delays.

3.3 Figures 3.10 and 3.11 illustrate the human interaction metaphor for the Ada rendezvous mechanism. However, they do not illustrate all the cases possible according to the graphical notation of Figures 3.2 and 3.3. Draw and explain new figures corresponding to 3.10 and 3.11 for conditional and timed entry calls and timed-out entry accepts.

3.4 With reference to Section 3.3.1, draw structure graphs depicting all possible forms of master/slave interaction and comment on the differences between them. Are there cases where a slave task could be replaced by a passive package? Explain.

3.5 With reference to the definitions of functional task types in Section 3.3.1, identify instances of these types in Figure 3.6(b). Is the secretary task in Figure 3.6(b) actually a secretary according to the definition of Section 3.3.1? What functional types are not present in Figure 3.6(b)? Can you see a role for them in completing the figure?

3.6 Consider Figure 3.14(c) showing an active stack package containing a nested scheduler task. Draw a complete structure diagram for a system of tasks using this package and then explain the fundamental differences at run-time between the nature of the tasks in this figure and the nature of the package. In what sense would it be fair to say that the package "disappears" at run-time, leaving only the tasks? In this sense, what role does the package play at run-time? In what sense is there no difference at run-time between the nested scheduler approach of Figure 3.14(c) and the separate scheduler approach of Figure 3.14(e)?

3.7 Consider Figure 3.17, showing indirect many-to-many interactions using a buffer task. Is there any significant efficiency difference between using a single buffer task as shown in the (d) part of the figure or using many buffer tasks (one per target) as shown in the (b) part of the figure?

3.8 Consider Figure 3.19, showing a priority server task. Explain how it is theoretically possible for entries to be accepted in other than priority order. What conditions in the underlying run-time system would make this possible?

3.9 Suppose one task calls the high priority entry of the server task of Figure 3.19, using a timed call, but many tasks call the medium and low priority entries. Provide a timing diagram showing the interleaved sequence of events among the calling tasks and the server task such that the server task would be unable to service callers of its medium and low priority entries even though the entry queue of the high priority entry is empty.

3.10 Draw timing diagrams showing the interleaved activities of the various tasks in the transport task structure of Figure 3.21(e) and the buffer task structure of Figure 3.21(h). Comment on the differences.

3.11 Suppose four tasks send items mutually to each other in all possible ways. Draw structure graphs showing the interaction structures for the transport task approach of Figure 3.21(e) and the buffer task approach of Figure 3.21(h). Compare the two approaches. Would your comparison of the two approaches be significantly different if the four tasks did not communicate with each other in all possible ways, but only in a pairwise fashion, in which each task communicates with only two other tasks?

3.12 Suppose that a system is being designed, composed of a number of tasks which must interact with each other to accomplish the work. Give examples showing that ad hoc combinations of different interaction structures from Figure 3.21 can lead to deadlock.

3.13 Write pseudocode showing how the SENDER task of Figure 3.22(b) would use the credit mechanism of the TARGET task.

3.14 Write pseudocode showing how the SENDER and TARGET tasks of Figure 3.22(c) would interact to accomplish the exchange of items and credit.

3.15 Give a structure graph and pseudocode for the bank example of Figures 3.23–3.25 to illustrate how tellers might acquire their wicket numbers from the dispatcher dynamically.

3.16 Given a pair of tasks, each with one entry, which make mutual calls, give pseudocode for the bodies of the tasks illustrating the two cases where they are guaranteed to deadlock and where they are guaranteed never to deadlock.

3.17 Suppose a particular task contains two entries. Explain clearly the different implications for callers of the following different acceptance mechanisms (use timing diagrams if appropriate):
- ordered acceptance of the entries;
- selective acceptance of entries;
- acceptance of one entry within the critical section of the other entry.

3.18 Write pseudocode for the different cases of Question 3.17.

CHAPTER 4

4.1 Figure 4.10 shows a CONTROL task interacting with a number of SLAVE tasks by two mechanisms, accepting calls from the SLAVES and making calls to the SLAVES. Under what circumstances could the SLAVE tasks be replaced by procedures, with resulting improvement in system efficiency? Under what circumstances is keeping the SLAVES as tasks more efficient?

4.2 Write appropriate pseudocode for the LIFE and KEYBOARD tasks of the LIFE system example. Include a type-ahead buffer in the KEYBOARD task.

4.3 Define appropriate array aggregates for the finite state machines of the LIFE system command decoder (Figure 4.17). Suggest a more efficient way of representing the finite state machines.

4.4 Develop new structure graphs for the LIFE example for the case where the design is based on a character stream command decoder instead of a word stream command decoder. Contrast this design with the one in Chapter 4.

4.5 Write pseudocode for the body of the FORMS system logical display management package and the nested field edit package.

4.6 Explain what modifications are required to the FORMS design to accommodate the dotted states and transitions in the command processor finite state machine of Figure 4.24.

4.7 Draw a timing diagram showing the interleaved sequence of events leading to the line printer task of the FORMS system being unable to print available lines until the operator hits a keystroke (see Figure 4.25(a) and the associated text).

4.8 Redesign the FORMS system using the buffer task approach of Figure 3.21(h) instead of the transport task approach used in Figure 4.25. Start with the idea that each main task in the system will have its own buffer task through which it will receive all its interactions from other tasks in the system. In the FORMS system, the two main tasks are the event decoder and the line printer. Contrast your design with the one presented in Chapter 4.

4.9 Write pseudocode for the command recognizer and command processor packages which are nested in the event decoder task of Figure 4.25.

4.10 Modify the FORMS system design so that concurrent printing and editing is achieved by double buffering. Two form buffers would be provided: one for data entry and editing and the other for background printing of a previously entered form. A print command would have to be added to the operator interface. Draw a structure graph corresponding to Figure 4.25(a) to show the new approach.

4.11 Draw a complete structure graph for the FORMS system as developed in Chapter 4, showing all components of the system on one figure. Include stored data as well as packages and tasks in your structure graph.

4.12 Draw a structure graph indicating how a file system interface might be added to the FORMS system.

4.13 Consider an expanded version of the FORMS system viewed as a number of subsystems, a console manager subsystem, a printer manager subsystem and a file manager subsystem. For modularity, it would be desirable to make each subsystem an active package. Draw a structure graph, showing what components would be so packaged, either (a) for the approach taken in Chapter 4, or (b) for the buffer task approach developed in Question 4.8. Explain how this structure could be used as a general one for embedded operating systems for personal workstations.

4.14 Consider the DIALOGUE system structure graph of Figure 4.32. Draw another structure graph based on this one showing how an inappropriate internal structure for the active message system interface package could result in deadlock. (*Hint*—what if the SEND_MESSAGE procedure of the package caused the caller to wait for room for the message?)

4.15 Would it be advantageous to redesign the DIALOGUE system as shown in Figure 4.32 based on the buffer task model of task interaction instead of the transport task model? Explain.

4.16 In the alternate structure graph of Figure 4.33 for the DIALOGUE system, there is no means for the event decoder task to control the flow of incoming messages. Devise a flow control mechanism based on the discussions in Chapter 3.

4.17 Develop the internal logic of the event decoder task of Figure 4.33, including an internal structure graph and pseudocode.

4.18 Draw a structure graph to implement the data flow graph of Figure 4.34.

CHAPTER 5

5.1 When a dispatcher allocates members of a pool of server tasks to user tasks, as in the BANK example of Figure 5.1, the possibility arises of races between tasks. The solutions shown in Figure 5.1 are free from such races, but only a slight modification would be needed to introduce the possibility of races. Suppose the dispatcher task provides two entries for tellers, one READY entry as shown in Figure 5.1(a), where tellers may declare themselves ready, and another WAIT__FOR__WORK entry, where tellers may wait until work is assigned. The WAIT__FOR__WORK entry would be guarded. Now the possibility exists of a race between tellers to call the WAIT__FOR__WORK entry after returning from the call to the READY entry. Draw a structure graph showing the dispatcher/teller interaction and explain the race, using a timing diagram.

5.2 Write pseudocode for the REQUEST__SERVICE procedure of the BANK package of Figure 5.1(a).

5.3 Design the body of the MAILROOM package of Figure 5.7.

5.4 Design the body of the MAILROOM package of Figure 5.8.

5.5 Consider the flow control mechanism suggested by the structure graphs of Figure 5.11. Write pseudocode for the body of the target tasks to implement the linear interaction structure of Figure 5.11(b), and the nonlinear structure of Figure 5.11(d). Contrast the two approaches. Comment on why the approach of Figure 5.11(d) does not provide a generalized block/wakeup mechanism.

5.6 Write pseudocode to implement the linear interaction structure for the final readers/writers solution of Figure 5.16, following the approach suggested in the discussion of that figure in the text.

5.7 Explain how the linear waiting solution for the agent pool example as shown in Figure 5.17(b) can result in a race which will give the customer an invalid agent number. Use a timing diagram. What slight modification of the logic of the problem (as depicted in Figure 5.17(a)) would render this race of no importance?

5.8 Suppose the race problem in Figure 5.17(b) was solved by providing a check entry in the dispatcher for use by an agent to check if it has been allocated. The agent would use this entry only if a customer called while the agent was in the unallocated state. What new problem does this solution introduce? Would a solution to this problem be to provide a list of allocated agent numbers global to the dispatcher task but local to the pool package, which could be consulted by agents? What additional new problem does this introduce?

5.9 Consider the problem of designing the body of the communications package for the reliability unit model of Figure 5.23. Suppose the package can be divided into two parts internally, one part of which supports export and import of "please call" messages for task entries and the other of which supports any kind of message communication between reliability units. Assume a suitable interface view of the inter-reliability unit messaging component of the package. Then design the entry call export/import part. This part of the package must arrange to make calls on entries of tasks in the same reliability unit; this could be done, for example, by using a pool of "partner" tasks to make the requested calls. Alternatively, conditional calls could be made by a call manager task. In either case, your design should take account of the possibility that entries may be closed by guards.

5.10 Study the treatment of generics in the Ada reference manual and comment on the desirability of including generics in the parts kit of Ada mechanisms available for design at the level of the examples in Chapters 2 through 5.

CHAPTER 6

6.1 The interface structure between the DIALOGUE and COMM systems shown in Figure 6.9 is based on the transport task canonical form for layered systems suggested by Figure 6.3(d). In this canonical form, the tasks of each layer are packaged. However, the tasks of the DIALOGUE system in Figure 6.9 are not packaged. Show how the complete DIALOGUE system could be packaged to fit the canonical structure.

6.2 Show how the DIALOGUE/COMM interface structure of Figure 6.9 could be redesigned to accommodate the buffer task canonical structure of Figure 6.4(c).

6.3 Redesign the logical frame management package of Figure 6.12 based on the buffer task canonical structure for layered systems of Figure 6.4(c).

6.4 Write pseudocode for the body of the F_PROTOCOL package of Figure 6.14, using tables for the finite state machines, following the approach taken for the LIFE system command decoder in Chapter 4.

6.5 Prepare pseudocode for the internal logic of the FS task, based on the ideas in Figures 6.13, 6.14 and 6.15.

6.6 Show how the physical frame mangement package of Figure 6.16 could be modified for use with a layered structure based on the buffer task canonical form.

6.7 Write pseudocode for the interrupt task of the physical frame management package of Figure 6.16.

6.8 In the COMM subsystem, suppose the body of the F package of Figure 6.12 must be modified, without changing the syntax or semantics of its specifications, so that it serves as an I/O package for a DMA (Direct Memory Access) device which manages all of the details of the frame protocol. Assume that the DMA device is a separate hardware device which copies outgoing data frames from frame buffers in the body of the F package into its own internal buffers, for subsequent transmission. Similarly, it copies incoming frames from its own internal buffers into frame buffers in the body of the F package. Completion of copying of buffers from or to the DMA device is signalled by separate interrupts. Assume that the DMA device performs all the frame protocol functions so that the only concern of the F package is to manage the transfer of frames to and from the DMA device and to and from the M package. In this sense, its responsibilities are similar to those of the old P package (which is no longer needed). Draw well-annotated data flow and structure graphs for the body of the new F package and explain its operation.

6.9 Figure 6.17 shows a checker task approach to reporting failures at the frame level to tasks at higher levels. Draw structure graphs showing specifically how this checker task could interface to the higher levels of the COMM and DIALOGUE systems.

6.10 Use the data flow graph of Figure 6.19 as the basis for redesigning the structure graphs for the COMM subsystem based on the buffer task canonical model for layered system interactions depicted in Figure 6.4(c).

CHAPTER 7

7.1 Races may occur in many ways between tasks. The X.25 packet layer package of Figure 7.5 presents us with a possible example. The possibility exists in this package of a race between a task attempting to CONNECT a call (after being assigned a VC# by the DISPATCHER) and the ROUTER__IN task attempting to PUT an incoming-call packet. Explain this race and its consequences, using a timing diagram. What recovery mechanism is implicit in Figure 7.5?

7.2 Give a simplified structure graph for the X.25 packet layer package of Figure 7.5 for the special case where the package supports only a single virtual circuit. Remove all features of Figure 7.5 which are not required for this case. Justify your simplifications.

7.3 Redraw the relevant parts of the structure graph for the X.25 packet layer package of Figure 7.5 to accommodate the following different approach to incoming call reception. When an incoming call packet arrives, the caller's address is extracted from this packet and passed on to the user at WAIT__FOR__CALL, who must confirm that the call is desired before a call accept packet will be sent. This is in contrast to the approach taken in Figure 7.5, where the VCM task sends the call accept packet immediately and forces the user to clear undesired calls. Consider the possibility of changes to the package interface, to the task responsibilities and to the task interactions to accommodate this different approach.

7.4 What changes should be made to the X.25 packet layer package of Figure 7.5 if VCM tasks do not manage fixed virtual circuits, but rather are assigned virtual circuit numbers dynamically? With this new approach, a particular VCM task may manage different virtual circuits at different times. Recall that incoming call packets, call request packets, and call accept packets all specify a virtual circuit number. In the approach of Figure 7.5, the virtual circuit number in an incoming-call packet identifies the appropriate VCM task uniquely. Therefore ROUTER__IN can use the number to direct the packet to the appropriate VCM task. With the dynamic allocation approach, this is no longer possible because, at the time of arrival of such a packet, ROUTER__IN does not know which VCM task will manage the virtual circuit. In general, a free VCM task must be given a new virtual circuit number every time an incoming-call packet arrives or a call is requested locally. This is in contrast to the approach of Figure 7.5 where a free VCM task gives its virtual circuit number to the dispatcher. (*Hint*— the agent pool example of Chapter 5 may provide clues on how to manage dynamic virtual circuit numbers).

7.5 What design changes would be required in Figure 7.5 for the multiple virtual circuit case if the buffer task is eliminated?

7.6 Design an appropriate message interface package, along the lines of the M package of Chapter 6, to provide a message sending and receiving interface above the X.25 package for use by higher system layers. Take into account the fact that, as designed, the packet layer package of Figure 7.5 does not provide a mechanism to wait for transmission credit. Recall that the design of Chapter 6 relied on such a mechanism.

7.7 Extend the structure graph of Figure 7.5 to include a waiting for credit mechanism similar to that included in the various packages of Chapter 6.

7.8 Provide pseudocode for the body of the dispatcher task of Figure 7.5.

7.9. Draw a structure graph showing how the message interface package of Question 7.6 might use the event reporting mechanism of Figure 7.7.

7.10 Draw a structure graph showing a different organization for the body of the X.25 package of Figure 7.5, in which there is only one main task to manage all the virtual circuits.

7.11 Draw a different structure graph for the body of the X.25 packet of Figure 7.5, in which a pair of main tasks is used, one to manage call control for all virtual circuits and the other to manage data transfer for all virtual circuits.

7.12 Write pseudocode for the body of the dispatcher task of Figure 7.5 for the case where the VCM tasks are dynamically created as needed (as suggested in Section 7.4.3).

7.13 Develop an alternative structure for the X.25 packet layer package, using the buffer task canonical interaction structure of Figure 6.4(c) as the starting point. Assume one VCM task per virtual circuit as before. A clean approach is to provide one buffer task shared among all the virtual circuit tasks and to provide a family of entries where the virtual circuit tasks can wait by virtual circuit number. Is the dispatcher still required, or can its function be incorporated in the buffer task? Contrast your design to that of Figure 7.5. With this approach, is it still useful to provide separate package procedures for each of the functions of the package? Or should the package interface be redesigned to provide only two procedures, one for transmission and one for reception, as suggested by Figure 6.4(c)?

Index